WAR AND PEACE

In the Life of the Prophet Muḥammad (peace be upon him)

ZAKARIA BASHIER

THE ISLAMIC FOUNDATION

Published by

The Islamic Foundation
Markfield Conference Centre
Ratby Lane, Markfield
Leicestershire, LE67 9SY, United Kingdom
Tel: 01530 244944/5, Fax: 01530 244946
E-mail: info@islamic-foundation.org.uk
publications@islamic-foundation.com
Website: www.islamic-foundation.org.uk

Quran House, P.O. Box 30611, Nairobi, Kenya

P.M.B. 3193, Kano, Nigeria

British Library Cataloguing-in-Publication Data

Bashier, Zakaria
War and peace in the life of Prophet Muhammad (peace be upon him)
1. Muhammad, Prophet, d.632 2. Muhammad, Prophet, d. 632 – Military leadership 3. War – Religious aspects – Islam 4.Peace – Religious aspects – Islam 5. Saudi Arabia – History, Military
I. Title II. Islamic Foundation (Great Britain)
297.6'3

ISBN 0 86037 520 X pbk
ISBN 0 86037 515 3 hbk

Cover/Book design & typeset: Nasir Cadir
Printed & bound in England by Antony Rowe Ltd, Chippenham, Wiltshire

بِسْمِ ٱللَّهِ ٱلرَّحْمَٰنِ ٱلرَّحِيمِ

Contents

Dedication

In all humbleness, I dedicate this work to the Gracious Soul of the Prophet, hoping to be counted one of his brothers, who will meet him at his Ḥawḍ

Transliteration Table

Arabic Consonants:

Initial, unexpressed medial and final:

ء	ʼ	د	d	ض	ḍ	ك	k
ب	b	ذ	dh	ط	ṭ	ل	l
ت	t	ر	r	ظ	ẓ	م	m
ث	th	ز	z	ع	ʻ	ن	n
ج	j	س	s	غ	gh	هـ	h
ح	ḥ	ش	sh	ف	f	و	w
خ	kh	ص	ṣ	ق	q	ي	y

Vowels, diphthongs, etc.

Short:	ـَ	a	ـِ	i	ـُ	u
Long:	ـَا	ā	ـُو	ū	ـِي	ī
Diphthongs:			ـَوْ	aw		
			ـَيْ	ay		

Foreword

We have great pleasure in publishing another valuable work on the illustrious life of the Prophet Muḥammad, by Dr Zakaria Bashier. His earlier titles in the series published by the Foundation, *Life of the Prophet in Makkah*, *Hijra*: *Story and Significance* and *Sunshine at Madinah*, have received wide acclaim from both scholars and general readers. All these titles draw on original Arabic sources and show wide familiarity with recent works in the field. In exploring effectively and energetically the various aspects and dimensions of the Prophet's life, Zakaria Bashier's focus is on establishing the relevance of the Prophet's role model for our lives. In so doing, his works transcend the ordinary writings on the subject which are concerned mainly with relating a factual account of the life and achivements of the Prophet. Zakaria Bashier's works draw us closer to this exemplary man, his life-enriching teachings, his noble Companions, and above all, the blessed mission of Islam. Reading these, one gets a fair idea of how the Qur'ān and the Prophet's guidance helped transform the notorious, lawless Arab bedouins into embodiments of virtues discipline and leadership. His writings bring into sharper focus the unassuming Prophet Muḥammad (peace be upon him) and his selfless Companions who never hesitate to sacrifice all that they had for the sake of Allah and for the cause of Islam.

This latest addition to the series entitled *War and Peace in the Life of the Prophet Muḥammad* (peace be upon him) whilst retaining all the best features of his earlier writings on *Sīrah*, has immediate relevance by way of its solid refutation of the misperception that Islam is inextricably linked with violence. More remarkably, this volume dismisses the Orientalists' claim about the disparity between the Prophet's Makkan and Madīnan phases of life. There was never any inconsistency in the Prophet's words and deeds, as he preached and practised the same ideals of co-existence and freedom of faith in Makkah as well as in Madīnah . This truth is brought home with greater force and clarity by Zakaria Bashier's insightful elucidation of verses 5 and 29 of *Sūrah al-Tawbah* which allow Muslims to wage war if necessary. The conclusion reached by him is that peaceful co-existence with other faiths is the rule in Islam and war is only an exception. Islam sanctions war only in self-defence or against tyrannical rulers. All the major battles in the early history of Islam are studied in the wider context of Islamic teachings on war and peace. In the same light peace treaties and delegations sent by the Prophet to various rulers are also examined. In sum, it is a substantial work on *Sīrah* for which Zakaria Bashier deserves our thanks and appreciation.

The present work could rightfully be regarded as the concluding volume of Zakaria Bashier's earlier three works on *Sīrah* and the reader will get a full picture of the extraordinary life and contribution of the Prophet Muḥammad (peace be upon him) if all the four volumes are studied in proper sequence.

I take this opportunity to thank the Foundation production team, especially Br Nasir Cadir for ensuring the publication of this title. May Allah reward all those who helped in its production and enable us to emulate the Prophet's role model. (Amin)

28 Ramadan 1426H
31 October 2005 CE

M. Manazir Ahsan
Director General

Author's Introduction

One of the major charges pressed against Islam is that it is a violent religion which was spread by the sword. Quite a few of the orientalists of old and new have pressed this charge to its extreme limits, in every field of their study of Islam, and it has now been given new vogue and momentum after the sorrowful events of September 11.

The orientalists claim that what had been a peaceful and dovish Islam, in its initial Makkan phase, had suddenly become aggressive and power-seeking, when it assumed statehood in its Madīnan Phase. The Prophet (peace be upon him) himself was accused of being inconsistent in his practices in Madīnah with what he used to preach in Makkah about tolerance and freedom of religious belief, and that there is no compulsion in religion.

Be that as it may, some recent studies of this topic appeared which tried to interpret this change in the course of Islam – i.e. from being peaceful and tolerant in Makkah, to being violent and aggressive in Madīnah – by making use of the concept of Qur'ānic verses which were abrogated by Allah, Himself. It is alleged, in these recent studies, that the early Makkan Qur'ānic verses calling for religious tolerance and peaceful coexistence with the adherents of other religious faiths, especially with the People of the Book, were abrogated by the so-called verses of the sword of *Sūrah al-Tawbah* (Repentance), i.e. verses numbers 5 and 29.

> *Then when the sacred months are drawn away, slay the idolaters wherever you find them; and take them, and confine them, and lie in wait for them at every place of ambush. But if they repent, and perform the prayer, and pay* zakāh *(alms), then let them go their way.* [*al-Tawbah* 9:5]

> *Fight those who believe not in God and the Last Day, and do not forbid what God and His Messenger have forbidden, such men as practise not the religion of truth, being of those who have been given the Book, until they pay* jizyah *with willing submission, and feel themselves subdued.* [*al-Tawbah* 9:29]

This reading of the situation, which inevitably depicts Islam as a hawkish, violent religion, seems to me to be plainly mistaken. The basic position of Islam is that religious convictions can only be disseminated by means of valid arguments and persuasive proofs. No man can be made to believe sincerely in any ideas or theories through compulsion or force. For a coerced person may pretend to believe under the force of fear and intimidation, but that is not genuine faith, since it will be forsaken at the earliest chance that freedom of thought presents itself.

The theory put forward in this study [*War and Peace in the life of the Prophet Muḥammad* (peace be upon him)] is that peace and peaceful coexistence with people of other faiths is the rule and custom in Islamic *sharīʿah* and Islamic way of life. Islam resorts to war only when it is compelled to defend itself against outside aggression. Almost all the historic wars waged by Islam can be construed as being just wars launched in self-defense, or against tyrant rulers and regimes under which men, women and children were oppressed and made powerless, be they Muslim or non-Muslim. Especially, war is construed as legitimate against tyrants and dictators who prevent the right of man to worship God Almighty freely and without fear or intimidation. It does not matter in Islam which religion these oppressed men, women and children are professing. They do not have to be Muslims; they could be Jews or Christians or followers of any other religious denomination, especially if it is deemed to be divinely revealed.

I started writing this manuscript in the summer of 1990, when I was visiting the Islamic Foundation, Markfield. But before I finished it, I had to return to Khartoum.

As life in Khartoum was so hectic and chaotic at that time, I could not resume work on this study for many years (more than seven years altogether). In 1997, I was appointed as Vice-Chancellor of Juba University, and as that was the first and only appointment I could secure under the National Salvation Government (NSG) of al-Bashier, I thought I could not afford to fail or underachieve. So I devoted all my energies to the new post and new challenge. Not only had the manuscript of the present study suffered more delay, but I was so dispirited and exhausted that I pondered giving up the whole project of finishing the book. Then my term of office as Vice-Chancellor of Juba university was terminated and I found myself jobless in Khartoum. As I was hard pressed financially, I had to look for a job outside the country. When I obtained a job as an expert in academic planning at the University of Qatar, I was too pleased to take it. That meant more delays in the writing and editing of this manuscript, which became the longest manuscript ever to remain in my hands. Every task and every achievement has a set and ordained time during which it would be completed (*Wa Li Kulli Ajalin Kitāb*).

Subḥānaka Allāhumma wa biḥamdika, Ash-hadu an lā ilāha illā anta. Astaghfiruka wa Atūbu ilayk! Wa uṣallī wa usallim ʿalā sayyidinā Muḥammad taslīman kathīran. Wa'l-ḥamdu lillāhi Rabbi'l-'Ālamīn.

30th August 2004

Zakaria Bashier
Markfield Institute of Higher Education
Markfield, Leicestershire, UK.

CHAPTER 1

From Oppression to Liberation

1. PROLOGUE

Throughout the Makkan phase of his mission, the Prophet (peace be upon him) endured the oppression and persecution of the polytheists of Makkah, with an ever-patient forbearance. He ordered his besieged and hard-pressed Companions and followers to do the same. So, for thirteen years, their strategy was one of peaceful resistance. They argued and reasoned, they explained the theses of Islam; the promise it holds for mankind in this life and in the next. The most they allowed themselves was to engage their interlocutors in polemic; wherein they attempted to substantiate their claims, and criticize the false beliefs of the polytheists and their foolish, irrational habits of idol-worship and glorifying their ancestors.

This line of action was, in fact, prescribed by God Almighty Himself. The Prophet (peace be upon him) was not given any mandate to fight back against his persecutors at that stage. The most he could do was to permit a number of those of his followers who were exposed to the worst persecution, on account of their lack of defenders and tribal allies, to make the first minor *hijrah* to Abyssinia.

However, as soon as the Prophet (peace be upon him) assumed political authority in Madīnah and Islam came into statehood, that policy of passive resistance was reversed. Very soon after the Prophet (peace be upon him) settled in Madīnah, he received clear and unequivocal Qur'ānic permission to fight back and not passively endure the aggression and malpractices of the polytheists against him and his followers. This new policy is expressed in verses 39-40 of *Sūrah al-Ḥajj* (Pilgrimage).[1]

These verses ushered in a new phase in the history of Islam. They were revealed at a very early stage of the Madīnan period, only a few months after the Prophet's arrival there, and initiated a wholly new orientation for the Prophet (peace be upon him) and the evolving society of Muslims. From then on, the newly formed Islamic regime was geared up to face the impending armed struggle with the polytheists, championed by the Quraysh from their base in Makkah. It was time to end the tyranny of the Quraysh, and destroy their power and influence. Not only were the Quraysh responsible for opposing the Muslims, and unjustly evicting them from their homes and lands, they were also a major obstacle in the way of Islam, preventing it from freely reaching the people of Arabia.

2. PERMISSION TO WAGE WAR

In effect, verses 39-40 of *Sūrah al-Ḥajj* not only made it permissible for the Prophet (peace be upon him) to fight back against his oppressors, they even suggest to him he should take up the challenge of armed resistance to polytheists in all earnest. This is implicit in the oblique promise, that God Almighty was capable of making the Muslims victorious over their enemies, despite the obvious disparity in their respective military strengths:

> *Leave is given to those against whom war has been waged (to fight back) because they have been wronged, surely Allah is capable of giving them victory – those who have been driven out of their homes without right, only because they said our Lord is Allah. For had it not been for Allah's repelling some people by means of others, then cloisters and churches, oratories and mosques, wherein the name of Allah is much mentioned, would assuredly have been destroyed. Surely Allah helps those who help Him; surely Allah is All-Powerful, All-Mighty.* [*Al-Ḥajj* 22:39-40]

The importance of these verses of *Sūrah al-Ḥajj* cannot be overstated. As well as launching a new period for the Prophet (peace be upon him) and the Muslims, that was destined to last for the next eight years up to the opening of Makkah, these verses give first expression to the philosophy of waging war in Islam, basically, in defence of Islam and justice. But the term defence here, we must state at the outset, is used in a broad sense that will be better understood as we proceed to explicate the dynamics of the campaigns; military actions in which the Prophet was engaged. In some cases, these actions were indeed in retaliation against attacks by enemy. In other cases, the Prophet (peace be upon him) initiated military actions, for example, against the unjust and oppressive regimes bordering Arabia, whose existence and flourishing influence constituted a threat to the nascent Islamic state in Madīnah. Also, punitive campaigns were initiated against the Bedouins surrounding Madīnah, in view of their bellicose disposition and traditions of predatory raiding: the only way to deter them was to demonstrate to them that the new state of Madīnah was not an easy prey; they had to be persuaded that it would be unwise for them to consider attacking the Muslims, in hope of plunder and booty.

The disposition of the Quraysh was obviously the central concern behind these verses of *Sūrah al-Ḥajj*. In a sense, these verses amounted to a declaration of war against the Quraysh. But the Quraysh was no insignificant enemy. If the Muslims were to fight them effectively, and in the hope of victory, all the proper preparations and plans needed to be made. Within an overall strategy, every action needed to be thought out ahead of time, and every risk carefully weighted. Contingencies had to be anticipated and Muslims trained to cope with them. The strategic objectives of individual actions and the campaign as a whole had to be well-defined, and necessary precautions and preparations made to ensure success. War is always a most serious endeavour, with the gravest implications for costs in life and property, but in this instance the future of the nascent Muslim society as a whole was at stake. Therefore, meeting the challenge of war against the Quraysh demanded commitment from Muslims and morale of the very highest quality.

Verse 41 of *Sūrah al-Ḥajj*, following the verses cited above, makes it both an obligation and a privilege for the Muslims to fight in the cause of justice, and to uphold the values and norms of Islam:

> *Those who, if we establish them in the land, seek to establish* ṣalāh *and to pay* zakāh, *and they enjoin goodness and forbid evil and corruption.* [*Al-Ḥajj* 22:41]

It is clear that it is almost a necessary condition and consequence of the Muslims being established in the land, that they fight to uphold good and to establish Islamic precepts, norms and ideals in the actual reality of their social order.

Thus, seen in its historical and sociological context, waging war by the Prophet of Islam was quite a natural development from the Makkan phase. The old Christian polemic that Islam is a war-like religion is misconceived. Islam does not condole war as such, nor condole arbitrary resort to it. If anything, warring for its own sake is abhorred in the Qur'ān. But religious persecution, injustice and oppression are regarded as more abhorrent. If war becomes a necessary means of repelling aggression and removing evil and oppression, then the Muslims should not shy away from it. The military campaigns that the Prophet (peace be upon him) and his Muslim followers waged against the Quraysh, during the first eight years of the *Hijrah* era, and which culminated in the conquest of Makkah, were essentially wars of liberation with the strategic aim of containing, and then putting an end to the abuses of authority and power of the oppressive and tyrannical Quraysh.

The Prophet (peace be upon him) drew up and put into practice comprehensive, thorough and meticulous plans to achieve that aim. These plans were meant to, and did, fit into a grand strategy of security and defence for the Madīnan community. The comprehensive and effective nature of this strategy showed that the Prophet (peace be upon him), was working with very sophisticated and broad concepts of security and defence, and that he displayed a very clear vision of things to come.

His strategy was multi-dimensional, with educational, political, economic, as well as intelligence and military components. He was fully aware of the psychological and ideological consequences of particular policies, and combined these with hard-headed military tactics. The practical measures adopted by the Prophet (peace be upon him), were chiefly intended to achieve two goals:

a. To enhance the security and status of Madīnah as a *ḥaram* or religious sanctuary;

b. To put pressures on the Quraysh, that would frustrate their aims, reduce their ability to incite the Bedouins around Madīnah against the Muslims, and weaken or destroy their commercial trading within and beyond the Arabian peninsula.

3. MILITARY EXPEDITIONS (*SARĀYĀ*)

The military expeditions were perhaps the first practical measures undertaken by the Prophet (peace be upon him) to implement the new orientation in policy, commanded by the verses of *Sūrah al-Ḥajj* cited earlier.

3.1 Ḥamzah's Expedition

The first expedition, led by Ḥamzah, was dispatched barely five months after the Prophet's arrival in Madīnah, on the 12th Rabī' al-Awwal, year 13, of his mission (24th July, 622). Ḥamzah's expedition took place in Ramaḍān of the first year of the *Hijrah* (December 622). Thirty Muslims took part in the expedition, all of them exclusively of the Muhājirīn or emigrants from Makkah. They succeeded in intercepting a large commercial caravan, belonging to the Quraysh, comprising of 300 camels and their riders, led by ʿAmr ibn Hishām (Abū Jahl). However, no fighting took place, as the two groups were separated, through the influence and good offices of an Arabian leader, by the name of Majdī ibn ʿAmr, in a place known as al-ʿĀṣ on the Red Sea coast.

3.2 The Expedition of ʿUbaydah ibn al-Ḥārith

The following month, that is to say, Shawwāl of the same year, ʿUbaydah ibn al-Ḥārith of the Banū Hāshim, a first cousin of the Prophet (peace be upon him), led a second expedition, comprising twice the number of men in Ḥamzah's expedition and also exclusively made of the Muhājirīn. They too succeeded in intercepting another commercial caravan of the Quraysh, led by Abū Sufyān himself, one of the Quraysh's foremost leaders. Abū Sufyān's force consisted of two hundred camels loaded with goods. The two forces met face to face, this time with no third party to intervene, at the valley of Rābigh, on the Red Sea coast between Makkah and Madīnah. A minor skirmish took place, during which the gallant Saʿd ibn Abī al-Waqqāṣ, who later distinguished himself in leading the Muslim armies to an astonishing victory against the Persians at Qādisiyyah, shot the first arrow in Islam, fatally wounding one of the polytheists of the Quraysh. However, no full scale military engagement followed, and the two parties departed to their respective destinations.

3.3 The Expedition of Saʿd ibn Abī al-Waqqāṣ

In the next month Dhū al-Qaʿdah (January 623), a third expedition was dispatched, comprising twenty men led by Saʿd ibn Abī al-Waqqāṣ himself. They pursued a small caravan of the Quraysh, but missed it.

3.4 The Expedition of ʿAbdullāh ibn Jaḥsh

This was the most worthwhile of all the expeditions, and perhaps had the most far-reaching consequences and repercussions. It was led by ʿAbdullāh ibn Jaḥsh, a cousin of the Prophet (peace be upon him), with a small force of twelve Muslims (some sources put their number as only eight), also exclusively from the Muhājirīn. The Prophet's instructions to Ibn Jaḥsh were quite different from his previous ones which indicated the uniqueness and special character of this expedition.

Ibn Jaḥsh and his men were to head southward in the direction of Makkah. He was given a letter, but ordered not to open it until the party had travelled for two complete days. He was also told that the mission was a voluntary one. No one should be obliged to take part in it. When Ibn Jaḥsh opened the secret letter, it read: 'If you read this letter, proceed until you descend the valley of Nakhlah, between Makkah and Ṭā'if. There, watch the Quraysh, and gather for us information about them.'

Ibn Jaḥsh responded to this instruction with: 'I hear and obey.' He then informed the others that, on the orders of the Prophet (peace be upon him), they were to proceed to Nakhlah, south of Makkah on the route from Ṭā'if. None was required to participate against his will. He also told them that he himself would act on the orders of the Prophet (peace be upon him), even if he had to go it alone. However, all of the men voiced their willingness to participate. And so the expedition proceeded to Nakhlah, deep in the territory of the enemy, the farthest any Muslim force had ventured to penetrate so far. It was indeed a mission fraught with grave dangers, owing to the proximity of Nakhlah to Makkah, the fact that it lay on the Makkans' trade route to Ṭā'if, and the smallness in number of the Muslims' force. That explains the Prophet's directive, that participation in the mission should wholly be voluntary.

This expedition took place in the sacred month of Rajab, in the second year of the *Hijrah*, about seven months after the expedition led by Saʿd ibn Abī al-Waqqāṣ. During these months, other expeditions did take place, including two led by the Prophet (peace be upon him) himself. But I have not included these expeditions in this group because it formed a unity in that all of the expeditions were directed against the commercial interests of the Quraysh. No sooner had Ibn Jaḥsh and his men descended the Valley of Nakhlah, than a Quraysh caravan, evidently coming from the south (Yemen), appeared, well stocked with goods and poorly guarded, because southern routes of Quraysh trade had never before been threatened by the Muslims. It was guarded by only four men. Ibn Jaḥsh and his company attacked the caravan, killing one man by the name of ʿAmr ibn al-Ḥaḍramī, and capturing two others, while the fourth fled to Makkah. Ibn Jaḥsh took the two captives and the caravan, and hastened northwards to Madīnah, lest the Quraysh should catch up with him.

When the Prophet (peace be upon him) saw the two captives and learned of the killing of ʿAmr al-Ḥaḍramī, he was visibly displeased and said to Ibn Jaḥsh: 'I did not order you to conduct any fighting in the sacred month!'

The emphasis of the Prophet (peace be upon him) was not on fighting as such, but on fighting in the holy month of Rajab. This incident proved a major embarrassment to the Prophet (peace be upon him) initially, since it was considered scandalous to Arabian customs to conduct fighting during four holy months, of which Rajab was one. The incident caused a great row throughout Arabia. The Quraysh made the most of it in their propaganda war against the Prophet (peace be upon him) and the Muslims! 'They claimed to be religious and now they are profaning the sacred months,' they were clamouring.

The Prophet (peace be upon him) initially disassociated himself from the affair, had his stance publicly known, and refused either to deal with the captives or to accept his *khums* (or fifth of the booty). Ibn Jaḥsh and his men found themselves in a very difficult situation, and the Muslims did not make it easier for them. They rebuked and criticized them for having caused the Prophet (peace be upon him) such embarrassment.

3.5 The Qur'ānic Revelation on the Nakhlah Incident

However, the crisis was relieved by God's Grace, in the following Qur'ānic revelation:

> *They question you concerning the sacred month, and fighting therein. Say: fighting therein is a great (sin). But to bar men from the way of Allah, And uphold disbelief in Him, and the Holy Mosque and expelling its people from it, that is indeed a greater (sin) in the sight of Allah. Indeed persecution* (fitnah) *is more heinous than killing people (in the sacred month)! They will not cease to fight with you till they turn you from your religion, if they could.* [*al-Baqarah* 2: 217]

The above verse constituted a valid and most effective reply to the polemics of the Quraysh, that the Muslims, despite their claims to piety, had violated the holy month, killing and plundering their adversaries. The Quraysh, of all people, had no right to talk about sacred obligations, since they had totally disregarded the Arabian code of chivalry, by persecuting the Prophet (peace be upon him) and his followers, for no cause other than their saying: 'God is our Lord.' They had shown no regard for the fact that the Prophet (peace be upon him) and many of his followers were close relatives of theirs, as well as being men of honour and integrity. Moreover, a just war had its own rules. The Prophet (peace be upon him) and the Muslims were brought, by the verses just cited, to understand that the Quraysh intended the total annihilation of the Muslims, and that they should think more about the importance of their survival than about rules to do with the holiness of particular times or places. Their faith and their own lives, the life of the Prophet (peace be upon him), the principle of freedom from religious persecution, and the whole future of Islam, were all at stake.

The Nakhlah expedition proved to be a decisive turning-point, marking the end of light skirmishing between the Quraysh and the Muslims. More than any other encounter before it, Nakhlah intensified the frustrations of the Quraysh to a high pitch. They felt that if they were to maintain their eminence in Arabia, then they must get out to destroy the power of Muḥammad. The Prophet (peace be upon him), too, knew that he had crossed his Rubicon in his relations with the Quraysh, that he could only expect the worst from them, and that harsh, prolonged wars were ahead of him, which he must win if he was to survive at all.

4. THE RESULTS OF THE EXPEDITIONS AGAINST THE QURAYSH

As we noted, those four expeditions are grouped together even though the last one of Ibn Jaḥsh took place much later, because they were all primarily directed against the Quraysh. We now ask: did they achieve what they were meant to achieve? What were the Prophet's major objectives in launching them in the first place? It would seem that these expeditions had very decisive and quick results on the following accounts:

a. Firstly, the once thriving international commerce of the Quraysh, the mainstay and backbone of their economic prosperity, was seriously disrupted. Their trade to Syria in the north, and Yemen in the south, were blocked and rendered unsafe. The Quraysh could do little to prevent this eventuality. As for the Muslims, they stood to lose nothing by effecting this blockade. Rather, they stood to perhaps gain some provisions and wealth in order to compensate for their lost wealth, and property at Makkah, which they had been forced to leave behind. In addition, this blockade made life difficult for the Quraysh.

b. Secondly, the Quraysh's prestige among the inhabitants of Arabia at large, especially among the Bedouin tribes, was severely damaged. Some tribes who were not particularly friendly with the Quraysh, for example, Khuzāʿah who had long-standing feuds with the Quraysh, rejoiced at the humiliation that these expeditions had inflicted on the Quraysh, and began to ponder the possibility of allying with the emerging power of the Muslim community in Madīnah.

c. Thirdly, these expeditions achieved a strategic aim for the Prophet (peace be upon him), namely provoking and inciting the Quraysh to the battlefield, where their political, religious and moral authority in Arabia might once and for all be tested and defeated. Whereas the Quraysh was quite oblivious to such considerations and totally ill-informed about the growing power and preparedness of the Prophet and his camp, the Prophet (peace be upon him) had the most up-to-date information about the whereabouts of the Quraysh and their commercial caravans. The superb network of informants and intelligence at the disposal of the Prophet (peace be upon him), can be inferred from the way he masterminded the expedition of Ibn Jaḥsh, in particular, its timing, its secrecy, the location to which it was directed, and the sense of danger and anticipation associated with it.

d. Fourthly, these expeditions helped to train Muslims for combat fitness and war-readiness that would be needed in the inevitable battles ahead. More importantly, the prestige of the Quraysh and their reputation for invulnerability, were thoroughly undermined, so that the Muslims no longer feared military confrontation with the Quraysh.

e. Finally, the Nakhlah expedition brought into the hands of Muhājirīn a considerable amount of money, food provisions and maybe some armaments, all of which they were in dire need, since they had left their wealth in Makkah when forced to migrate. Those four expeditions were not the only expeditions against the Quraysh, but they were the only ones before Badr.[2]

5. EXPEDITIONS LED BY THE PROPHET IN PERSON

The Prophet (peace be upon him) is said to have led in person at least two major expeditions in those early days of Islam in Madīnah.

a. The Expedition of Waddān: This was directed chiefly at the Bedouins of Banū Ḍamrah, who as a result of this expedition were duly impressed by the personality of the Prophet (peace be upon him), and by his political and military power. They decided to become the allies of the Prophet (peace be upon him), concluded a *Muwādaʿah* (peace treaty) with him, and the Muslims returned to Madīnah, without encountering any hardship.

b. The Expedition of al–ʿAshīrah: Like that of Waddān, this expedition was directed chiefly at the Bedouins, though both expeditions had implications for the Quraysh, and it too ended in the conclusion of a *Muwādaʿah* with the Bedouin tribe of Banū Mudlij, thus, it is safe to infer that the primary motive of the expeditions, led by the Prophet (peace be upon him) in person, was not military, but political; hence the need for his presence as head of state. The presence of the tribal head or *shaykh* was required by the custom of the Bedouins, in order to dignify and secure inter-tribal agreements. For them, the Prophet (peace be upon him) was the head of the Muslim tribe, and therefore it was necessary that he be present for treaties to be concluded. The Prophet (peace be upon him) attached considerable importance to the matter of securing alliances with any power that could help defend the Muslims against their enemies. At no stage of his mission, was the Prophet (peace be upon him) without liable allies: in Makkah, it will be recalled, he was first allied to the Banū Hāshim and Banū ʿAbd al-Muṭṭalib, led by his own uncle Abū Ṭālib. When Abū Ṭālib passed away, the Prophet (peace be upon him) became temporarily allied with al-Muṭʿim ibn ʿUdayy, a non-Muslim, but a man of considerable courage and integrity, with a large and effective tribal following. Then, before the *hijrah*, the Prophet (peace be upon him) took the Pledges of the Two ʿAqabas. Very soon after he settled in Madīnah, he concluded the momentous *Ṣaḥīfah* Pact between the Anṣārs, the Muhājirīn and the Jewish tribes of Madīnah.

c. The Jewish tribes of Madīnah: When war with the Quraysh became inevitable, the Prophet (peace be upon him) actively sought new allies among the powerful tribes of the Bedouins around Madīnah. To this end, by means of the expeditions mentioned and other methods, further alliances were secured with Khuzāʿah, Banū Ḍamrah and Banū Mudlij. Over time, the numbers of the Prophet's followers were to increase tremendously. Thus it is clear that the concluding of alliances was a major element of his diplomatic policy as well as being a powerful instrument of his *daʿwah*. The Prophet (peace be upon him) was keenly aware of how and where political power lay in Arabia. He had a clear vision of how and why it should become a unified, unitary power. Within his unwavering commitment to the cause of Islam, and to the ennobling of his followers through Islam, he handled political issues with extraordinary skill and acumen.

5.1 Results of the Expeditions led by the Prophet

a. By going out to meet with the tribal chiefs, the Prophet (peace be upon him) projected himself as the political and military leader. An Arabs' chief had to make public appearances, meet frequently with his counterparts, make his person felt and his view widely known. To be able to take a public role, and to sit in public council, was considered by the Arabs of the time as an indication of good lineage and excellent manners. However, Muḥammad (peace be upon him) was not just a tribal chief or a mere statesman, he was a Prophet and the Messenger of God. His mission was to call the people to the service, and worship of the One, True God, Allah. It is his claim to Prophethood that was a reason for the Arabs around Madīnah to be drawn to him, to take a glance of him and assess his person at first hand. Many of them were instantly won over by his noble looks. Many went around affirming: 'I have seen Muḥammad, and by God, his face is decidedly not the face of a liar or an impostor,' they said.

b. The Bedouins were very appreciative of power and might. They would only respect and fear a powerful chief; they would not respect a weak or meek chief. But when they saw the great love and esteem the Prophet (peace be upon him) enjoyed among his followers, they were duly impressed, and only desired to be allied with him.

c. Those who did not choose to ally themselves with the Prophet (peace be upon him) were, nonetheless, persuaded that they should not choose to make him an enemy. We can be sure that the Prophet (peace be upon him) intended to deter those tough and war-like Bedouins accustomed to raiding and plunder as a way of life.

d. Most particularly, the Prophet (peace be upon him) aimed to secure alliances with or, failing that, the neutrality of those Bedouin tribes who lived and roamed in the area that lay between the Muslims and the Quraysh. This policy, implemented through the campaigns and expeditions led by the Prophet (peace be upon him) in person, and those led by his commanders, was an essential preparation for the impending war with the Quraysh.

e. Last but not least, these expeditions were a very powerful tool for the dissemination of information about the new state and authority of Madīnah, about its leading figures, about the nature and high purpose of its mission and its institutions. As news travels fast in the desert by word of mouth, Bedouins tribes, far and wide, came to hear about the Prophet's marches. At the very best, they began to fear and respect him, for that they were not to raid the Muslims or to ally with the Quraysh against Muslims. In this way, the image and prestige of the Quraysh was further tarnished, just as the star of the nascent Islamic society shone ever more brightly.

6. OTHER EXPEDITIONS

There were minor expeditions, but of an inconclusive nature and therefore not meriting very detailed study in the present context. Two of these minor expeditions were led by the Prophet (peace be upon him) himself. In the expedition of Bawāt, he led a contingent of two hundred Anṣārs as well as Muhājirīn, and tried, unsuccessfully, to intercept a caravan led by Umayyah ibn Khalaf. He stopped at Bawāt and then returned to Madīnah.

He led a second expedition against Kurz ibn Jābir al-Fihrī, who had raided the outskirts of Madīnah and managed to get away with some camels belonging to the Muslims. The Prophet (peace be upon him) set out immediately in hot pursuit of Kurz who was, however, able to make good his escape. When the Muslims got to the valley of Ṣafwān, in the vicinity of the wells of Badr, they stopped and camped for a few days. For this reason, some Muslim historians call this expedition, even though it involved no fighting, the first Battle of Badr.

7. THE FINAL OUTCOME OF THESE EXPEDITIONS (*SARĀYĀ*)

We can now give a clearer account of the outcome of these expeditions and their implications for:

a. The Muslim home front.
b. The standing of the Quraysh.
c. Relations with Bedouins.

a. On the home front: Through these expeditions, the Muslims learnt a new military vigorous discipline, and combat fitness. The *jihād* became instilled into them. Alongside a mobilization of resources and of the people, a great increase in solidarity was achieved, as every single Muslim acquired thorough knowledge of the terrain around Madīnah, and as far south as Nakhlah. They gained vital experience in the techniques of preparing and fighting battles, in the logistics of manpower and provisions, and the tactics of pursuit and engagement. They also got ample opportunity to know the demography of the Madīnah area, and habits, characters and disposition of the various Bedouin tribes in the vicinity and of some of the areas of desert that separated them from the Quraysh. Moreover the Muslims were able to win many strong, reliable allies, and to deter others from offensive action against them.

b. With regard to the Quraysh, the Muslims managed to amount an effective threat to the trade routes upon which the Quraysh depended, and were eventually able to disrupt about half of their trade. The standing and prestige of the Quraysh among the Arabs was thoroughly undermined, obliging them to contemplate open battle with the Muslims. Little by little the Quraysh were separated from their former allies and supporters, many of whom were won over to the Prophet (peace be upon him) and his cause. Their status as overlords in Arabia was compromised, and their reputation as models of the Arab traditions of honour and chivalry permanently eroded by their unjust and hysterical hostility towards the Muslims, and especially by their persecution of the Prophet (peace be upon him).

c. With regard to the Bedouins, the expeditions helped to win some of them as allies of the Prophet (peace be upon him), to deter others from attacking the Muslims and to deter still others from supporting the Quraysh.

In general, the Prophet (peace be upon him) set the highest ideal of a tough fighter, who was both resourceful and vigorous and also absolutely sincere and disinterested in his devotion to the cause of Islam. His superb skill as a commander and his readiness for combat, both physically and psychologically, at the advanced age of over fifty, were astonishing, and excited the highest admiration. The expeditions put the Muslims firmly on the road to victory. They afforded them ample opportunity to perfect their military skills, and to gather considerable military forces. They gained from the wealth of the Quraysh provisions as well as armaments. They became well-versed in the techniques of managing and winning battles, and acquired valuable expertise and experience in such matters as field intelligence and the management of information and psychological advantage. They had the chance to test the quality of their faith in what the power, and help of God could achieve for them. When fighting, a Muslim expected to realize either of two objectives:

a. Total victory over an unjust and belligerent enemy, or;

b. *Shahādah* (martyrdom) in the way of God knowing fully that his death is not brought on by the risk of military engagement, but only if the destined end of his fate has been reached.

8. THE PHILOSOPHY OF FIGHTING IN ISLAM

Fighting in Islam is only sanctioned within the context of *da'wah* or a calling to Islam. This means in part that it fits within a certain conceptual system, alongside religious faith, ethical norms and a world-view based on recognition and worship of the True God, Allah. Seen within that framework, fighting or waging war is not the primary concept nor is it the first priority. There are more fundamental concepts and more important priorities which must be clarified before one can meaningfully talk about war or fighting in Islam. We have already seen that the concept of fighting or waging war was totally absent during the whole of the Makkan period. Only after the *Hijrah*, and the setting up of the Islamic State in Madīnah, was fighting in the way of God prescribed and sanctioned.

Islam calls on mankind to submit to the authority of God Almighty Alone, and warns them not to associate partners with Him. The Prophet Muḥammad (peace be upon him) was commanded to exert himself to the utmost, invoking the Qur'ān, in the pursuit of this goal. This command came in one of the early Makkan revelations in which the word *jihād* is explicitly used:

> *So obey not the unbelievers but strive against them with your utmost effort, making use of the Qur'ān.* [*al-Furqān* 25:52].

Fighting in the way of God is one phase of *jihād*, a phase that was only sanctioned in the Madīnan stage, thirteen years after the commencement of the Islamic *da'wah*. Thus war or fighting is the subsidiary function of *jihād*, and *jihād* is a function of the *da'wah* to Islam. It stems from the Arabic '*jāhada*' which means 'emptying' or 'exhausting'. A man is said to have '*jihād al-nafs*' when he has exhausted his utmost effort. Thus the injunction to make *Jihād* in the way of God is basically the injunction that a Muslim should exert himself to the utmost in his efforts to bring that state of affairs described in the Qur'ān as, 'when the word of Allah is supreme'... '*ḥattā takūna kalimatu Allāhi hiya al-'ulyā*,'' not in a particular region, but the world over:

> *And fight them (the unbelievers) until religious persecution is no more, and religion is all for Allah. But if they cease, then surely Allah is Seer of what they do.* [*al-Anfāl* 8:39].

The Arabic phrase used in the above verse to refer to the enforcement of God's authority is: '*Wa yakūna al-dīnu kulluhu lil'lāh.*' This could be interpreted as the condition when non-Muslim powers accept the principle of religious freedom and totally desist from religious persecution and agree, in principle and practice that all people at any time have the full right to convert to Islam, or any other divine religion for that matter, and desist from placing any obstacles in the way of religious freedom.

Thus, in the light of this interpretation, waging war against a non-Muslim state, would only be justifiable in Islam, if that non-Muslim state resorts to oppression and practises religious persecution against its people. War will also be justified if that state seeks to impose a religion or ideology against the will of its people, because there is no compulsion in religion.

In the light of the above Qur'ānic verse, Islam seems to be committed to the view that armed resistance to injustice and oppression is sanctioned. It is the duty of the Muslims to help alleviate the suffering of the *mustaḍ'afīn* (the powerless) wherever they exist, be they Muslims or non-Muslims. By implication, a truly Muslim state will make it one of the pillars of its foreign policy to help promote the cause of liberty and justice where and wherever it can. This commitment is bound to set that Muslim state at variance with unjust and tyrannical regimes, should they exist. The odds are that it will find itself in conflict or outright war with such regimes.

Could a Muslim state be charged with aggression or belligerence on this account? If such an accusation is made it would be unjustified. If in fact a Muslim state does champion the cause of liberty and justice, could it be said, on this account, that a Muslim state can never coexist peacefully with non-Muslim states? It is conceded that a truly Muslim state would indeed be in conflict with unjust, tyrannical and oppressive regimes. But this conflict need not, at all times, assume the proportion of armed conflict or war. It is conceivable that the conflict could take the form of a cold war of words and ideology. It may, for example, take the form of severing of trade or diplomatic ties. Be that as it may, outright war cannot be ruled out. But war can be evaded if the oppressive regimes declared their willingness to improve their commitment to basic human rights and to be more sensitive to the demands of religious freedom and human dignity. Also, a Muslim state may best serve the goals of upholding the ideals of justice and liberty by embarking on policies of dialogue and negotiations, rather than war and confrontation. If the Muslims' overriding goal is the spread of the true faith in the One True God, Allah, then this cannot be brought about by war and hostilities. The only road to influence the convictions of mankind is across the bridge of dialogue and persuasion. 'There is no compulsion in religion,' declares the Qur'ān, and the power of war and coercion of mankind is very limited indeed. It is very difficult to see how humanity can be persuaded that there is just One, True God, Allah, through the use of force and coercion.

The foregoing interpretation which we suggest for the Arabic phrase: *ḥattā lā takūna fitnatan, wa yakūna ad-Dīnu kulluhu lil'lāh* is supported by other verses from the Qur'ān, which we will cite presently. But, on the other hand, it seems to be opposed by the so called '*Āyat al-Sayf*' (the verses of the sword). We will first give those verses which seem to support peaceful coexistence between Muslim and non-Muslim nations and powers, and which advocate basic human rights and liberties, before we proceed to discuss the verses of the sword, so called.

First of all, there is a group of Qur'ānic verses which clearly enjoin the Muslims to be fair-minded and peace oriented in their dealings with non-Muslims, even if the latter are lacking in justice. Moreover, these verses unequivocally shun aggression and the initiation of hostilities by the Muslims: God says in the Qur'ān:

> *Fight in the way of Allah those who fight you, but do not begin hostilities. Surely Allah loves not the aggressors. And slay them, whenever you find them, and drive them out of the places whence they drove you out, for persecution is worse than slaughter. And fight not with them at the sacred Mosque, until they first fight you, but if they fight you therein then slay them. Such is the reward of the unbelievers.* [*al-Baqarah* 2:190-191]

> *And fight them until persecution is no more, and religion is all for Allah. But if they desist, then let there be no hostility except against wrongdoers.* [*al-Baqarah* 2:193]

> *You who believe! Stand out firmly for Allah, witnesses to fair dealing. And let not the hatred of others for you make you swerve to wrong and depart from justice. But be just, that is nearest to piety.* [*al-Mā'idah* 5:8]

> *You who believe! Enter peace all of you and follow not the steps of Satan.* [*al-Baqarah* 2:208]

> *And if they incline to peace, so incline you to it, and trust in Allah.* [*al-Anfāl* 8:61]

> *Reconciliation (and settlement) is better for you.* [*al-Nisā'* 4:128]

There is also a group of Qur'ānic verses which seem to be addressed to the Prophet (peace be upon him), reminding him that religious freedom is a matter ordained by God Himself. The implications of these verses is that it is both morally wrong and practically futile to try to change the religious convictions of people by force or by waging war. There is no need for the Prophet (peace be upon him) to organize or to be excessively domineering over the recalcitrance of the unbelievers:

And if your Lord willed, all who are on the earth would have believed together. Would you (Muḥammad) *compel men until they become believers?* [*Yūnus* 10:99]

So remind them! You are but a reminder, you are not a controller over them. [*al-Ghāshiyah* 88:21-22]

The methods of the Prophet (peace be upon him), in seeking to spread his faith, did not include coercion or intimidation, manipulation or domination. His methods were essentially reasoning by varied ways and convincing arguments, and all available means of legitimate persuasion. He could appeal to common sense, to ethical ideals which are highly cherished and valued by all decent human beings, or he could appeal to noble and positive passions. It is dubious techniques of manipulating the affairs of men, exploiting their illegitimate desires, interests, fears or animosities, playing up rivalries and unwarranted ambitions, that he should totally shun. Nor did his methods embrace domination, exploitation and control. It was not his ultimate goal to seize power and authority for their own sake, but to use it to transform people's souls and lives so that they would form a community and society of brotherhood and equity, to bring about and realize God's Will and Purpose for mankind.

8.1 The Fight to Liberate the Oppressed

The Qur'ānic command, that religious belief can not be changed by the use of force or by waging war, is not incompatible with the policy of declaring war against tyrannical and oppressive regimes. As a matter of fact, the Muslims were commanded by God to fight in the cause of human liberty and dignity. They were even reminded of the days when they themselves were powerless and oppressed. It was through God's Help and Grace that they became victorious over their former oppressors. Would they not then desire to fight for the sake of *al-mustaḍʿafin* (the powerless)? It would indeed be very strange and unacceptable that those who had suffered aggression, and tasted the bitterness of injustice, should not or would not come to the aid of the oppressed; even more unthinkable that they themselves turn to aggression or oppression should they assume political power and authority.

God, in the Qur'ān, enjoins the Muslims to fight in the cause of human emancipation:

> *How is it with you that you do not fight in the way of God, and the abased, feeble men, women and children who say: Our Lord, bring us forth from this city, whose people are unjust, and appoint to us protector from You, and appoint to us from You a help.* [*al-Nisā'* 4:75]

The fight to oppose religious persecution is deemed essential for the progress and well-being of humanity at large. Hence the duty of the Muslims to be involved in it. This notion is presented in the Qur'ān in the context of survival of human civilization and progress. The will to fight in this cause is deemed, in the Qur'ān, essential if evil and destructive powers, inculcated in the dark side of human passions, are to be thwarted.

> *For had it not been for Allah's repelling some men by means of others, cloisters and churches, oratories and mosques, wherein the name Allah is much mentioned, would assuredly have been pulled down.* [*al-Ḥajj* 22:40]

This verse highlights the fact that war is justifiable as a means of survival, a means of repelling and combating much worse possibilities. As the Qur'ān had indicated, persecution and discriminating against people on account of their religions, is a greater evil than war. Also the domination of evil, tyrannical powers is a greater evil than war. The Qur'ān told the Muslims, in clear unequivocal language, that if they lacked the will to fight against injustice and oppression, then a great *fitnah* (religious oppression) and corruption would spread on the surface of the earth. It even went so far as to threaten them of dire consequences, both in this life and in the next, if they fail to meet the commandment to answer the call to *jihād*:

> *O you who believe, what is the matter with you? That when it is said to you 'go forth in the way of Allah', You sink down heavily to the earth, do you prefer the life of this world to the Hereafter? But little is the comfort if this life, as compared with the hereafter. Unless you go forth, He will punish you with a grievous punishment. And instead of you, He will substitute another people and you will not hurt Him anything. For Allah is Powerful over everything.* [*al-Tawbah* 9:38-39]

In *Sūrah al-Tawbah* (Repentance), we find another Qur'ānic verse which threatens the Muslims that if they prefer their comfort and that of their families and friends, and so become unresponsive to the call to *jihād*, then they might expect the worst from God:

> *Say* (O Muḥammad): *If your fathers, your sons, your brothers, your clan, and the wealth you have acquired, and the goods for which you fear that there will be no sale, and the dwellings you love – if these are dearer to you than Allah and His way, then wait till Allah brings His command. Allah guide not the people of ungodliness.* [*al-Tawbah* 9:24]

The way of *jihād* has always been depicted as the Muslims' way to success and succour in this world and the next. It has also been commended by countless sayings of the Prophet (peace be upon him) and his rightly guided Caliphs. The Qur'ān commands the way of *jihād* in forceful and vivid language, which takes account of the fact that many of the early Muslims were traders:

> *O you who believe! Shall I lead you to a commerce that shall deliver you from a painful chastisement? You shall believe in Allah and His Messenger, and struggle in the way of Allah with your wealth and yourselves. That will be better for you if you but knew.* [*al-Ṣaff* 61:10-11]

In the foregoing we hope to have shown that *jihād* and fighting in the way of God is not just meant to safeguard the Muslims' homeland and defend their rights to live in freedom and dignity, worshipping the One True God, Allah, without fear of molestation. It is also commanded in order to defend the same rights for mankind, the two objectives, internal and external, are by no means contradictory; rather, they are complementary. Should the Muslim states allow unjust and tyrannical regimes which deny their people religious freedom to thrive around their boundaries unchecked, then its very security, defence and indeed its survival would be seriously threatened and jeopardized. Taking the offensive against such regimes, if the situation so demands, is part and parcel of the overall defence commitment of the Muslim state.

The above interpretation of the doctrine of *jihād* would appear to be incompatible with the so-called *Āyat al-Sayf*, to which we referred earlier. As a matter of fact, there is a school of Muslim thinkers who believe that *Āyat al-Sayf* (the verse of the sword) were revealed in *Sūrah al-Tawbah*, much later than the other *sūrahs* in which other *jihād* verses are found, so they have abrogated or otherwise superseded all earlier Qur'ānic verses on the issue.

8.2 Āyat al-Sayf (Verses of the Sword)

The verses of the sword (*Āyat al-Sayf*) are interpreted as predominant and overriding by the hard-liners among Muslim thinkers, as also by some orientalists who favour this interpretation because they give substance to the view which they are inclined to hold, that Islam is a militant religion, prone to violence and aggression. Let us first give the text of these verses: one of them is verse number 29 of *Sūrah al-Tawbah*.

> *Fight those who believe not in Allah and the Last Day, and do not forbid what Allah and His Messenger have forbidden – such men as practice not the religion of Truth, from amongst the people of the Book, until they pay Jizya with willing submission, and feel themselves subdued.* [*al-Tawbah* 9:29]

Some Orientalists[3] have taken this verse as signifying the impossibility of peaceful coexistence and co-operation between Islam and the outside world. They see it as implying that a Muslim state is committed to be in constant war with non-Muslim forces until they (a) accept Islam, or (b) pay *jizyah* (a defence tax, against Non-Muslims) and thus become subdued, or (c) are utterly defeated and destroyed.[4]

On the other hand, the hardliners among Muslim thinkers claim that this verse of the sword is overriding because it is part of *Sūrah al-Tawbah* which is one of the very last *sūrahs* to be revealed. They claim that earlier verses reflect earlier stages in the history of Islamic *daʿwah*, stages which had subsequently been superseded by the prevalence of new circumstances and new legislation. But this line of argument seems quite untenable, if pressed in every case, and without producing tangible evidence that a change in the direction of legislation had been made, either by abrogation or otherwise modifying the previous legislation. It would indeed be very damaging to the Islamic *daʿwah* if the above line of argument is pressed without further evidence. One of the consequences of adopting the above line of thinking would be the cancellation of all the *sharīʿah*, excepting those aspects of it revealed in the very last days of the Prophet (peace be upon him). To evade such a possibility, the Prophet (peace be upon him) used to point out promptly and very clearly any verse of the Qur'ān which God had abrogated. The practice of verse abrogation was governed by very exact and specific rules, and it is one of those topics with respect to which independent personal opinion has no role to play. Succession in time alone does not constitute a valid reason for abrogation. The difference in the content of Qur'ānic verses dealing with the same issues, e.g. fighting in the way of God or *jihād*, revealed at different times in succession, is to be understood by jurists in the light of (a) the principles and ultimate goals of the *sharīʿah* (b) previous Qur'ānic revelation unless abrogation had been explicitly pointed out, the requirement here being that of harmony and consistency, (c) the reason behind the revelation (*asbāb nuzūl al-Āyah*), (d) the change in the situation and times especially when these tend to militate against the reasons and wisdom behind the earlier revelation in the historical development of the Islamic society and state. The mild verses revealed before the verses of the sword could be viewed as alternative policies and strategies that continue to be valid and which are to be practised should the circumstances require a less militant handling than the verse of the sword. Moreover, some of these mild verses consist of valid and very broad principles of universal applicability, and therefore need not be abrogated just because some stronger verse was revealed later, unless otherwise explicitly stated.

Indeed, the situation with regard to *jihād* and war is not a typical one in that it appears to consist of two apparently contrary tendencies: one towards fighting and waging war in the way of God, the other towards kindness, mercy and tolerance. In many major issues, this same feature of *sharīʿah* seems to be present: there are always two strands of attitude, apparently contradictory but actually fused into a harmonious whole; perhaps comparable to two electrical poles, one negative, the other positive, which working together supply useful energy. Thus, in *sharīʿah*, there is always the passing temporal aspect of any legislation and also the positive, eternal one. The temporal one is needed to cater for the changing, earthly human conditions reflective of man's weakness, evil intentions and his base passions of envy, greed and aggression, while the eternal, more permanent aspect embodies the Divine will and purpose for man, stating as it does normally universal principles.

In the issue of war and peace, these two aspects are there. They complement each other, and they naturally fuse together to give a consistent policy of war and peace. Yet peace is clearly the more basic, more permanent option in Islam, while war is only necessitated by man's unavoidable passions for aggression and injustice. That peace is the foremost overriding option in Islam is clearly demonstrated by the following considerations:

a. *As-Salām* (or peace) is one of the Beautiful Names of God.

b. It is well known that *salām* (peace) is the ordinary salutation of the Muslims, every time they meet or depart. *Salām* is also the salutation of the Muslims in the Hereafter.

c. After each of the five obligatory daily prayers, a Muslim's supplication and *du'ā'* is:

'O Lord! You are the Peace.
All peace proceeds from You.
All peace returns unto You.
Help us to live in peace, O our Lord.
Allow us to enter the Paradise which is Your lodge, the lodge of peace.'

d. Paradise itself is depicted essentially as the abode of peace, in the gracious Qur'ān:

Surely this is the path of Your Lord, Straight, We have detailed the verses (thereof); For those people who take heed For them is the abode of peace with their Lord. And He is their Protector for that they were doing... [*al-An'ām* 6:126-127]

The ultimate goal to which Islam is calling humanity is to lead them to the abode of peace. God says in the Qur'ān:

And Allah calls to the abode of peace, and leads whom He will to the straight path. [*Yūnus* 10:25]

War as envisaged in the verses of the sword, and indeed in many other contexts, is far from diminishing this fundamental, unshakable commitment to peace as the permanent, ultimately desirable reality, as a necessary means to ensure and secure the right of everyone to live in peace. But peace cannot be achieved if tyrannical powers, and agents of oppression, evil and ungodly religions and cults are allowed a free hand over the affairs of men. Where such evil powers tend to prevail, then it is the sacred duty of Muslims to resist them and indeed engage them in the battlefield, with the aim of destroying them and their power bases.[5]

9. THE VERSES OF THE SWORD AND THE PEOPLE OF THE BOOK

We have alluded to the two aspects of the *sharīʿah*, the temporal and the eternal. Through its temporal aspect it remains in touch with, concerned with, and interacting with, the changing, fluid human condition of this life. But through the eternal aspect, the *sharīʿah* expresses God's last will and purpose for man. Thus it would be a gross mistake to hold the view either that all of *sharīʿah* rules and injunctions are absolute or that they are all relative in the sense of being history-bound. The right view is the balanced one that both aspects are there together always, thus making it uniquely possible for the *sharīʿah* to be both the eternal, unchangeable will of God Almighty, and at the same time malleable and flexible, suited to the changing conditions and circumstances of human development on this earth.

What is shocking to many regarding the verses of the sword is that one of them is not directed against the Arab polytheists, towards whom the Qur'ān had adopted a hard, uncompromising attitude from the start, but against the People of the Book, i.e. Jews, Christians and Magians. The prevailing attitude towards *Ahl al-Kitāb* (People of the Book) is one of tolerance and magnanimity. The Qur'ān enjoins that they be allowed to live in peace, practise their religions in freedom and that they be protected by the Muslims, if they opt to come under the protection of Muslims, by paying a special tax towards that end called *al-jizyah*. Moreover, the Qur'ān has in fact enjoined pro-active tolerance, charity and love to be shown to those People of the Book, who showed themselves to be peacefully inclined towards the Muslims, and did not initiate any hatred or hostilities against them. This line of policy regarding the People of the Book, is expressed in many verses of the Qur'ān:

> *God forbids you not, with regard to those who did not fight you on account of your faith, nor did they drive you out of your homes, that you may deal kindly and justly with them. For God loves those who are prone to justice…* [*al-Mumtaḥinah* 60:8]

> *If they withdraw from you and do not fight you, and offer you peace, then Allah has opened no way for you against them.* [*al-Nisā'* 4:90]

Far from permitting the Muslims to wage war against the People of the Book, the Qur'ān forbids the Muslims even to utter harsh words, when engaged with them in arguments or polemics.

> *And argue not with people of the Scripture, save in the fairer manner, except for those of them that do wrong, and say 'We believe in what has been sent down to us, and has been sent down to you; And our God and your God is one, and unto Him we have surrendered.'* [*al-ʿAnkabūt* 29:46]

Qur'ānic verses, such as the ones cited above, are expressive of the permanent, overriding norms and rules that govern the relation of Muslims with the People of the Book. The verse of the sword, number 29 of *Sūrah al-Tawbah*, is thus a departure from those fundamental, permanent norms. The hardened attitude of this verse of the sword pertains more to the temporal aspect of *sharīʿah*, in the context of inter-communal relations with the People of the Book. This is not to be taken to mean that the verse of the sword is relative. It is perfectly universal; enforceable whenever circumstances demand its enforcement and application. It is an exception to fight the People of the Book rather than the rule. Verse 46 of *Sūrah al-ʿAnkabūt* above, clearly envisages such as exception… 'except for those of them that do wrong.'

When the Prophet (peace be upon him) first descended on Madīnah, his relations with the People of the Book, namely the Jews, since no Christians or Magians lived there, were very cordial. But soon afterwards they began to sour and tensions began to mount. Then tribe after tribe of the Jews of Madīnah became hostile to the Prophet (peace be upon him), as they saw him rise in power and prosperity, and succeed in spreading the message of Islam far and wide, scoring decisive victories over his enemies. Their place of pride and eminence in Madīnah, and in Arabia at large, were compromised and later undermined. They then embarked on the road of confrontation, and became involved in intrigues and conspiracies against the Prophet (peace be upon him) and the Muslims. Not only this, but they waged a war of slant and slander against the Muslims, and ultimately joined hands with the polytheists of the Quraysh in waging direct war against the Muslims, during the Battle of the Trench (al-Khandaq). Thus, the rules of the game were changed, the Prophet (peace be upon him) unsheathed the sword against them, because that was the path they chose to follow in their relations with the Muslims, in total disregard for the friendly approach and kindness which the Prophet (peace be upon him) had shown towards them, and despite the pact (*ṣaḥīfat al-Madīnah*) which they signed with him.

The theory proposed by some militant Muslim thinkers on the issue, namely that the verse of the sword in question (No. 29 of *al-Tawbah*) is in fact overriding, on account of its being revealed later in time than the other more lenient verses, is clearly untenable:

First of all, the verse of the sword indicates that it is directed, not against all the People of the Book without discrimination, but against those whom war is to be waged who are carefully delineated as:

a. Not believing in God and the Hereafter.
b. They do not forbid what God has forbidden.
c. They do not accept the true religion.
d. Furthermore they are pointed out as a group within *Ahl al-Kitāb* '*min Ahl al-Kitāb*'.

The Arabic article (*min*) clearly indicates 'some', thus, not all the People of the Book are being meant by the verse of the sword.

This line of interpretation is borne out by the actual practice of the Prophet (peace be upon him) in his conflict with the People of the Book.

a. Firstly, he never waged war, nor even threatened war against the Christians of Arabia, especially the Christian Arabian tribe of

Banū Taghlub in northern Arabia. It is doubtful if he threatened the Christians of Najrān by the use of force if they did not pay *jizyah*, although, of course, he had asked for it and they agreed to pay. However, the case with Banu Taghlub was different in this respect, in that they were not even asked to pay *jizyah*.

b. Secondly, even when open hostilities with the Jews of Madīnah broke out the Prophet (peace be upon him) never attacked them, all at once, nor did he attack them arbitrarily and without a reason. In every case, he attacked only a particular group, in retaliation against their misdeeds and aggressive designs against himself, while sparing the other peaceful groups. There was never an all-out war against all the Jews indiscriminately, let alone such a war against all the People of the Book, in general, Jews as well as Christians!

Thus, this verse of the sword could not, under any interpretation, be taken as warranting an all-out war against the People of the Book. Nor could it be interpreted, as some orientalists and some militant Muslims would like it to be interpreted, as an abrogation of all previous legislation concerning the relationship of Muslims with the People of the Book. The dominant norms governing that relationship were ones of pro-active tolerance and cordiality, as long as they abided by the spirit of peaceful co-operation and coexistence. Muslims and the People of the Book have thereafter, coexisted peacefully together for many centuries. This is a testimony of the tolerant views expressed about them in the Qur'ān and the *sunnah*. If the twentieth century has been characterized by tensions and conflicts between Muslims and the People of the Book in such places as Palestine, India, Philippines and Lebanon, it is because evil and sinister forces were stirring things up and instigating enmity and hatred between Muslims and their non-Muslim compatriots from amongst the People of the Book. Otherwise, the Muslims and the People of the Book, especially the Christians, would have lived together, visiting each other's homes, intermarrying and mingling together for social, cultural and commercial purposes. Last but not least, the verses of the Sword reflected a special historical stage in the relationship of the Muslims with the Jews of Madīnah and later on against the Byzantine Christians of the Roman empire, when they started to amass their soldiers at the northern frontiers of the Muslim state. It was never directed against the peaceful groups: (a) the Christians of Abyssinia, (b) the Christians of Najrān, (c) or the Christians of the northern Arabia tribe of Banū Taghlub.

Thus, the verses of the sword, though of course an eternally valid and universal Qur'ānic revelation, is reflective of a temporal phase in the relationship of the Muslims with the People of the Book; it is not an overriding rule applicable irrespective of whether or not the People of the Book were peaceful or otherwise.

10. EPILOGUE: THE PROPHET OF MERCY AND THE PROPHET OF WAR

The Prophet Muḥammad (peace be upon him) is described as '*Nabīy al-raḥmah wa nabīy al-malḥamah*,' i.e. the Prophet of mercy and the Prophet of combat. As we have explained, in the arguments above, these two epithets are not necessarily contradictory: rather, they are complementary. The wars which the Prophet (peace be upon him) launched during his life were means of *daʿwah* and were carried out in the context of his religious and spiritual mission to liberate humanity from the tyranny of false gods, and oppression of unjust systems and regimes. The wars of the Prophet (peace be upon him) were almost all defensive, in the broad sense of the word (defensive), to which we have been alluding.

These wars were never fought in the spirit of personal or national glory, nor were they carried out with a view to material gains. They were fought in the way of God, so that religious persecution was no more and religion became totally a godly affair. Religion could not be exploited by the force of tyranny or superstitions. The Muslims were commanded, by the Qur'ān, to go to war if need be, so as to remove the obstacles of tyranny and oppression, and clear the way for the freedom of man to worship God Almighty Alone.

That Prophet Muḥammad is '*Nabīy al-raḥmah*' is attested to by no lesser testimony than the Qur'ān itself. God said: '*We have not sent you save as mercy unto mankind.*' [*al-Anbiyā*' 21:107]

However, no equivalent Qur'ānic text exists to the effect that the Prophet (peace be upon him) is also a warrior Prophet. But Qur'ānic exhortations to the Prophet (peace be upon him) to fight in the way of God and to wage all-out war against the Arabian polytheists are abound in the Qur'ān. Yet the discrepancy in the relative weight of the two epithets of '*Nabīy al-raḥmah*' and '*Nabīy al-malḥamah*' is not to be lost. We venture to say that the first epithet is the more fundamental and the more expressive of the essence of Muḥammad's mission, personality and career. It is the more permanent, everlasting definition of his essence and reality.

Thus war is merely a passing, temporary instrument of his *daʿwah* and policy. War had been necessitated by certain circumstances and contingencies. If these circumstances and contingencies ceased to exist, so would war become obsolete, according to the prevalence of altogether new conditions. The concept of a warrior Prophet is not alien to the Judaic tradition or history (witness the careers of David and Solomon). Nor was it abhorrent to the Abrahamic tradition. It was only uncongenial to the particular mission of Jesus and of his immediate predecessors, John the Baptist and Zachariah of the Holy Altar. They were passive victims of the violent, soulless Israelites of the time.

The murdering of Zachariah and his son John, and the attempt on the life of Jesus by the forces of evil amply showed, I think, that changing times and human conditions both demanded and called for the resumption of the Prophet-warrior tradition of Judaism. However, the concepts of mercy, love and tolerance emphasized in the mission of Jesus were neither lost nor wasted. They were incorporated in the eternal mission of Muḥammad (pbuh), in his superior capacity as '*Nabīy al-raḥmah*' (i.e. The Prophet of Mercy).

It is indeed remarkable that a man of such gentle nature, of such pacific and friendly disposition, as Muḥammad was during his whole life until the age of fifty-three, should suddenly take to the battlefield and become involved in military challenges and conflicts, and even more remarkable that he emerged victorious. With the possible exception of the Battle of Uḥud, which was not a decisive defeat, the Prophet (peace be upon him) was a victor throughout his military career. Nevertheless, it is the portrait of the Prophet (peace be upon him) as the gentlest and mildest of all men that has survived in the *sīrah* sources (i.e. Life of the Prophet) and is narrated over and over again. The violent phase of his life and career did not overshadow or compromise his most gentle nature:

> He was neither gruff, nor impolite nor was he taken to raising his voice like a hawker in the market-place. If he passed by, a flaming candle would no more than flicker owing to the serenity of gait; and if he walked over reeds, not a sound would come from below his feet. He never used obscene language. Through Him, the Almighty God opened eyes that were blind, ears that were deaf, and hearts that were sealed.[6]

Not only is it clear that he was quite averse to war and violence by disposition and style for the greater part of his life, it is also perfectly clear that he never used war as a tool of personal ambitions, aggrandisement or other material interests. The conclusion, therefore, inescapable that, in waging the wars he did, he was constrained into doing so by the realities and necessities of his religious and political mission, that is, by the need and obligation to fulfil God's commandments and achieve His will and purpose for man at the time. Moreover, the forces of evil would not leave the Muslims alone, but were adamant in their determination to destroy them.

That eventually also made military confrontation inescapable. Throughout the last three centuries that witnessed the decline of Muslim religious and political power, the military dimension of the Prophet (peace be upon him) was totally ignored. Through decline and weakness, the Muslims of modern times came very close to losing their hearts and spirits. They clamoured for peace at any cost or any price, even if that meant a dishonourable and unconditional surrender to a cruel and ruthless enemy. They failed to see that, in certain circumstances, preparing for a possible war and demonstrably possessing the will to fight is the Muslims' best defence against their enemy. Otherwise, the Muslims will be easy targets for the aggressive attacks of their enemies; 'sitting ducks' for the enemy to shoot at, to use a phrase which Shaykh Ahmad Deedat, the celebrated Muslim thinker and lecturer, was very fond of repeating. The Qur'ān has repeatedly warned the Muslims against such slackening and failure of spirit vis-à-vis their enemies, warned them against neglecting the exhortation to *jihād* and being content with dishonourable peace.

> *So do not faint and call for peace, when you should be the uppermost, and Allah is with you and He will not deprive you of your labours.* [*Muḥammad* 47:35]

Muslims today are subjected to the worst sorts of victimization, oppression and domination, yet they fail to resort to *jihād*, with the exception of a few cases, and thus continue to be the target of the aggression of their enemies. Worse still, the malicious, but very powerful and effective propaganda machines of these enemies are portraying them as terrorists and aggressors. So powerful and so effective is this campaign of the anti-Islamic mass media, that the Muslims are cowed into a passive defensive posture. Had they heeded the repeated calls of the Qur'ān to the legitimacy of *jihād* for the purposes of self-defence, and in defence of justice and liberty, and had they emulated the Prophet Muḥammad (peace be upon him), they could not have found themselves in the pitiful state of affairs in which they are now living.

We end this chapter with the general conclusion to be drawn from the above discussion. Far from being apologetic or polemical, our construal of the Islamic theory of *jihād* and peace is that it should be considered the normal state of affairs for Muslims to peacefully coexist with the People of the Book in honour, dignity, mutual trust and reciprocated equality and friendship. But should the People of the Book revert to aggression and enmity, then it would be quite cowardly and reprehensible for the Muslims to shy away from the prospects of military engagement and confrontation. To clamour for peace in these circumstances is tantamount to an unconditional and cowardly surrender. It is in the light of such unfavourable conditions that we should understand the Qur'ān's repeated calls to the Muslims, never to abandon the preparations for the engagement of their enemy under all circumstances of war and peace:

> *Make ready against them all that you can of (armed) force, and of horses tethered, that you may terrify thereby the enemy of Allah and your enemy, and others besides them that you know not.* [*al-Anfāl* 8:60]

Thus, *jihād*, in the broad sense of the word, which means to exert oneself to the utmost of one's effort and ability, is a way of life for a Muslim community. It is to be followed in times of war and times of peace – particularly times of peace because it is an essential prerequisite of waging *jihād* in the narrow military sense. It is also a method for successful nation-building, which is based on the solid foundation of totally developed, trained and mobilized individuals. Underscoring this interpretation, the Prophet (peace be upon him) said:

> Whosoever died and he never participated in a military campaign, nor told himself of such participation, he would die and a residue of hypocrisy still in his heart.[7]

The Prophet (peace be upon him) is also reported to have said:

> Whenever a group of Muslims abandoned *jihād*, and became totally absorbed in cultivating the land and the raising of cattle, then God would impose humiliation and abasement upon them, and would not remove it, until they return to their religion, and be ready for *jihād* in self-defence.[8]

CHAPTER 2

The Great Epic of Badr: An Astounding Victory of Islam

1. BADR, THE FIRST TASTE OF DECISIVE VICTORY

Badr, was no ordinary historical incident, nor was it an isolated event in the Prophet's career. In a sense, no Islamic struggle will be complete or manage to achieve its final goal of victory over the forces of evil and unbelief without finding its Badr. Thus viewed, Badr becomes a permanent feature of the Prophetic paradigm of *jihād*, or struggle, in the way of God Almighty. In other words, Badr, is an essential stage in any genuine and successful Islamic struggle.

In order to help the reader grasp and appreciate the importance of Badr in the Prophet's career, we must try to answer the following questions:

a. What were the reasons and causes that led to the Battle of Badr?

b. How did Badr take place?

c. What were the striking features of that fateful encounter with the Quraysh at Badr?

d. Why did the Muslims emerge victorious, and the Quraysh and the unbelievers defeated and humiliated?

e. What were the most decisive consequences of that battle?

f. What lessons and morals can the student of history draw from it?

2. THE CAUSES OF BADR

As to the causes that made Badr inevitable, they are not difficult to seek. Badr was the logical culmination of the Islamic *daʿwah* and movement, initiated by the Prophet (peace be upon him) some fourteen hundred years ago in Makkah. Every event and development in the struggle that ensued between the Muslims and the Quraysh, because of the inception of Islam, was building in the direction of Badr: the challenge and provocation posed by the new Islamic world-view to the vested interests of the Quraysh, and to their vantage position in pre-Islamic Arabia; the conflict that ensued between the two parties; the eviction of the Muslims from Makkah; together with the appropriation of their wealth and homes; the *hijrah* to Madīnah; and last but not least, the Qur'ānic permission for the Muslims to fight back, revealed immediately after the *hijrah* to Madīnah; all these events were building up towards Badr. Before the granting of permission, the Muslims could not engage their adversaries in the battlefield. The permission to fight back was immediately followed by other Qur'ānic verses, exhorting Muslims to fight back in self defence and instituting *jihād* as a permanent major strategy of the Muslims' struggle against evil and unbelief. These other Qur'ānic revelation verses made it clear, that evil and unbelief were not passing features of reality, but a permanent one. Moreover, the encounter with evil is inevitable, because evil forces are, by their very nature, aggressive, uncompromising and provocative. They seek to eradicate goodness and godliness from life by every possible means in their possession. The efforts to avoid a showdown with evil forces are futile, because they sooner or later will enforce such a showdown, unless the forces of righteousness surrender to them; God forbid.

The Prophet's expeditions and *sarāyā*, which are discussed in the first chapter, perfectly prepared the ground for Badr. The trade routes of the Quraysh were effectively blocked or interrupted. With the Quraysh commerce disrupted, many Bedouin tribes, especially the powerful Khuzāʿah, though still unbelievers, were won over to the side of the Prophet (peace be upon him), as allies against the Quraysh.

Meanwhile, the Muslims' exodus from Makkah was successfully completed and their nascent state in Madīnah was secured, not merely as a set of rules or laws, or even as a set of formal institutions and policies, but firmly established in the hearts and minds of the vast majority of the inhabitants of the city, notwithstanding the enmity of the Madīnan Jews and Hypocrites.

However, the immediate cause of the Battle of Badr was the Muslims' pursuit of a Quraysh commercial caravan, coming from Syria, and led by none other than Abū Sufyān himself. Abū Sufyān, the head of the Quraysh opposition to Islam, managed to dodge his Muslim pursuers and arrived safely, with the caravan intact, in Makkah.

When he arrived in Makkah, Abū Sufyān found the Makkans fully alerted, and mobilized for war against the Muslims, having received news about the Muslim offensive against their caravan. He was there in time to join the army, in fact to assume its command.

3. HOW DID THE BATTLE TAKE PLACE?

The original pledge the Madīnans gave to the Prophet (peace be upon him) was just to defend him against any attack. The situation had changed. So, the Prophet (peace be upon him) called a *Shūrā* Council. He asked: 'O People! Give me your counsel.' One by one, the leaders of Muhājirīn spoke supporting the Prophet (peace be upon him), and assuring him of their ability to fight the Quraysh and defeat them. Abū Bakr, ʿUmar and al-Miqdād ibn ʿAmr, all of them spoke very enthusiastically in support of the proposal that they should engage their Quraysh adversaries. But the Prophet (peace be upon him) again repeated: 'Give me your counsel, O people!'

Saʿd ibn Muʿādh, the celebrated Anṣār leader, sprang to his feet and said: 'Perhaps we are the men you mean, O Messenger of God.' 'Yes,' said the Prophet (peace be upon him). 'We have faith in you, and we believe what you have told us is the truth, and we have testified to that; and we have given our firm pledge to hear and obey!' So do what you will, and we will be with you. For by Him Who has sent you with the truth, if you were to plunge into that sea, we would do the same, not a single man amongst us would stay behind," said Saʿd ibn Muʿādh.

The Prophet (peace be upon him) was indeed very pleased to hear the speech of Saʿd ibn Muʿādh, the foremost chief of the Aws, and the most gallant amongst them.

The holding of this council, amidst the unusual atmosphere of the impending threat of war, is both a tribute to the Prophet's resoluteness and keenness of purpose, and also a hallmark of that unmistakable prophetic genius and acumen in leadership and statesmanship. By this act of *shūrā* (consultation), the Prophet (peace be upon him) had both underwritten and strongly emphasized the principle of mutual consultation and *shūrā* and at the same time consolidated his home front vis-à-vis the advancing enemy from Makkah. By eliciting the Anṣār's support for his military strategy of taking the offensive against the Quraysh, the Prophet (peace be upon him) managed to supersede the merely defensive pledge to which the Anṣārs had agreed in signing the Second 'Aqabah Pledge'.

Thus, having consolidated the home front, the Prophet (peace be upon him) managed to achieve, from the outset, a tremendous tactical advantage over his enemy, which was divided and in discord, due to the heterogeneous nature of its supreme military command, vacillating between the hawkishness of Abū Jahl and dovishness of 'Utbah ibn Rabīʿah and Abū Sufyān ibn Ḥarb'. The Prophet's leadership, in peace and war, was profoundly mindful of the need of the leader to accommodate and incorporate the best of his followers' opinions, thoughts and aspirations. The mode of the Prophet's leadership was decisively collective and pluralistic. The heterogeneous ideas and opinions of the community of the faithful were thus woven and integrated in the final outcome of a general *shūrā* or consultation.

3.1 Al-Ḥubāb's Objection to the Stationing of the Troops

As soon as the Prophet (peace be upon him) moved forward, and stationed his troops in the valley of Badr, another occasion presented itself for more extended and more intensive practice of the *shūrā*. This time, the exchange of opinions was initiated, not by the Prophet (peace be upon him) as leader and commander-in-chief of the Muslim army, but by an ordinary soldier, by the name of Al-Ḥubāb ibn al-Mundhir: Al-Ḥubāb disapproved of the way the Prophet (peace be upon him) had stationed the Muslims' army in the valley of Badr.

'Is this a position which God has commanded you to take, or is it merely of your opinion and of the tactics and ruses of war?' asked ibn al-Mundhir.

'It is merely of my opinion and of the tactics and ruses of war.' replied the Prophet (peace be upon him).

'Then, this is not a good stationing of the troops! A better stationing will be further down the valley, around the nearest well to the enemy. We shall destroy all the wells behind us and station our troops around the nearest well to the enemy. This way, we drink while we deprive the enemy of any source of water,' advised al-Ḥubāb ibn al-Mundhir.

The Prophet (peace be upon him) immediately saw the soundness of al-Ḥubāb's expert opinion and acted upon it. It proved a tremendous success. This incident validated the necessity of the *shūrā*, as a safeguard against the fallibility of human judgment albeit Muḥammad's judgment, in his capacity as a human being.

Moreover, *shūrā* is also envisaged, within the Islamic scheme of policy and ideology, as a check against the tyranny and despotic tendencies of leaders and commanders. *Shūrā* is also commended because, in a community where it is practised, men come together as equals and brothers, and thus become united in mind and heart. The leaders behave with humility, and the rank and file become active participants in the whole affairs of the community. In this way everybody becomes part of the decision-making process of the community.

3.2 Shūrā and Equality

In one aspect of it, *shūrā* is a derivative rule that can be subsumed, under the more comprehensive Islamic principle of equality, of the faithful in the sight of God. The only legitimate criterion of discrimination is that of *taqwā* (piety). *Prima facie* all believers are equal in their right to voice their opinions, and are equally entitled to have them heard with respect, dignity and brotherly regard, all other things being equal. Of course, if a Muslim commits a crime, or in some way falls short of the Islamic moral standards, or is judged lacking in his commitment or obligations, then his right of equal opportunity to participate in the *shūrā* practice at any level could be jeopardised, at his own risk and responsibility.

Also illustrative of the general moral norm of equality in Islam is the Prophet's insistence, en route to Badr, on being treated exactly as an ordinary soldier, as far as the facility of transportation was concerned. At the rather advanced age of fifty-four, he insisted on having an equal share in walking beside or riding the camel that he was sharing with two of his Companions:

'You are not more capable of marching than I, and I am not less in need for other-worldly reward than you!' insisted the Prophet (peace be upon him).

The fortitude, high spirit and fitness of the Prophet (peace be upon him) were indeed remarkable, comparable if not, surpassing those of ʿAlī ibn Abī Ṭālib, at that time in his early twenties, and Marthad Ibn Abī Marthad al-Ghanawī, also a powerful young man of extraordinary physique, who worked as a blacksmith. But more important, and more significant than the Prophet's physical fitness at fifty-four, was his keenness to put into practice the principles which were integral parts, central to his Prophetic teaching, the norms and values he ardently advocated. The hardship which the gracious Prophet (peace be upon him) took upon himself in his insistence on giving a practical example, could be grasped and appreciated, if we remember that the march towards Badr was started on the 8th of Ramaḍān, of the second year of the *Hijrah*. The distance between Madīnah and the valley of Badr, which is approximately 80 miles, took the Muslims about seven or eight days, since the battle took place on the 17th of Ramaḍān.

3.3 How did the Battle Take Place?

In attempting to answer this question, no elaborate details will be given, because they are available in most of the standard texts on the *sīrah*. However, for the sake of completeness in the present account, a sketchy account of the event will be attempted, while the main emphasis will continue to be on gaining better understanding and appreciation of the phenomenon of Badr and its significance in Islamic history.

When the Muslims learned of the escape of the caravan and the presence of a powerful the Quraysh force at the other end of the valley of Badr, some of them were obviously disappointed. They had been asked to come out in pursuit of a commercial caravan, with the prospects of booty and inflicting a loss on their adversaries, the Quraysh. Then, those prospects were replaced by the possibility of having to fight that powerful force: some of the Muslims were not yet psychologically prepared to engage so formidable an enemy, especially in view of the great discrepancy in the relative numerical strength of the two forces.

The Muslims' army consisted altogether of three hundred and five men, seventy camels, and two horses. Of the men, eighty-three were Muhājirīn, sixty-one were of the Aws and the rest were of the Khazraj. The army of the Quraysh consisted of almost a thousand soldiers, well equipped, many of whom were on horseback. Most of the gallant leaders of the Quraysh were there.

At first, there was some hesitation and anxiety in the Muslims' camp. But God and the gracious Prophet (peace be upon him) assured them of God's backing and of the imminent victory over the enemy.

3.4 The Qur'ān's Depiction of the Situation

The Qur'ān depicted the condition of the Muslims army as follows:

> *Even as your lord caused you to go forth from your home, with the Truth, and surely a party of the believers were averse (to this). They argue with you of the truth, after it has been explained to them, as if they have been driven to death, with their eyes wide open. And*

> *when God promised you one of the two bands (of the enemy) that it would be yours, and you longed that other than the armed one might be yours. But God willed that the truth should triumph by His words and that He would eradicate the unbelievers.* [*al-Anfāl* 8:5-7]

The Muslim Companions of the Prophet (peace be upon him) were a superior band of men and women, yet they remained men of flesh and blood, because some of them, at some times, showed visible signs of human weakness and frailty. God had accepted their best offering, and had forgiven their weakness and failings. In the frank, honest and truthful style of the Qur'ān, nothing is concealed, no embarrassment is meant, only to display and take cognizance of all the facts of the situation. The above Qur'ānic verses of *al-Anfāl* make it very clear that the timing of the Battle of Badr was determined by God alone. Other Qur'ānic verses convey the same impression.

> *When you were in the near hill (of the valley) and they were on the farther and the caravan was below you (on the coast plain). And had you made an appointment to meet one another, you surely would have failed to keep the appointment, but (it happened, as it did, without the forethought of either of you), that Allah might conclude a thing that must be done; that he who perished (on that day) might perish by a clear sign, and he who lived, might live by a clear sign. Surely Allah is All-Hearing, All-Knowing. When Allah showed you them, in your dream, as few, and had He shown them as many, you would have lost heart; and quarrelled about the matter but Allah saved (you). He is surely knowing of what is in the breasts (of man). And when He showed them, when you encountered, in your eyes (Muslims) as few and made you few in their eyes, that Allah may conclude a matter that must be done. Unto Allah all matters are returned.* [*al-Anfāl* 8:42-44]

Thus, the impression is further confirmed that Badr had been exclusively conceived and meticulously executed by God alone; that the Prophet, the Muslims and the Quraysh unbelievers were all drawn into it by various devices of Divine making. Moreover, God prepared the stage for the battle, and eventually sent His soldiers of the angels, dressed like Arabs, with white turbans, and led by Gabriel himself (in yellow).

The Qur'ān gives minute details of God's involvement and the help He rendered to the Muslims, and the defeat which He inflicted upon their enemy:

> *When you were crying and calling upon your Lord for help, and He answered you: I will reinforce you with a thousand angels, riding behind you… Allah wrought this not, save as good tidings, and that your hearts thereby might be at rest. Victory comes only from Allah. Surely Allah is All-Mighty, All-Wise. When He was causing slumber to fall upon you, as a reassurance from Him, and sent down water from the sky upon you, that thereby He might purify you, and remove from you the defilement of Satan, and to strengthen your heart, and to confirm your feet. When your Lord was revealing to the angels, 'I am with you', so confirm the believers, I shall cast into the hearts of the unbelievers terror; so smite upon the necks, and smite every finger of them.* [*al-Anfāl* 8:9-12]

Notwithstanding all these demonstrations from the Qur'ān, that God was Himself commanding the Muslims' side on the Battle of Badr, the Qur'ān, at the same time, makes it amply clear that God's succour was not meted out arbitrarily. In some sense, it was succour well-deserved by the Muslims, because they had been severely tried, and they had withstood the trial for almost fifteen years, since the beginning of the call to Islam in Makkah. Badr itself was yet another such tremendous trial, and they had succeeded in it, when they were few in numbers and poorly armed, half-hungry, and with no previous experience in combat. They fought gallantly, and they successfully challenged the might of the Quraysh.

The Qur'ānic text went straight to emphasize this aspect of the matter:

> *Those only are the believers who, when God is mentioned, their hearts quake, and when His verses recited to them, it increases them in*

faith, and in their Lord they put their trust. Those who perform the prayer, and expend of what We have provided them, those are the true believers; for them are degrees (of honour) with their Lord, and forgiveness and generous provision. [*al-Anfāl* 8:2-4]

In order that God's victory would be complete for them, the Qur'ān exhorted the Muslims of Badr to live up to what was expected of them, when they met their enemy on the battlefield. This was their role, which they had to fulfil, if they were to qualify, in the decisive last moments, for God's victory, which was already close at hand:

O believers, when you encounter the unbelievers marching to battle, turn not your backs to them. Whoever turns his back to them on that day, unless manoeuvring for battle, or intent to join another host, he has truly incurred anger from Allah, and his abode will be Hell, and evil homecoming. [*al-Anfāl* 8:15-16]

The two armies met in the early morning of Friday, 17th Ramaḍān. Before they marched to the battleground, the army of the Quraysh was hidden from the eyes of the Muslims by the hill of 'Aqanqal'. That morning, the Quraysh army crossed that hill and came down its slope, into the valley of Badr to face the Muslims. When the Prophet (peace be upon him) caught sight of them, he prayed passionately:

O Lord! Here are Quraysh: they have come in their arrogance and their vanity, opposing You, and belying Your Messenger. Lord! Your victory which you have promised me! Lord! should this (Muslim) company perish today You will not be worshipped on this earth. O Lord! This morning destroy them!

When the two armies met, the Angels and other soldieries of God were already at work, setting the stage of the battleground in such a way that it would be advantageous to the Muslims, and disadvantageous to the unbelievers:

a. The sky rained heavily making the grounds transverse where the unbelievers stood, muddy and heavy and very difficult to walk upon. The nature of the soil where the Quraysh troops were stationed was such that rain had that kind of effect upon it. While the nature of soil where the Muslims stood was sandy and the rain had a very congenial effect upon it, making it firmer and easier to move upon.

b. The weather became cool, and a pleasant breeze swept across the Muslims' faces. They became drowsy, as they stood there, to the extent that the swords fell out of the hands of some of them. They would pick them up to drop them once more. This strange state of affairs continued for a few minutes just before the melee took place! But it had a wonderful refreshing effect upon them. They became relaxed, their hearts relieved from fears and anxieties, their heads became cool and clear, and their energy and stamina revived.

c. Due to the fatigue, many of them experienced orgasm and rain water cleansed and purified them from *janābah* (i.e. the state of being unclean after experiencing orgasm). It also cleansed them from the dirt and dust they incurred, during the week-long journey from Madīnah.

d. God caused their hearts to be reassured, their minds to be at rest, and the enemy was belittled in their eyes.

e. Terror was one of God's formidable hosts and soldiers, one that was the Prophet's privilege to always have at his side. He was supported by it 'I have been helped and made victorious with *Ru'b*' (i.e. Terror), the Gracious Prophet (peace be upon him) used to say.

f. Last but not least, the angels were there, ready to join the battle at the right moment.

g. Moreover, the Prophet, while imploring his Lord passionately went into a trance and was actually shown the outcome of the Battle, with the Muslims achieving a clean and decisive victory over their Quraysh adversaries. The Prophet (peace be upon him) conveyed this to the Muslim troops, and their morale was boosted greatly. He told them he was shown who and where many of the Quraysh nobles would fall and be killed. This was an outstanding miracle of the Prophet (peace be upon him), because those whom he had said would be killed of the Quraysh nobles were indeed killed on that day, and fell precisely on the spots he had indicated for them.

4. STRIKING FEATURES OF BADR

As we have seen, Badr was accompanied by many phenomena that could be described as supernatural; such as we have referred to above. On the other hand, it was also marked by actions and events, which could be described, as superhuman. Some of what the Muslims did and said seemed truly superhuman.

a. First and foremost, we have seen the fortitude and stamina of the Prophet (peace be upon him), walking at the age of fifty-four, at least two-thirds of the distance between Madīnah and Badr, a distance of more than eighty miles, during Ramaḍān and the hot season. We have seen his humility and modesty, his compassion for his Companions, and his regard and respect for their opinions and wishes.

b. Then we must praise the high mindedness and the utter devotion and dedication of the Muhājirīn. They joined the campaign almost to a man, none opting to stay behind, despite the long struggle, the suffering and the hardships they had been through, since the inception of Islam.

c. We must also praise the high-mindedness of the Anṣār, who were not confused or deterred by the changing situation, and who were ready and willing to amend their contractual obligation to support and defend the Prophet (peace be upon him). We must also praise the Anṣār for honouring the commitment made on their behalf by their chief, Saʿd ibn Muʿādh, even though they had not been consulted on the matter.

d. There was the example of ʿUmayr of Banū Zahrah of the Muhājirīn, who was only fifteen years old, and who implored the Prophet (peace be upon him) to let him participate in the fight, and who had stood on his toe in order to appear taller than he was.

e. There was the case of Sawād ibn Ghazīyah of the Anṣār, who received a light pinch from the Prophet's arrow in his belly, because he was standing outside the line. Sawād protested that he had been hurt and wanted to have retaliation from the person of the Prophet (peace be upon him). The Prophet (peace be upon him) immediately agreed and uncovered his gracious body so that Sawād could give him a prick, tit for tat. However, Sawād had something totally different in mind; for his real motive was to have a chance to kiss the body of the Prophet, lest he might fall a martyr. We also take note of the Prophet's keen sense of justice, his humility, his compassion for his Companions and his disregard for his personal rights and privileges, his complete disinterestedness and absolute altruism.

f. There was the story of ʿUmayr ibn al-Humām, of Banū Salamah, who was eating some dates out of his hand when he heard the Prophet (peace be upon him) saying: 'No man shall fight them today with forbearance and for God's sake, going forward against them and get killed, save that he will be taken to Paradise." ʿUmayr, hearing that, said: '*Bakhin*! *Bakhin*! Is it not the case that nothing stands between me and Paradise except those people killing me?' Then he threw away those dates and fought until he was killed.

g. Another Muslim, by the name of ʿAwf ibn al-Ḥārith asked the Prophet (peace be upon him): 'What is it that makes God quite pleased with his servant?' (Literally: What makes God laugh out of pleasure with his servant). 'For him to fight bare-bodied against the unbelievers,' replied the Prophet (peace be upon him). 'Awf ibn al-Ḥārith took off his armour and fought the enemy, bare-bodied until he was killed.

h. There was also the example of Abū Bakr, the most tender hearted of the Companions of the Prophet (peace be upon him). He fought his own son 'Abd al-Raḥmān who chose to side with the Quraysh: 'What happened to my money (in Makkah) evil-hearted man.' 'It has all gone! O old man,' replied 'Abd al-Raḥmān. Later 'Abd al-Raḥmān became a Muslim and once mentioned the battle of Badr. 'You know, father, I could have killed you at Badr, because I had more than one chance of doing that but I spared you.' Said 'Abd al-Raḥmān. 'By Him in whose hands is my soul, had I found one chance of killing you, I wouldn't have spared you,' reported Abū Bakr.

5. WHY WERE THE QURAYSH DEFEATED?

Despite their superior military strength, the Quraysh were defeated for the following reasons:

a. First of all, they had no just cause. If the Prophet (peace be upon him) took the offensive against them at Badr, attacking their commercial caravan, they had before that committed many acts of aggression against the interests of the Muslims, not least among these was the appropriation of the Muslim's wealth and property at Makkah during the Hijrah.

b. The Quraysh lacked a unified command, and they had no unity of purpose. Actually they were divided on the issue of resorting to fighting, when their caravan reached Makkah safely. There were 'hawks' and 'doves' among them.

c. God was against them, and so were the hosts of God and the angels. How could they win a war against God?

d. The Muslims were united, determined to uphold the banner of Islam, and settle scores with their foes. Moreover, there was the prospect of entering Paradise if they achieved martyrdom. They had a mission and a divine call, and they were eager to see the word of God rule supreme. The Quraysh had no such goals or ambitions.

6. WHAT WERE THE MAIN RESULTS OF BADR?

Badr represented the sweetest of the Muslims' victories. It represented a turning point in the history of Islam, when the hard times experienced by the Muslims began to change for the better. It was a battle with the most far-reaching consequences.[1]

a. Quraysh military might was largely destroyed!

b. Their image in Arabia, especially among the power-conscious Bedouins, was considerably tarnished.

c. The Muslims of Madīnah gained tremendously in recognition and prestige, and were put in a much stronger position to pursue further the task of building a community and *Ummah* dedicated to the worship of God alone, as well as the realization of the ideals of brotherhood, justice and equality.

d. Although Badr did not mark the end of the military power of the Quraysh, nor even the end of their capacity to start fresh military hostilities, yet it considerably weakened their resolve and morale. The weakening of their general military strength would become apparent in their coming offensives against the Muslims.

e. The loss of such prominent Quraysh leaders such as Abū Jahl and ʿUtbah would be keenly felt, when the Quraysh planned the next expedition against the Muslims. Abū Jahl represented the motive force for the Quraysh whereas ʿUtbah represented their brainpower.

f. Moreover, the life-line of Quraysh trade was cut by the battle of Badr. No caravan could, after Badr, venture outside of Makkah. Yet the trade with Syria and the Mediterranean ports constituted the bulk of the Quraysh trade, an eventuality which also meant that their economic power was considerably weakened in the wake of Badr.

g. One of the important lessons of Badr is that the sheer number of troops is not the decisive factor in achieving victory. The Quraysh troops were three times as many as the Muslim troops. They were by far the better equipped and the better trained in the arts of warfare.

h. Although supernatural phenomena attended Badr, and God and His hosts and His angels were clearly on the Muslims' side, yet that divine help and succour was not arbitrarily given. It was, in some sense, a consequence of the total dedication and steadfastness of the Muslims. It was a contingent of their faith, trust and total dependence upon their Lord. Their offerings, obedience and the love of God and His Messengers were important reasons why God's help and victory, promised in the Qur'ān, were quite at hand, once the Muslims managed to come forward to the battleground of *jihād*.

i. Last but not least, Badr provides an example of a situation when war, ugly as it is, becomes absolutely justifiable. It becomes the ultimate measure and ultimate escape for the oppressed and the downtrodden. It provides them with their last chance to emancipate themselves, and get rid of their enemies and oppressors. A justifiable war is both a natural[2] and decisive way to resolve a long drawn out struggle, when that struggle has reached an impasse and resists every attempt to resolve it peacefully.

7. THE AFTERMATH OF BADR

As the dust of the Battle of Badr settled, the astounding victory of the Muslims became clear, and the terrible defeat of the Quraysh was a material reality. The Muslims rejoiced, while the Quraysh wept profoundly over the demise of their best fighting force and the death of some of their most cherished leaders:

- ʿAmr ibn Hishām, leader of Banū Makhzūm.
- ʿUtbah ibn Rabīʿah, leader of Banū ʿAbd al-Dār, the father of Hind and father-in-law of Abū Sufyān.
- Al-Walīd ibn ʿUtbah, brother of Hind.
- Shaybah ibn Rabīʿah, brother of ʿUtbah.
- Umayyah ibn Khalaf, an outstanding leader and elder statesman of the Quraysh.
- And many others.

The total number of those killed on the side of the Quraysh was seventy, according to Al-Wāqidī[3] including the two men executed on the orders of the Prophet (peace be upon him) himself. Others fell captive to the Muslims, because they had committed the heinous crime of cursing the Messenger of God. The executed men were ʿUtbah ibn Abī Muʿādh and al-Naḍr ibn al-Ḥārith.

ʿUtbah ibn Abī Muʿādh was the immediate neighbour of the Prophet (peace be upon him) at Makkah, before the Hijrah. He was the source of constant harassment to the Prophet(peace be upon him), and his Muslim Companions. He even forced his sons to divorce the daughters of the Prophet. He used to put dirt on the threshold of the Prophet, and one day, finding the Prophet (peace be upon him) prostrating in prayer, he put the afterbirth from a sheep on his head. He was generally active in the campaign to persecute and oppress the Muslims at Makkah. Likewise, al-Naḍr ibn al-Ḥārith did a lot to hurt the Prophet (peace be upon him) and his Companions at Makkah, before the Hijrah. He was a poet-propagandist who composed vile and vicious verses about the Prophet (peace be upon him) and his Companions.

7.1 The Captives Well-Treated

Apart from these two cases, the Prophet (peace be upon him) ordered the Muslims to treat the captives well, especially his uncle al-ʿAbbās. Al-ʿAbbās, a long time friend of the Muslims and chief of Banū Hāshim, the traditional protectors of the Muslims at Makkah, had been forced to join the army of the Quraysh, marching to Badr. ʿUmar ibn al-Khaṭṭāb asked the Prophet's permission to break the front teeth of Suhayl ibn ʿAmr, another vicious propagandist, who had given the Muslims a very hard time at Makkah. The Prophet (peace be upon him) refused to give such permission, saying: 'I shall not mutilate anyone under any circumstances, lest God should mutilate me, even though I am His Prophet.'

7.2 Controversy Over the Captives of Badr

What to do about the captives of Badr, numbering about seventy, developed in an open controversy. On the one hand, the Prophet (peace be upon him) and Abū Bakr al-Ṣiddīq favoured the view that the captives should be spared and ransom money accepted for their release. On the other hand, ʿUmar advocated that they should be killed. They were combatants of considerable strength, and if they were set free, what was the guarantee that they would not take the field against the Muslims once more, argued ʿUmar ibn al-Khaṭṭāb. But the tender-hearted Prophet (peace be upon him), and his principal minister and friend Abū Bakr, being of a very similar disposition himself, both abhorred the possibility of bloodshed. Further, many of the captives were related to the Prophet (peace be upon him) and his larger family Banū Hāshim. There were al-ʿAbbās, his uncle, and Abū al-ʿĀṣ ibn al-Rabīʿ his own son in-law, the husband of his beloved Zaynab. The Prophet's compassion towards the Hashimites was not primarily a matter of nepotism or favouritism, it was prompted and dictated by such factual considerations as:

a. The favour which the Muslims owed to Hashimites who had protected and sided with them during their difficult and prolonged ordeal at Makkah.

b. The Prophet (peace be upon him) knew very well and appreciated the potential of the Quraysh, both as a military and as a diplomatic force in Arabia. He hoped and prayed that one day he would be able to use that potential in the battlefield to pacify Arabia and defend it once it swung under the control of Islam. The Prophet (peace be upon him) prophesied that the emergence of the political power of Islam in Arabia would provoke the enmity and opposition of the two superpowers of the day, 'The Romans and the Persians.' When that happened, as it was destined to happen, he would be in need of the power and the human resources of the Arab elite of the Quraysh.

c. Moreover, the money that they would get as a ransom was much needed and could be put to some very useful purposes.

d. Kind treatment and sparing the captives of the Quraysh was more conducive to the pacification of the Quraysh than their slaughter.

e. Having decided to spare the captives, the Prophet (peace be upon him) put them to the useful purpose of teaching the Muslims how to read and write. He accepted money as ransom from some of them, but asked the Muslims' permission to set his son-in-law free without ransom, because he had nothing to offer except a necklace, which his wife, Zaynab, managed to produce, but which originally belonged to Khadījah, the Prophet's much beloved senior wife.

The whole affair of the captives was settled in accordance with the Prophet's opinion, and they were all set free, eventually. But the matter was not let to rest, at that level. Qur'ānic verses were revealed later (see below) which, in effect, approved of ʿUmar's position that all the combatants among the captives be killed, with the exception of the Hashimites relatives of the Prophet (peace be upon him), especially al-ʿAbbās, because of their earlier service to Muslims.

7.3 The Qur'ān Comments on the Issue of War Captives

The Qur'ānic comment on the captives' question is as follows:

> *It does not behave a Prophet to hold war captives, until he makes wide slaughter in the land; you desire the passing goods of this world, and Allah desires (for you) the Hereafter, and Allah is All-Mighty, All-wise.* [*al-Anfāl* 8:67]

This verse must have been severe for the Muslims, because it had in clear and unambiguous language exposed a typical human weakness in some of the Badr fighters, namely the love of the passing goods of this world. That some of the Badr referees suffered from this typical human weakness, was amply demonstrated in two occasions during the march to Badr.

a. Firstly, some of them strongly disliked the possibility of having to clash with the Quraysh in the battlefield, as if they are being driven to death, their eyes wide open.

b. Secondly, there was the wrangling over the question of how war spoils were to be distributed, a matter which gave a noble *sūrah* of the Qur'ān its name: namely *Sūrah al-Anfāl*, whose opening verses dealt with this verse.

c. The opening verse of *Sūrah al-Anfāl* should be noted for its frankness, not only criticising the Prophet (peace be upon him) and rebuking the Muslims' wrangling over the war spoils, but also for its stern threat that such wrangling over material things of this world did not behove them, and might even lead to God's severe chastisement against them!

d. The verse strongly hints to the Muslims that they should not, as indeed did the Jews, assume the favour of their Lord God. God does not favour the Muslims out of mere prejudice for them. They must ensure that their behaviour is righteous, and their dealings fair and straightforward, true to the ideals and norms of the Qur'ān.

The severe attitude of the Qur'ānic verse on the captives issue holds several important lessons:

a. Firstly, it opposes the opinion of the Prophet (peace be upon him) and Abū Bakr, and is more in line with 'Umar's. The fact that it does so, together with the familiar Qur'ānic tendency to criticize, blame, rebuke or even threaten the Prophet (peace be upon him) at times, is a proof that Muḥammad could not have been the author of the Qur'ān.

b. Secondly, the concern over the material welfare of the Muslims as a community is not the overriding Qur'ānic concern. More important is the issue of the supremacy of God's word and the salvation of the Muslims in the Hereafter.

c. The militant tone of this verse is justifiable by the need to vanquish and punish the mischief and aggression of the Quraysh, by destroying their manpower. The Quraysh not only disbelieved the Messenger of God (peace be upon him) and opposed God Himself, they forced the Muslims out of their homes.

d. However, this verse and the one that immediately came after it, display that characteristic pragmatism and tolerance of the Qur'ān: The Muslims, as ordinary human beings were expected at times to display aspects of the weakness and frailties of human nature. In other words, to love the world and its beautiful ornaments is a characteristic human weakness that cannot be totally eradicated. Yet the Muslims were exhorted to resist it to their utmost power. At the same time, the above Qur'ānic verse assured the Muslims of God's forgiveness. It even called upon them to enjoy the victory achieved at Badr. The threatening tone of awful doom gave way to a more cheerful one of enjoy what you have won: Says God, in the Qur'ān:

> *Had it not been a prior ordinance of God, an awful doom could have come upon you, on account of what you have taken. Now, eat of what you have earned as booty is lawful and good and fear Allah, for surely Allah is All-Forgiving, All-Compassionate.* [*al-Anfāl* 8:68-69]

8. EPILOGUE ON BADR – A CONCLUDING NOTE: COLOURS AND SOUNDS

8.1 The Banners of Badr

The Muslims' army carried three banners. The one carried by Muṣʿab ibn ʿUmayr, the renowned *Dāʿiyah* and first Muslim ambassador to Yathrib, was white in colour. The other two banners were black, and they were carried right in front of the Prophet (peace be upon him). One called ʿal-ʿUqābʾ carried by ʿAlī ibn Abī Ṭālib, the Prophet's cousin and son-in-law and the second by one of the Anṣārs.

The war cry of the Muslims was *Aḥad, Aḥad*; One, One, God is One, and *Yā Manṣūr amit;* Allāhu Akbar, God Almighty is the Greatest.

8.2 The Colours of Angels

Angels appeared at Badr in white costumes, wearing white turbans, which extended behind their back, with Gabriel wearing a yellow turban. They were all on horseback. Gabriel was seen by some descending through the clouds, on that rainy day leading his horse, known as Ḥayzūm. Just before the two armies clashed, the Prophet (peace be upon him) filled his hand with pebbles and threw them at the enemy, saying:

'Defamed are those faces.' To this act of the Prophet (peace be upon him), the Qur'ān refers: *You did not throw, when you threw, but it was Allah who threw*. [*al-Anfāl* 8: 17]

The descent of the angels from heaven was accompanied by a tremendous sound. One of the unbelievers heard a voice in the clouds saying: 'Go forward, Ḥayzūm!'

8.3 Quraysh in Dispute

The Quraysh disputed hotly among themselves, just before the start of the war. There were two camps: The 'doves' represented by Ḥakīm ibn Hishām, and ʿUtbah ibn Rabīʿah. These wanted the Quraysh to return home and not engage the Muslims in battle. Their caravan had arrived safely in Makkah and, after all, Muḥammad (peace be upon him) and the Muslims, especially the Muhājirīn, were their own kith and kin. Should they engage them in war, the result would be the unpleasant one of killing each other, and the Quraysh side would become bitter and divided, as some of them would have killed their fathers and brothers. If Muḥammad (peace be upon him) became victorious, then his glory is the glory of the Quraysh and if the other Arabs prevailed over him, that was what they wanted. But the 'hawks', represented by ʿAmr ibn Hishām (Abū Jahl), accused ʿUtbah and Ḥakīm ibn Hishām of cowardice and vowed not to go back to Makkah until Muḥammad and the Muslims had been routed.

8.4 Bilāl Versus Umayyah ibn Khalaf

Bilāl, seeing his former master and oppressor Umayyah ibn Khalaf, shouted as they charged against him: 'Umayyah ibn Khalaf the head of disbelief, I may not live if he lives!' Bilāl dealt a fatal blow to Umayyah who, together with his son, was captured by ʿAbd al-Raḥmān ibn ʿAwf. But Bilāl would not allow his old enemy to escape alive that day, while he was still on the battleground.

8.5 ʻUkāshah going forward to Paradise

ʻUkāshah ibn Miḥsan lost his sword on the day of Badr, because it was broken into two halves during the fighting. He called to the Prophet (peace be upon him): 'I have lost my sword!' The Prophet (peace be upon him) gave him a long piece of wood. When ʻUkāshah shook it in his hand, it became a real sword of steel, yet another miracle of the Prophet (peace be upon him) on that fateful day.

The Prophet (peace be upon him) said: 'Some men of my *Ummah*, fifty thousand of them, will enter paradise, their faces shining like the full moon,' ʻUkāshah said: 'O Prophet of God, pray that I am one of them.' 'You are one of them, O ʻUkāshah.' Another man came forward and asked: 'May I be of them?' 'No, ʻUkāshah has preceded you in that,' said the Prophet (peace be upon him).

8.6 O People of the Grave!

In the evening of the day of Badr, when the corpses of the unbelievers had been buried, the Prophet (peace be upon him) stood over the ditch, where they were collectively buried, and called out to them; 'O people of the ditch, have you found what God has promised you to be true? For I have found what God has promised me to be true!' The Muslims protested: 'O Messenger of God, how do you address dead people?' 'You do not hear better than they! Only they can not reply!' said the Prophet(peace be upon him).

8.7 ʻAbdullāh ibn Masʻūd versus Abū Jahl

The killing of Umayyah ibn Khalaf by the former Abyssinian slave, Sayyidunā Bilāl signalled a major shift in the balance of power in Arabia. The Quraysh were no longer the dominant power. The Muslims had just come into that position. Umayyah ibn Khalaf represented the old, now vanquished power, of the aristocracy of the Quraysh, its prestige, arrogance, vanity and military and commercial strength. Now it was people like Bilāl and ʻAbdullāh ibn Masʻūd, who was an ordinary Arab employed as a shepherd by Abū Jahl, who emerged as the new elite. On the day of Badr, ibn Musʿūd killed Abū Jahl. Later, he distinguished himself as a governor of Baṣrah, and was a renowned scholar of Qur'ānic exegesis, and renowned also for his melodious recitation of the Qur'ān. The Prophet (peace be upon him) used to comment on Ibn Masʿūd's manner of the recitation of the Qur'ān: 'Whoever desires to hear the Qur'ān as it has been revealed to me, let him listen to the recitation of ibn ʿAbd,' (meaning ʿAbdullāh ibn Masʿūd).

ʿAbdullāh ibn Masʿūd was the foremost among the Muslim activists in Makkah. Of a small, slight frame, he was to be seen everywhere in Makkah, during those early days. For this reason, he had borne a great deal of the wrath of the Quraysh, and their persecution. His employer, Abū Jahl, had been particularly severe upon him. On the day of Badr, the scores were set even. Having managed to kill Abū Jahl, who was of a great physical stature, and also had great marshal courage, ibn Masʿūd climbed on the top of the towering figure of his enemy. Abū Jahl, who was dying, opened his eyes and recognized ibn Masʿūd, sitting on his chest. He said: 'Ibn Masʿūd, the little shepherd of our sheep, you have indeed climbed a difficult climb!' Then he closed his eyes and died.

When the Prophet (peace be upon him) entered Madīnah, the next day, people met him at the outskirts to salute and congratulate him. One Muslim soldier boasted: 'On what do you congratulate us! We met a group of old, hairless persons, and we easily cut them.' 'Wait a minute, son of my brother,' protested the Prophet (peace be upon him),[4] 'those were the *Mala*'.' Those were the *Mala*', meaning that the people defeated at Badr were the notables and chiefs of Arabia, people of honour, prestige and wealth. That Muslim soldier who made the naïve comment about the power of the Quraysh, whom the Muslims had just vanquished, had clearly failed to see the significance of the events of that day. That is why the Prophet (peace be upon him) intervened to correct him.

8.8 The Full Significance of Badr

We have already said that Badr was not an isolated event in the history of Islam. Rather, it was the culmination of unusual events that were taking shape in Arabia, in rapid succession, and constituting a major process in which history was made and remade. Badr was the logical outcome of the struggle initiated by the Prophet's call to pure monotheism. Moreover, Badr had its monumental consequences in the history of Islam, launching the new power of the Muslim state of al-Madīnah, and terminating the hegemony of the Quraysh.

But it is the significance of Badr as a permanent feature of the methodology of Islamic *daʿwah* that must be highlighted here. For Badr is a major sign-post in the way of bringing about an Islamic transformation, and the re-ordering of a particular setting of human reality, whereby this reality will submit and conform to the pattern ordained by God, to which the Qur'ān refers. No Islamic transformation can be effected without a Badr stage; because it is, in the very nature of things, that evil powers would attempt to obstruct the Islamic project. God has told us, in the Qur'ān, that the strife and struggle between belief and unbelief is inevitable. It is a matter divinely ordained to test the Muslims' will, on the one hand, and to vanquish and destroy evil, on the other hand. Thus every successful Islamic movement, every true Muslim community, must find its Badr and win it. Thus Badr is part of God's grand design for Muslims and any Islamic movement. The Qur'ān comments on the inevitability of Badr in the following way: *Succour comes only from Allah, the All-Mighty, All-Wise and that He may cut off a part of those who disbelieve or overwhelm them, that they turn in their tracks unsuccessful.* [*Āl ʿImrān* 3:126-127]

Moreover, verses 38-41 of *Sūrah al-Ḥajj*, make it very clear that the permission which God gave to the Muslims, to fight back in self-defence, was given with an eye to Badr in particular. If this reading is correct, then Badr must be seen as an idea, a device and a strategy which was God-ordained to achieve the objectives mentioned in those verses, namely to redress the injustices suffered, to destroy the enemies of Islam, to confirm the Muslims in their homes and land and to make them feel contented, peaceful, secure and well established in the land. That waging war (i.e. just war) was not merely seen as an exercise in vendetta, but much more substantially, it was seen as an effective tool and device by means of which the enemy was led to its destruction, so that it would no longer obstruct the road to supremacy of God's word and grand design for humanity. But so long as there is good and evil, the conflict between them is inevitable, and the side of goodness must not shy away from doing whatever it takes to defeat evil and establish goodness and godliness on earth!

An Islamic movement which is presented with the opportunity to find its Badr, but hesitates and loses that chance, will not be successful in its endeavour. It will stagnate or be destroyed by its enemies, having missed its Badr. This type of Islamic movement would be a spent force which, having missed its Badr would not be able to transform from the Badr to post-Badr, stage. At most, its existence will be a kind of arrested growth, fossilized and senile. On the other hand, an Islamic movement which rushes its pre-Badr stage, and moves to a stage of confrontation too early, without fulfilling its prerequisites and before allowing conditions for a successful confrontation, will be destroyed, and its growth will be aborted, thus suffering defeat or annihilation prematurely. A third type of Islamic movement may fail to reach the Badr stage because its growth has been arrested or prevented, or because its membership do not possess the necessary energy or the know-how which would enable them to develop and progress. In so far as the Islamic process of social change, leading to a total Islamic transformation, is a dynamic process, a genuine Islamic movement that follows the true Prophetic model of *daʿwah* and *jihād*, in the wide sense of adopting the right resources and right methodology, will, by its very nature, move forward to its destined Badr stage in a reasonable time, most probably during the lifetime of its authentic leader, and its true and dedicated rank and file.

One sure indicator that an Islamic movement has matured, and reached its Badr stage, will be the readiness of its leader, as well as its rank and file, to take the calculated risk of challenging their adversaries on the battlefield, when they have become reasonably sure that they enjoy a clear advantage over them. The Qur'ān[5] describes the Companions of the Prophet at Badr as possessing tremendous willpower, and physical as well as moral courage, to fight the enemy. The strength of one believer was the equal to that of the combined strength of ten unbelievers. When later, the Muslims became weakened by their desire for worldly things, their valour was reduced to just double that of the unbelievers. The Qur'ān also described the Muslims as God-fearing, patient and dedicated to the cause of upholding God's word, and of loving God, and His Messenger more than they loved themselves. It was these characteristics which made them merit and deserve God's help and succour, rendered to them by the sending of His angels to fight along their side. These characteristics were summed up in the opening verses of *Sūrah al-Anfāl* in which the story of the Battle of Badr is given in considerable detail:

> *Those only are the true believers who when God is mentioned, their hearts quake, and when His verses are recited to them, they increase them in faith, and in their Lord they put their trust, those who perform the prayer (Ṣalāt) expend of what we have provided of them. These are the true believers. They have high degrees with their Lord and forgiveness and generous provision.* [*al-Anfāl* 8:2-4]

9. EPILOGUE

Our conclusion deals with the issue of religious persecution. The Qur'ān does not accept any excuse or justification from a Muslim for willingly allowing himself to suffer religious oppression. If a Muslim is not literally imprisoned or materially held down, then he is not to be reprieved or excused if he passively submits and bows down to oppression. This issue was high in the agenda, featuring in the discussions among Muslims, in the wake of Badr, when some of those killed fighting with the Quraysh were in fact Muslims who had failed to make the *hijrah* to Madīnah and were caught up in the hostilities between the Muslims and the Quraysh. This was the case of some

Muslim members of Banū Hāshim, who had been forced to join the army of the Quraysh.[6] A decisive Qur'ānic verse was revealed to the Prophet (peace be upon him), and the matter was sealed, that one who fails to rise up against religious oppression does so at the risk of his own faith and life:

> *Lo: Surely for those whom the angels cause to die, while still they are wronging themselves, they (the angels) say 'in what have you been engaged?' They will say: 'We were oppressed in the land.' The angles will say: 'But was not the earth of Allah wide enough, so that you might have emigrated in it?' Such men, their abode will be Hell-an evil homecoming! Except the feeble among men, and the women, and the children, who are unable to devise a plan, and are not shown a way out.* [*al-Nisā'* 4:97-98]

Thus the Qur'ān[7] consoled the Muslims that they were not responsible for the death of those Muslims, who, through their failure to act in earnest, to make the *hijrah* to Madīnah, found themselves compelled by their situation to fight alongside the unbelievers at Badr. The Muslims were not to blame for the sad and tragic fate of those negligent Muslims. The issues relating to the wider question of the Pax Islamica have been discussed in a preceding book.[8] They are part and parcel of the wider issue of *Muwālāt* (allegiance to Muslims) which is a necessary condition for extending the *Pax Islamica* to Muslims, not living in the land of Islam. Thus a Muslim who lives permanently in a land which is not under Islamic rule, nor a land of *Amān*, i.e. a Land in treaty with a land under Islamic rule, does so at his own peril, risking both his life and quality of his faith.

CHAPTER 3

The Battle of Uḥud: A Temporary Setback

1. PROLOGUE

It is said that every war has its seeds in some preceding war or conflict. This maxim could not have been more true than it was in the Battle of Uḥud. Thus Uḥud was, in effect, a direct consequence of the Battle of Badr.

The first reaction of the Quraysh to the news coming from Badr was one of disbelief, as they were so shocked by their defeat at the hands of the by far inferior force of the Muslims. Indeed it is very hard now, as it was then, to offer a materialistic or purely empirical explanation of superior performance of the Muslim army at Badr. This is a further proof of the Qur'ānic explanation that the Muslims were aided by supernatural powers. As a matter of fact, both Muslims and the Quraysh agreed that the battle of Badr was decided rather swiftly, and that mysterious figures, dressed in white costumes and piebald horses, participated in the fighting.[1]

2. QURAYSH MOURN THEIR DEAD

At first, Quraysh vowed not to mourn their dead, lest the Prophet (peace be upon him) and the Muslims should delight over their grief. But they could not maintain this posture, as the tide of their grief and anger rose day by day. As the terrible scale of their defeat became more manifest, they started to mourn with the most profound sorrow and lamentation. Of all the Quraysh, none grieved so much as Hind bint ʿUtbah ibn Rabīʿah, wife of Abū Sufyān ibn Ḥarb, the head of the Quraysh opposition. Hind lost her father, her brother, and her uncle in the Battle of Badr. As the days passed, her grief grew into hatred and enmity, and the determination for revenge. Revenge-seeking, typical of the pre-Islamic Arabian personality, became a consummate obsession for Hind. Hind vowed not to touch ointment or perfumes, not allow her husband to approach her until she had avenged her dead at Badr, and until such time as she witnessed Muḥammad defeated in the battleground. Her husband, Abū Sufyān ibn Ḥarb, vowed not to cleanse himself until he made the scores even with Muḥammad on the battleground.

3. THE JEWS OF BANŪ QAYNUQĀʿ BREAK COVENANT

The situation was further complicated by a grave development that poisoned the relationship between the Muslims and the Jews, which had generally been pacific up to that event, because of the covenant of peace that existed between them and the Muslims.[2] A Muslim woman went to a jeweller who happened to be a Jew, in the market of the city of Madīnah, situated in the Jewish quarters of Banū Qaynuqāʿ. The Madīnan Jews enjoyed substantial monopoly of the trade and commerce there. The Muslim woman was covered up, in her Muslim *ḥijāb*. The Jewish jeweller tried to seduce her and asked her to uncover her face. When she refused, he resorted to an indecent trick. He tipped off his assistant to pin the lower part of her dress to her back so that when she rose to get out, she was exposed. She shouted in horror and shame as the two Jews laughed. A Muslim passer-by heard and saw what happened. He leapt at the Jews, killing one of them. The Jews of the market-place crowded around the Muslim and managed to kill him. The Muslims of Madīnah heard of the incident and the Muslims and Jews were, for the first time, on the verge of armed conflict. The Prophet (peace be upon him) tried to solve the situation peacefully. He rebuked the Jews of Banū Qaynuqāʿ for having broken their covenant with him, and asked them to pay ransom for the killed Muslim. But the Jews were defiant: 'O Muḥammad! Do not fall under the illusion that you are invincible. The people whom you met at Badr had no knowledge of warfare. By God, if you were to wage war upon us, you would find us a formidable enemy.'[3]

Failing to sway them to peace, the Prophet (peace be upon him) resorted to a more drastic measure. He quickly mobilized the Muslims, and the Banū Qaynuqāʿ found themselves blocked in their quarter. The blockade lasted for fifteen days, at the end of which they surrendered. The Prophet (peace be upon him) ruled that they were to vacate the city of Madīnah. They were not to take their armaments or their machinery, but only such light personal effects as they could carry. They moved north and settled in Adhriʿāt, near southern boundaries of Palestine.

Of course, the incident of the Muslim woman, who was maltreated by the Jewish jeweller and his assistant, was not an isolated one. For the Jewish reaction to the victory of the Muslims at Badr, was one of open resentment and anger, mixed with increasing sense of insecurity, and anxiety for their status in Madīnah. But above all, they were angry to see Muḥammad (peace be upon him) growing in power and prestige. Their community was rife with resentment, and they talked ill of Muḥammad and the Muslims. Due to their nearness to the Muslims, since they lived in the city centre, and because they mixed freely with the Muslims in the market place, some of their ill-talk reached the Muslims. Moreover, the Qur'ān had informed the Prophet (peace be upon him) of their state of mind and warned him against them, and their scheming. The Prophet (peace be upon him) was strongly urged, in the Qur'ān, not to hesitate to sever his covenant with them:

> *Say (O Muḥammad) unto those who disbelieve: you shall be defeated, and gathered unto Hell, an evil cradling. There has already been a sign for you in the two parties that encountered: one party fighting in the way of God, and another unbelieving, they saw them twice their (real) number, clearly with their own eyes. Thus God supports*

with His Help whom He wills. Surely in that is a lesson for those with understanding. [*Āl ʿImrān* 3:12-13]

Obviously, this Qur'ānic verse must have been revealed in the interim period between the meeting in the market place, inside the quarters of Banū Qaynuqāʿ and the time of the blockade.

Other Qur'ānic verses, revealed to the Prophet (peace be upon him) at about this time, with obvious allusions to the affair of Banū Qaynuqāʿ, sought to inform the Prophet (peace be upon him) and the Muslims of the real motives, and the real mood of the Madīnan Jews in general, and Banū Qaynuqāʿ in particular, so as to educate those who, among the Muslims, still harboured illusions about the possibility of continued friendship and alliance with the Jews. These who still wanted to maintain cordial relations with the Jews included their age-long allies: Saʿd ibn ʿUbādah, Chief of the Khazraj, and Saʿd ibn Muʿādh, chief of the Aws, not to speak of their staunch supporter and their friend, ʿAbdullāh ibn Ubayy ibn Salūl. God revealed, concerning the Madīnan Jews and the hypocrites the following verses, in the wake of Badr:

> *O you who believe, take not for your intimates others outside yourselves such men who spare nothing to ruin you: they yearn that you suffer; hatred has already shown itself in the (utterances) of their mouths, but that which they already hide in their breasts even greater. Now, we have made clear to you the revealed verse, if you understand. Ha, there you are, you love them, and they love you not, and you believe in all the Scripture, and when they meet you, they say: 'we believe', but when they go apart, they bit their fingers tips at you in rage. Say (O Muḥammad), 'Die in your rage! Surely God is aware of what is hidden in (your) breast. If you are visited by good fortune, it vexes them, but if you are smitten by evil, they rejoice at it. Yet if you are patient and God-fearing, then their guile will hurt you nothing. Surely God encompassed all the things they do.* [*Āl ʿImrān:* 3:118-120]

Al-Ṭabarī, in his voluminous commentary on the Qur'ān, says on the authority of Qatādah, that the above verses refer not to the hypocrites, but to the People of the Book living in Madīnah, not far from the Muslims, because the hypocrites did not show open hatred to the Muslims. But that some of those People of the Book used to openly speak ill of them. Sayyid Quṭb,[5] in his *Fī-Ẓilāl al-Qur'ān*, also confirms the view that the reference in these verses is to the People of the Book in Madīnah at that time. Yet, in Quṭb's view, the import of these verses is perfectly general.

Thus, these verses must have also been revealed at a time when Muslim-Jewish relations in Madīnah were taking a sharp turn for the worse. It is interesting that even so, the Muslim camp still harboured some love and sympathy for their Jewish compatriots, uninformed of the latter's guiles and scheming against them, and completely unaware of the Madīnah Jews' increasing violations of the Madīnah peace covenant. Especially vocal in his criticism and vilification of the Muslims, was Ka῾b ibn al-Ashraf, and two other poets among the Jews of Madīnah. Ka῾b ibn al-Ashraf of the Jews of Banū al-Naḍīr, could not contain his anger, when he learned about the defeat of the Quraysh at Badr, and openly remarked: 'Those were the nobles of Arabia, and kings of mankind. By God, if Muḥammad has slain these men, then the interior of the earth is a better dwelling place for us than the top of it.'[8]

Ka῾b ibn al-Ashraf was so incensed by the news of the victory of the Muslims at Badr, that he even left Madīnah before the Prophet's return therein from Badr. Arriving at Makkah, he composed poetry in memory of those killed, and he offered his condolences to their families. However, the main purpose of his trip was to urge the Makkans to seek revenge against Muḥammad (peace be upon him) and the Muslims, and he promised Jewish help to that end. Moreover, he vilified the Prophet (peace be upon him), insulted and cursed him in very foul language, and incensed and provoked the Muslims by composing indecent poetry about their women.

Two men, executed on the order of the Prophet (peace be upon him), Abū Afk of Banū ῾Āmir and Asmā' bint Marwān, had both composed poetry insulting and cursing the Prophet and the (peace be upon him) Muslims. These killings had led to further deterioration in Muslim-Jewish relations. From that time on, it was plain war between the two groups. It must be about this time that the Affair of Banū Qaynuqāʿ took place, and it is against the background of these grave and sinister developments that we must seek to understand the conflict between the two groups. These developments were no doubt compounded by the new atmosphere of competition, which was fast developing into an all-out war of survival between them. At the bottom of the conflict was no doubt a profound and total clash between two cultural identities; the Muslims seeing themselves in the light of Qur'ānic directives, as the vicegerents of God Almighty, while the Jews of Madīnah were priding themselves on the legacy of Judah, and that they were of the pure lineage of Abraham. They were of the seed of Jacob, son of Isaac, son of Abraham whereas the Arabs and the Muslims were Hagarites. In the words of the leaders of Banū Qaynuqāʿ, in the heat of the conflict between them and the Prophet (peace be upon him), the Madīnan Jews saw themselves as '*naḥnu al-Nās*.'[7] i.e. 'We are the men, the people that really counted.' They were God's Chosen People! It was during this time that Qur'ānic verses must have been revealed which cautioned the Muslims against the scheming of the Jews, and which forbade them to take the Jews in confidence.

4. THE PACIFICATION OF BEDOUINS AROUND MADĪNAH

The incident of Kaʿb ibn al-Ashraf, and the slaying of the leaders of the Quraysh at Badr created unrest among the Bedouins of Madīnah. These consisted of a vast network of tribes, extending westward to the coast of the Red Sea, eastward to Iraq and southwards to the vicinity of Makkah. They were greatly alarmed by the events of Badr, and the uncertainty that preceded and followed it. Before Badr, it was the Prophet (peace be upon him) who seized the initiative by contacting them, and securing the alliance of the powerful Banū Khuzāʿah, in his efforts to strike at the commercial interest of the Quraysh. But after Badr, it was the Quraysh and their Jewish allies who took the first step, capitalizing, no doubt, on the economic plight of the Bedouins, brought by the collapse of the Quraysh commerce and economy, in which they were partners and middlemen. They used to extend their protection to these caravans, and to receive fees in return. They also obtained their life needs and food and grains from these caravans. Now that no caravans were coming by, due to the Muslim blockade, the Bedouins were understandably restless. Some of them were already part of the new order, and they stood to benefit from it in various ways. Their economic needs were obviously taken care of; maybe from their share of the booty, as they fought alongside the Muslims, or even from *Zakāt* being of the category of 'those whose hearts are to be won.' This inference is inescapable, in view of the fact that the Banū Khuzāʿah managed to maintain their alliance with the Muslims through the difficult phase of the blockade against the Quraysh, during which they had undoubtedly incurred great financial losses. Unless there was some system of reparation and compensation, it would indeed be difficult to explain how they had managed to stick to their alliance with Muḥammad (peace be upon him), when that alliance was in direct conflict with their vital interest. An explanation that hinges on questions of religion or morality alone was not tenable, as they, the Khuzāʿites, were not then Muslims, but only allies of the Muslims. No doubt their long standing rivalry with the Banū Bakr, who were traditional allies of the Quraysh, helped a little to sway them to the side of the Muslims. Whether this sheer rivalry that was the main stay of their alliance with the Muslims must be discounted, because sheer emotion, no matter how strong it is, cannot provide solutions to the mundane demands of everyday living. Thus the stirring of the Bedouins around Madīnah was concentrated away from the land of Khuzāʿah, which remained pacific, that is in the lands to the east and south-east of Madīnah.

4.1 The Pacification of the Banū Sulaym

Banū Sulaym and their traditional allies of Banū Ghaṭafān were the chief Bedouin tribes around Madīnah to cause concern and insecurity to the Muslims. They were formidable fighters, and of cruel-hearted disposition, and confirmed in unbelief and hypocrisy. The Qur'ānic denunciation of the Bedouins cannot be interpreted as universally applicable to all of them, because the Qur'ān also speaks kindly of those Bedouins who expended in the way of God.[8] Thus the denunciation can only refer to particular groups of them. Among these, the Bedouins of Banū Sulaym and Ghaṭafān were a prime example. They caused the Muslims of Madīnah considerable worries, and were the privy to their defeat in the battle of Ḥunayn.[9]

It is of Bedouins of this brand and breed that the Qur'ān spoke of as:

> *Being most confirmed in unbelief and hypocrisy and they deserved not to learn of the* ḥudūd *(limits) of what God has revealed unto His Messenger.* [*al-Tawbah* 9:97][10]

News reached the Prophet (peace be upon him), through his informants among the Bedouins, of the stirrings of the formidable Ghaṭafān and Sulaym. As was his work to do, he took this news very seriously, and acted upon it, decisively and swiftly. Before those Bedouins could march against Madīnah, the Prophet (peace be upon him), once more, put his superior war strategy of general mobilization and permanent combat-readiness into action. In a few days of marching, hiding by day, marching by night, the Muslims' army, commanded by the Prophet (peace be upon him) himself, reached the heartland of Ghaṭafān and Sulaym. When they camped at a place known as Qarqarat al-Kudr, the Prophet (peace be upon him) learned that Sulaym and Ghaṭafān had fled, in every direction to the furthest extremity of their valley, and into the wide open desert. They were in such disarray, because the speed and strength of the Muslim response had taken them completely by surprise. Evidence of their disarray was indicated by the fact that they left behind almost all of their animal wealth, amounting to 500 camels. Anyone familiar with the great love which the Bedouins harbour for their camel herds, will easily infer that those Bedouins were struck by terrible fear of the

Muslims' reprisal against their aggressive scheming, which had been wholly unprovoked.

The Prophet (peace be upon him) and the Muslims, likewise, conducted expeditions against Banū Thaʿlabah and Banū Muḥārib at Dhū ʿAmr. Those again, like Banū Sulaym and Ghaṭafān, ran away to remote mountains in Najd, and the Prophet (peace be upon him) and his force returned safely to Madīnah, with the booty they had come into from their encounter with Sulaym and Ghaṭafān. No booty, however, was captured from Thaʿlabah, and Muḥārib.

5. THE MUSLIM BLOCKADE OF THE WESTERN CARAVAN ROUTE

The Quraysh did not only suffer the terrible humiliation and defeat at Badr, but they also suffered no less affliction due to the Muslim blockade of their vital commerce routes to the north and south. They deliberated about ways and means of dodging the blockade at great length. Eventually, they thought that they could revive the eastern route that passed through Iraq, long abandoned because of its harshness, its remoteness, and the scarcity of water wells on the route. But they had no choice but to try the eastern route. One Ṣafwān ibn Umayyah volunteered to command a trial trip to Syria, through the eastern route traversing Iraq. The caravan would carefully make its way through the friendly territory of Bakr ibn Wā'il, traditional allies of the Quraysh. The scarcity of water could be dealt with as, it being winter time, demand for water would be minimal. However, the Prophet (peace be upon him) was informe that a caravan was ambushed by the Muslims at a place called al-Qaradah. The Muslim commander, the celebrated Zayd ibn Ḥārithah (formerly Zayd ibn Muḥammad), returned with the caravan, worth one hundred thousand Dirhams completely intact. Thus the agony and indignation of the Quraysh and their resolve to wage their war of vengeance reached a climax. War was inevitable, as the Muslim challenge would neither pass away, nor could be evaded.

6. THE MAKKAH MARCH TO UḤUD

The stage was set for a new and bloody confrontation at the battlefield. The Quraysh mobilized every possible means and every possible resource they could muster for this decisive battle, in which they sought to avenge their dead and other losses at Badr. A huge army was drawn together, numbering about three thousand soldiers, of whom seven hundred were in full armour, and two hundred on horseback. They were accompanied by three thousand camels for riding, not counting other camels used for transport. At the insistence of Hind, the women of the Quraysh joined the expedition in great colours and musical companies, singing and dancing. Some of the Abyssinians of the Quraysh joined in the expedition, thus greatly adding to its colours and might. Al-ʿAbbās, uncle of the Prophet, was fearful for the fate of his nephew and the Muslims. It was al-ʿAbbās who hired a man from Makkah to warn the Prophet (peace be upon him) of the advancing army.

6.1 News of Quraysh's March reaches the Prophet

As the grim news reached the Prophet (peace be upon him) of the new Quraysh offensive – news which can hardly have been a surprise, in view of the effective economic blockade which the Muslims enforced against the Quraysh, he quickly called a public meeting, to which all Muslims were invited. The hypocrites were not excluded. The meeting debated the best way to meet the advancing army. The Prophet (peace be upon him) was of the view that it was best to let the encounter take place in the city itself. The Muslims would be entrenched in the houses of Madīnah, as the fighting would be in the streets and from house to house. This way, the Quraysh force would be deprived of two major advantages – its relatively large cavalry contingent, and its superiority in numbers –since the whole force would have to act in small units, to engage in hand-to-hand street fighting. ʿAbdullāh ibn Abī Salūl, chief of the hypocrites, was of the same opinion as the Prophet (peace be upon him). He argued that this was the way in which Madīnah had traditionally and successfully defended itself in the past.

6.2 The Prophet Holds a Shūrā Council

The younger Muslims, however, were of a different opinion. They wanted to march out to meet the enemy, fearful that fighting inside the city would be interpreted as cowardice, and moreover would entail destruction of what they were seeking to defend. These younger Muslims, many of whom had missed the opportunity to participate in Badr, and were keen to make up for it, were the more vocal party. The ultimate resolution was that the Muslim army would march out to meet the advancing enemy, outside Madīnah.

It is significant to note here the consistency of the Prophet's use of the *shūrā* institution. Particularly noteworthy here is his ready willingness to abide by the outcome of the consultation, even though it was contrary to his own considered opinion. The Prophet (peace be upon him), as was typical of his style of leadership, moved quickly to put the agreed resolution into practice. Having performed ʿAṣr prayer, he went into his house, and aided by Abū Bakr and ʿUmar, his two principal aides, put on his war armour. Meanwhile, those young Muslims became apprehensive, lest they had persuaded the gracious Prophet (peace be upon him) against his better judgment. To them, it was clear enough that the Prophet's opinion was not a matter of divine revelation, otherwise they would not have challenged it, still they felt guilty that they had challenged the Prophet (peace be upon him). So, they approached Him and expressed some apology for challenging him. However, the Prophet (peace be upon him) firmly refused to reconsider a decision that had been agreed upon by a vast majority of the *Shūrā* Council, only a short while before. He said: 'It would not behove a Prophet, when he puts his armour on, to take it off, until God had decided between him and his enemy.'

6.3 The Muslim Army Marches to Uḥud

The Prophet (peace be upon him) then set out in the direction of Uḥud. It was a Friday, late afternoon. The Prophet's refusal to reconsider the *Shūrā* Council's decision to go out to meet the enemy had angered Ibn Salūl. Among the other senior Muslims, also of the opinion that the encounter be inside Madīnah, were Saʿd ibn Muʿādh leader of Aws, and Saʿd ibn ʿUbādah, leader of Khazraj. But being devout Muslims, they accepted the decision with good heart and spirit, in contrast to Ibn Salūl, who continued to be dissatisfied. After the *ʿAṣr* prayer, the Muslim army moved in the direction of Uḥud. It was approximately one thousand men strong. The Prophet (peace be upon him) was on horseback and in full armour. The two gallant Saʿds of the Aws and Khazraj were in the vanguard ahead of him. The army camped at al-Shaykhān, just outside the city in the direction of Uḥud, whereas the Quraysh army was known to have camped at the middle of the valley of Uḥud. The Prophet (peace be upon him) knew very well that the Quraysh on that day enjoyed two major strategic advantages:

a. Their number was at least three times that of the Muslims.

b. They had a sizeable cavalry.

It was these two advantages which he had thought to offset by fighting within the city.

He now had to come up with a different strategy. This was to move quickly and quietly under the cover of darkness, in the small hours of Saturday, to a position just at the foot of the mountain of Uḥud, and station his troops between the enemy to the south and the mountain of Uḥud to the north. In this way, his army would have its back to the mount of Uḥud, and the enemy would lie exposed in front of him. This strategy was carried out, with the help of some Madīnan Bedouins, who knew the terrain of Madīnah very well.

6.4 Developments at al-Shaykhān

Al-Wāqidī[11] states that the Prophet encamped at a place called al-Shaykhān, near Ḥarrah, on the eastern side of Madīnah, on the road to Uḥud. Ibn Hishām, however, says that the Prophet's encampment was at a place called al-Shawṭ. Maybe, these were different names for the same place. There the Prophet (peace be upon him) inspected his army, prayed the *Maghrib* and *ʿIshā'* prayers and decided on a number of important issues. Al-Wāqidī states that a small contingent of Jews, allies of Ibn Salūl, turned up at al-Shaykhān, and wanted to join the Muslim army. But the Prophet (peace be upon him) turned them back, no doubt because of the souring of Muslim-Jewish relations, in the wake of the Banū Qaynuqāʿ affair. However, Ibn Hishām's version, merely mentions that Ibn Salūl sought the Prophet's permission to bring forward his Jewish allies, a request which the Prophet (peace be upon him) sharply declined, much to the exasperation of Ibn Salūl, who was still simmering over the rejection, by the *Shūrā* Council, of his strategy of meeting the enemy inside the city. It must have been this development which prompted him to return to Madīnah with almost one third of the army, followed no doubt by the hypocrites, and those whose feeble hearts had faltered. The dissension of Ibn Salūl, and the split he had caused in the Muslim ranks at that critical moment, when they were getting ready to meet their enemy, should have been depressing and demoralizing. However, it did not seem to affect the Muslims' spirits, which remained very high indeed. Two incidents give a sure indication of the steadfastness and morale of the Muslims:

a. A group of Muslim youth of very tender age stealthily joined the army, apparently without seeking the Prophet's permission. They were eleven in number altogether. Two of them, namely Rāfiʿ ibn Khadīj and Samurah ibn Jundub were fifteen years old and the rest were all thirteen years old. At first, the Prophet (pbuh) permitted Rāfiʿ to join the expedition, on the account of his reputation as a marksman. Then Samurah and his guardian protested that if Rāfiʿ was a good marksman, Samurah could overcome him in wrestling. A measure of the light heartedness of the gracious Prophet (peace be upon him), and his good cheer at a time of crisis was provided when he joyfully replied to the protestation of Samurah: 'You say you can win a wrestling contest with Rāfiʿ then let us have one.'

Indeed, Samurah easily put Rāfiʿ down in wrestling, while the Muslims cheered. The Prophet (peace be upon him) was pleased by the gallantry of the two boys and their high-mindedness, and felt assured that such a company of men could not easily be defeated in battle. In his Friday sermon at the mosque that day, the Prophet (peace be upon him) told the Muslims that victory, in the impending battle of Uḥud, would be theirs, on the condition that they were patient, and forbearing and obeyed his orders. The insistence of these two boys on joining the expedition at the young age of fifteen was indeed a good omen, and a heartening event. Still more heartening, was the insistence of nine other boys, who were only thirteen years old. These the Prophet (peace be upon him) did turn down, and insisted that they should return to the city. However, he did allow them to join the next battle of al-Khandaq, when they were fifteen years old.

The names of those gallant boys, as given by al-Wāqidī[12] were:

1. ʿAbdullāh ibn ʿUmar ibn al-Khaṭṭāb: Muhājir
2. Usāmah ibn Zayd ibn al-Ḥārith: Muhājir
3. Zayd ibn al-Arqam ibn abī al-Arqam: Muhājir
4. Zayd ibn Thābit: Anṣār.
5. Al-Nuʿmān ibn Bashīr: Anṣār
6. Al-Barā' ibn ʿĀzib: Anṣār
7. Usayd ibn Zuhayr: Anṣār
8. Urbah ibn Aws: Anṣār
9. Abū Saʿīd al-Khudrī: Anṣār

b. The second incident, which indicates the high morale and high spirits of the Muslim army, is provided by Zakwān ibn ʿAbd Qays:[13] The Prophet (peace be upon him) wanted a bodyguard. He said:

> 'Who will guard us tonight?'
> 'I will, O Messenger of God!'
> 'But who are you?'
> Zakwān ibn ʿAbd Qays.

> 'Sit down,' said the Prophet (peace be upon him), and repeated his request for a bodyguard:
> 'I will O Messenger of God!'
> 'But who are you?' Enquired the Prophet (peace be upon him).
> 'I am Ibn 'Abd Qays.'
> The Prophet (peace be upon him), then repeated his request for the third time. Again it was the same man who answered, with a different name!
> The Prophet was silent for a while, then he said: 'All right, the three of you shall be my bodyguards.'
> At that point Zakwān came forward:
> 'But where are your two companions?'
> 'There are none, it was only me who answered you in three times, O Messenger of God,' said Zakwān.
> All right, said the Prophet (peace be upon him), then you shall be my bodyguard,
> May God preserve you.

Then the general night guard for the whole army was selected. It consisted of fifty men, commanded by Muḥammad ibn Maslamah, who succeeded in keeping the Quraysh Cavalry at bay for the whole night, though they came quite near to the Muslim encampment at Ḥarrah.

In the early morning, while still dark, the Prophet (peace be upon him) made his way to the foot of Uḥud, as we described above, while Ubayy ibn Salūl, and presumably his Jewish allies, made it back to Madīnah. If the presence of this Jewish contingent, mentioned by al-Wāqidī, and ignored by Ibn Hishām, was authentic, then it meant that they were not representative of the generality of the Jews, who by then were quite opposed to the Prophet (peace be upon him) and his Muslim state. The return of Ibn Salūl was from al-Shawṭ (al-Shaykhān) according to Ibn Hishām,[14] but al-Wāqidī[15] states that Ibn Salūl went all the way with the Prophet (peace be upon him) to Uḥud, before returning to Madīnah. In the very nature of things, Ibn Hishām's account seems more credible, because a hesitant fighter would not go all the way to the battlefield, and when the enemy was in sight, allow himself, or would be allowed, to return back. It is more credible that he turned back at the midway point of al-Shaykhān, and probably during the night.

7. THE BATTLE OF UḤUD, EVENTS OF A FEARFUL DAY

After the dawn prayer, the Prophet (peace be upon him) set his army and organized it in rows, just as he did when praying, with Uḥud at their back, and the Quraysh between them and Makkah. He placed the archers on top of Uḥud to his left, and appointed their commander as ʿAbdullāh ibn Jubayr of Banū ʿĀmir ibn ʿAwf. He told them emphatically:

> Keep the cavalry of Quraysh back, make sure they do not overrun us from behind! Do not, under any circumistances, leave your position at the top of the hill, be we victorious or be we defeated. Stay put in your places in all circumstances. Make sure that they do not overrun as from your direction,[16] said the Prophet (peace be upon him) most emphatically.

Then the Prophet (peace be upon him) passed the Banner, as at Badr, to Muṣʿab ibn ʿUmayr, no doubt because he was of Makhzūm ibn ʿAbd al-Dār, the traditional Banner-bearers of the Quraysh, since the days of *Jāhiliyyah*. The Prophet (peace be upon him) then strictly ordered the Muslims not to start shooting until he gave his orders. The battle cry of Uḥud was 'Amit…Amit,' Kill! Kill! Kill the enemy!

Then the events of that day poured forth like a torrent or hurricane. It was by far the longest and the most trying day in the history of Islam, a day of sorrow, grief and suffering, the like of which had never happened before. The noble, gracious Muḥammad (peace be upon him), through no mistake of his, witnessed and suffered untold grief and hardship; he witnessed his army move from certain victory to defeat, through the negligence and disobedience of the archers, on the top of the mountain. He saw his Companions cut into pieces and slain. Worst of all, his best friend, his beloved uncle, the most gallant of men, Ḥamzah, was killed by an Abyssinian slave, by the name of Waḥshī. Later on, the Prophet (peace be upon him) stood over the body of Ḥamzah, horribly mutilated by the then callous, unbeliever, Hind bint ʿUtbah, wife of Abū Sufyān. Tears gushed from his beautiful, radiant face, marred by the wounds and cuts, he had suffered that day. 'Never have I been more angry in my whole life! If God would give me victory over the Quraysh, I vow by Him I will mutilate thirty of their dead,'[17] the Prophet (peace be upon him) cried out.

Yet God revealed to him that this vow is not a sound one, and he was duly educated with the best guidance on this issue, indeed a manifest Qur'ānic miracle. Thus Muḥammad (peace be upon him) couldn't be the author of the Qur'ān, since no one would rebuke himself and reverse his position in such circumstances. The Qur'ānic revelation reads:

> *If you inflict punishment, then inflict only so much as you have suffered; but should you endure patiently, that is even better for the patient.* [*The Bees:* 16:126]

When the gracious Prophet (peace be upon him) received this Qur'ānic revelation, he repented and vowed that he would never have any of the dead mutilated.

Yet the grief of the Prophet (peace be upon him) over the martyrdom of his most beloved uncle, who was also his long-time companion, actually never abated. Such was the profundity of his sense of bereavement at the loss of the gallant Ḥamzah that, when he returned to Madīnah that day and found the women of the Anṣār weeping over their martyred husbands and fathers, he could not contain himself, but loudly lamented: 'What about Ḥamzah! What about Hamzah! No one seems to be weeping over his death today,' the Prophet's gracious eyes were again filled with copious tears.

Years later, when the Prophet (peace be upon him) first set his eyes on Wahṣhī, the slayer of Ḥamzah, who then declared his Islam, and thus escaping the death penalty passed upon him, he was overcome with grief and sat down to ask him in a trembling, sobbing voice: 'Will you, Waḥshī, just narrate to me how you killed him?' When Waḥshī had told his story, the Prophet (peace be upon him) turned his face from him, as was his habit when angry or greatly upset, 'Vanish from my sight!' He said, or 'I do not ever want to see you again.'

Thereafter Waḥshī would hide when the Prophet (peace be upon him) passed by, lest the sight of him should cause the Prophet (peace be upon him) hurt. He became a good Muslim and joined the Muslim army against the apostates. It is said that it was Waḥshī who actually killed Musaylimah the Liar, head of the apostates of Najd.

8. THE PROPHET SUFFERED SERIOUS WOUNDS

The defeat of the Muslims, and the deaths of Ḥamzah, and the beloved Muṣʿab ibn ʿUmayr were not the only calamities which the Prophet (peace be upon him) suffered that day at Uḥud. His own person for the first time suffered serious injuries. A certain ʿUtbah ibn Abī Waqqāṣ (brother of Saʿd ibn Abī Waqqāṣ) hit him very hard with a stone, which cut a deep wound in his gracious face and cut his lower lip, broke his front teeth, and threw him to the ground. The Prophet (peace be upon him) rose, his face covered with blood. But he fell again, this time into a hole, dug by one of the polytheists, by the name of Abu ʿAmr, as a trap. Last but not least, a certain ʿAbdulllāh ibn Shihāb inflicted a second wound on his forehead, and a certain ibn Qamī'ah, who vowed to kill the Prophet (peace be upon him), dealt a blow at the Prophet's head, which was diverted a little bit by one of the Muslims, yet resulted in wounding his two cheeks, pushing his helmet deep into them. More blood was then gushing from the Prophet's face, yet the Prophet (peace be upon him) was in good cheer, indeed shouting to the small band of men, who gathered around him, to fight hard, saying that his own injuries were just minor wounds, in a brave attempt to keep up their morale.

9. THE MUSLIMS DEFEND THE PROPHET

The extent of the Muslim's losses at Uḥud were devastating. About seventy of them lay dead, including Ḥamzah, and Muṣ'ab ibn 'Umayr; the Muslims were in random, unprecedented flight in the face of their enemies. So great was the magnitude of their defeat, after their initial victory, that some prominent Companions of the Prophet ran for their lives, leaving the Prophet (peace be upon him) alone on the battlefield. 'Umar ibn al-khaṭṭāb, and Ṭalḥah ibn 'Ubaydullāh did not run away. However, on hearing the cry that Muḥammad was killed, they lost heart completely, and threw down their weapons and sat down on the ground, disconsolate. Anas ibn al-Naḍr found them in that pitiful state. 'Why are you sitting like this?' asked Anas. They said: 'Alas! The Prophet has been killed.' 'Then die as he has died for the sake of Islam,' shouted Anas, vividly annoyed.

By saying this, Anas ibn al-Naḍr apparently brought these great Muslims to their senses. As for himself, he plunged deep into the fray, fighting gallantly until he fell with more than seventy cuts on his body. Indeed, his body was so defamed by wounds, that only his sister could recognize him by a dye on his fingertips (henna).

10. ANAS IBN AL-NAḌR

The brave showing of Anas ibn an-Naḍr, a relative of Anas ibn Mālik, personal attendant of the Prophet (peace be upon him), was not an isolated case that day. It was, in fact, because of the bravery and heroism of a small band of Muslims, who defended the Prophet (peace be upon him) with their lives, that the unbelievers were not able to kill him. Again and again they tried to kill him, and every time they were driven back. Of these men, the most prominent were:

1. Abū Dujānah, the red-banded knight.
2. 'Alī ibn Abī Ṭālib.
3. 'Umar ibn al-Khaṭṭāb.

4. Abū Bakr al-Ṣiddīq.
5. Saʿd ibn Abī Waqqāṣ (muhājir), who shielded the Prophet (peace be upon him) with his body.
6. Nusaybah bint Kaʿb – Umm ʿUmārah (the famous woman-knight).
7. Muṣʿab ibn ʿUmayr, the holder of the main white banner, (who was later killed) and became a martyr.
8. Ḥamzah ibn ʿAbd al-Muṭṭalib (martyred).
9. Usayd ibn Ḥuḍayr, the holder of the Aws banner.
10. Saʿd ibn ʿUbādah, the holder of the Khazraj banner.
11. Saʿd ibn Muʿādh, Anṣār, the head of Aws tribe.
12. Muḥammad ibn Maslamah, Anṣār.
13. Ṭalḥah ibn ʿUbaydullāh, Muhājir.
14. Al-Ḥubāb ibn al-Mundhir, Anṣār.
15. Abū ʿUbaydah ibn al-Jarrāḥ, Muhājir.
16. Al-Zubayr ibn al-ʿAwwām, Muhājir.
17. ʿAṣim ibn Thābit, Anṣār.
18. Al-Ḥārith ibn al-Simmah, Anṣār.
19. Sahl ibn Ḥunayf, Anṣār.
20. Umm Ayman, Barakah, the Abyssinian governess of the Prophet and mother of Usāmah ibn Zayd.
21. ʿUmārah ibn Ziyād ibn as-Sakan, Anṣār, who died on the Prophet's lap having defended him heroically, sustaining more than fourteen wounds.
22. Qatādah ibn al-Nuʿmān, Anṣār, who lost one eye defending the Prophet, and it was he who had kept the Prophet's broken bow as a relic.

The youthful Qatādah ibn al-Nuʿmān, narrates al-Wāqidī, came to the Prophet (peace be upon him): Messenger of God and said:

> 'You see I lost my eye, and I have a young and beautiful wife, whom I love so much, and she likewise loves me. But I am fearful, that now she would be put off by my blind eye.'

Qatādah said that the Prophet (peace be upon him) took the ball of his eye, which Qatādah was still carrying in his hand, and put it back in its place, and blessing it with his gracious hand, it became as if it had never been hurt. That eye never gave Qatādah any more trouble, and was the better of his two eyes in old age, told Qatādah.

The above list of men and women, who stood their ground in Uḥud, and did not run away, is not exhaustive. Though he gives only fourteen names, al-Wāqidī himself implicitly concedes that his list is not exhaustive, because he immediately afterwards mentions, on the authority of Yaʿqūb ibn ʿAmr ibn Qatādah, that the men who stood their ground, when the Muslims were defeated and took to fight in Uḥud, were thirty in number. They all said: 'O Messenger of God, our faces will defend your face, and our bodies, your body. May peace be with you, not bidding you goodbye, *Inshā' Allāh*. It is astonishing that al-Wāqidī's list of fourteen, did not include ʿUmar ibn Al-Khaṭṭāb or indeed such men as ʿUmārah ibn al-Sakan, Qatādah ibn al-Nuʿmān or Muṣʿab ibn ʿUmayr, who might have been martyred early in the day. Al-Wāqidī's list also failed to mention the two Muslim women who also stood their ground around the Prophet (peace be upon him), and defended him, although he mentioned them elsewhere.

The Prophet (peace be upon him) himself fought gallantly, and ferociously until his bow was broken and never moved backward an inch, nor at any point lost his heart or high spirit. In the darkest moment, when all the fighting was just around him, and he was the prime target of the Quraysh, and though his own Companions were in flight, despite his repeated shouts to them, he sat down and put the head of the dying ʿUmārah ibn al-Sakan on his lap, and did not get up until ʿUmārah had passed away peacefully.[18]

Then the Prophet (peace be upon him) gave his order to retreat towards Uḥud, in the direction of al-Mihras, a well at the edge of Uḥud. Retreating with him, were most of the men we gave in the above list of 22 names. To these, we must now add some men who were returning to the Prophet, as he made it towards the hill, with the Quraysh in hot pursuit shouting 'O al-ʿUzzā, O Hubal!' The names of the new comers were:

23. Abū Ṭalḥah, who shielded the Prophet (peace be upon him) with his body, just as did Saʿd ibn Abī Waqqāṣ and Abū Dujānah.
24. Zayd ibn Ḥārithah (not mentioned in al-Wāqidī's original list, which is surprising, due to the intimacy of Zayd to the Prophet).
25. Al-Miqdād ibn ʿAmr.
26. Al-Sā'ib ibn Uthmān ibn Maẓʿūn.
27. Ḥāṭib ibn Abī Baltaʿah, the man who sent a warning to the Quraysh before the *fatḥ* of Makkah.
28. ʿUtbah ibn Ghazwān (who confessed that he was just fighting in defence of his homeland, Yathrib).
29. Khirāsh ibn al-Simmah.
30. Qurbah ibn ʿAmr.
31. Bishr ibn al-Barā' ibn Maʿrūr.
32. Abū Nā'ilah, Silkān ibn Salamah.
33. Abū Ruḥm al-Ghifārī.

Thus the number of men and women who stood their ground in the wake of defeat at Uḥud was even greater than thirty, exceeding the number given in the version of Yaʿqūb ibn ʿAmr ibn Qatādah. This is not unreasonable, since they managed to repulse the attacks of the Quraysh, again and again. In the confusion and chaos of the day, it would have been difficult for anyone to keep an exact record of just how many Muslims managed to hold their ground with the Prophet (peace be upon him). It is not unreasonable to suppose that there were, in fact, more than thirty men and women. To the above lists, we may now add the name of:

34. Mālik ibn Anas, Anṣār, mentioned by Ibn Hishām[19] to have sucked the blood from the face of the Prophet, in an effort to stop the bleeding.

However, the Prophet (peace be upon him) managed to complete his retreat safely to the foot of Uḥud, shielded by such men as Abū Dujānah, until he was killed, ʿUmārah ibn al-Sakan, also killed, Saʿd ibn Abī Waqqās, Abū Bakr, ʿUmar, Zayd ibn Ḥārith, Nusaybah bint Kaʿb, ʿAlī ibn Abī Ṭālib, al-Zubayr ibn Al-ʿAwwām, Ṭalḥah ibn ʿUbaydullāh, al-Ḥārith ibn Abī al-Simmah, etc. As the Prophet (peace be upon him) reached the foot of the mountain, Ubayy ibn Khalaf, long time enemy of the Prophet (peace be upon him) since Makkah days, who used to threaten him before Hijrah, got word that Muḥammad (peace be upon him) was still alive. He then came charging up to kill him: 'O Muḥammad,' he shouted, 'may I not live, if you live today.' The Muslim force defending the Prophet got ready to intercept him, when the Prophet (peace be upon him) pushed them aside, and jumped forward with such force and determination that some of them fell to the ground.[20] He (peace be upon him) shouted, 'let him come, let him come!'

Then the Prophet (peace be upon him) snatched a spear from the hands of al-Ḥārith ibn al-Simmah, took a step forward and threw it with terrific force against the attacker. The spear struck him in the neck; he turned his horse and ran away. He died on the way to Makkah.

The story of Ubayy ibn Khalaf is very significant. Here was a man with tremendous hatred towards the Prophet (peace be upon him), who continually harassed him at Makkah, and used to threaten his life. He once said to the Prophet (peace be upon him): 'I have this terrific horse, its name is al-ʿAwadh, I will feed it plenty of Dhurrah, because one day I am going to kill you with it,' (meaning in war).[21]

The Prophet (peace be upon him) answered: 'It is I who is going to kill you, one day, O Ubayy ibn Khalaf.' So just as Ubayy made good his promise of attempting to kill the Prophet (peace be upon him), so the Prophet made good this promise. This explains his curious insistence, that he be let alone to deal with Ubayy, unaided by anyone. It was customary of the Prophet (peace be upon him) that, when he set his mind to do something, a strange singleness of purpose and resolve set on his demeanour, and his face would glow like fire and glitter like solid pure steel (so that none would look like him, when he was earnest).[22] When Umayyah ibn Khalaf returned to the Quraysh wounded, his morale was crushed: 'Oh! I am going to die,' he would say. 'No, your wound is but a slight one,' the Quraysh would answer. 'But he has vowed, since the days of Makkah, that he would kill me. For, by God, if he so much as spat on me, he would kill me,' said Umayyah, frightened at the prospect of his imminent death. Indeed, the man died a few days later!

11. THE HEROES OF UḤUD

1.1 The Prophet Himself[23]

Foremost among the heroes of Uḥud is the Prophet (peace be upon him) himself, who managed to withdraw in an orderly manner, and thus achieve two major goals:

a. He managed to come out alive, and to save his army from complete destruction, which was a distinct possibility, but for God's mercy and His favour for the Muslims. The total number of Muslims killed at Uḥud was four or five from the Muhājirīn, and seventy from the Anṣār. Thus the bulk of the Muslim army returned safely to Madīnah. The Prophet's inventive and energetic thinking contributed, in no smaller measure, to the final outcome of the battle. The army of the Quraysh was still in the vicinity of Madīnah. So the Prophet (peace be upon him), though utterly exhausted so that he led the noon prayer that day seated, quickly regrouped and reorganized his army, and ordered a hot pursuit of the Quraysh. The Prophet (peace be upon him) himself took personal command of the army, and the Muslims joined in good cheer, and with a great deal of enthusiasm. The Muslim army marched on Sunday; the battle of Uḥud was on Saturday. Abū Sufyan and the Quraysh were pondering a fresh attack against the Muslims, to eradicate them. When they heard of the Prophet's renewed march, they hastily made their way back in the direction of Makkah. The casualties from the Quraysh were relatively light, twenty-two of them were killed.

b. Other heroes of Uḥud included:

1. Ḥamzah
2. Muṣʿab ibn ʿUmayr
3. Abū Dujānah
4. ʿUmārah ibn al-Sakan
5. Anas ibn Abī Ṭālib
6. ʿAlī ibn Abī Waqqāṣ
7. Ṭalḥah ibn ʿUbaydullāh
8. Nusaybah bint Kaʿb
9. ʿAbdullāh ibn Jaḥsh [cousin of the Prophet (peace be upon him)]

And many others.

Yet the list of the Uḥud heroes will not be complete without giving the extraordinary story of Ḥanẓalah, Ghasīlu al-Malā'ikah (i.e. he whom the angels had washed), and that of Abū Dujānah (the red-banded hero).

11.2 The Story of Ḥanẓalah (the Martyr washed by the angels)

Ḥanẓalah was a young, energetic Anṣārī, who was supposed to get married that Friday to a beautiful Anṣārī girl, whom he loved very much, and to whom he had been betrothed for a long time. But that was the very Friday on which the Muslims were to march out to meet their enemy at Uḥud. Ḥanzalah's predicament was acute. He experienced a great conflict in his heart, between his love and commitment to the cause of Islam and his chivalrous Arabic sense of Murū'ah on the one hand, and on the other hand the desire of his heart to get married to the girl he loved so dearly; an event he had awaited and looked forward to for so long. He went to see the Prophet (peace be upon him) and said:

> 'O Messenger of God, I am getting married today, and I don't like to be left behind by you.'
> 'It is all right. Get married today, spend the night with your bride, and join us tomorrow morning at Uḥud,' said the Prophet (peace be upon him).[24]

Ḥanẓalah ibn Abī ʿĀmir, was on that day wedded to Jamīlah bint ʿAbdullāh ibn Ubayy ibn Salūl, head of the hypocrites of Madīnah, a Madīnan of considerable wealth and prominence, before the inception of Islam. He spent the night with her, washed himself from *janābah*, and was ready to set out for the battleground when his bride clung to him fearing that he would be martyred, as she had seen in her dreams, Ḥanẓalah again slept with her. But this time he hurried forth to the battlefield, without washing from *janābah*. There was simply no time for that, else he would miss the battle and be of the *Khawālif* (those left behind), a status which amounted to the terrible crime of deserting not only the honour of defending the homeland, but that of deserting the faith of Islam, and of letting down the Prophet (peace be upon him) and the Muslims. So Ḥanẓalah rushed forth to the battlefield. He arrived in time to take part in the battle. When the Prophet (peace be upon him) was exposed, he fought gallantly, recklessly risking his life. He was killed after having a duel with Abū Sufyān, the commander-in-chief of the Makkan army at Uḥud. He came very close to killing Abū Sufyān, but the latter shouted as Ḥanẓalah threw him and sat on top of him, but a Makkan soldier overpowered Ḥanẓalah and managed to kill him.

The Prophet (peace be upon him) later said: 'Ḥanẓalah is being washed by the angels! Ask his wife what was the matter with him.'[25] They later asked her, and she said that when Ḥanẓalah heard the battle cries, he went out *junuban*, i.e. without washing from *janābah*, which is a religious obligation for a Muslim after having sex with a woman!

11.3 The Story of Abū Dujānah: (The red-banded hero)

A well-known knight of the Anṣār, by the name of Simāk ibn Kharashah, better known as Abū Dujānah. (The man with a red-head-band), was a formidable fighter feared by everyone. He converted to Islam, the Prophet (peace be upon him) appeared at the front of the Muslim army. He raised his sword high, and dished it saying:

> 'Who will take this sword of mine with its right?'
> ʿUmar ibn al-Khaṭṭāb rose and claimed the sword, but he was denied by the Prophet (peace be upon him). Then al-Zubayr ibn al-ʿAwwām rose to take it, but he, too, was rejected.
> The two noble Companions were much mortified.
> Then Abū Dujānah rose and asked:
> 'What is its right, O Messenger of God?'
> 'Its right is to smite the enemy with it until it breaks,' replied the Prophet (peace be upon him).
> 'I will take it by its right, O Messenger of God,' said Abū Dujānah.

Abū Dujānah and his red scarf have become a symbol of heroism and dedication to the cause of Islam, in contemporary times. Muslim freedom fighters everywhere, especially the young among them, can be seen wearing those red scarves around their heads, when marching to the front lines of the battlefield, symbolizing their resolve to fight until victory or martyrdom. This phenomenon has been observed in Bosnia, Afghanistan and among the *mujāhidūn* of the Sudan, marching to meet invaders from Eriterea, Ethiopia and Uganda in recent times. Abū Dujānah's example, his sacrifice and dedication for the cause of God, has been eternalized, in fulfilment of God's promise, in the Qur'ān, that martyrs are not dead, but ever living.

> *Think not of those killed in the cause of God as dead, Nay, they are alive, receiving their sustenance in the presence of their Lord.* [*ʿĀl ʿĪmrān* 3:169]

12. EPILOGUE: THE LESSONS OF UḤUD

12.1 Victory from Allah, Defeat from Satan

No battle in the history of Islam has received the kind of elaborate commentary that Uḥud has received in the Qur'ān. It is true that the Battle of Badr is referred to a number of times in the Qur'ān. But in each case, the Qur'ānic references to Badr indicate that the victory which the Muslims achieved was from God alone, who sent down His angels and His hosts to make it possible. The Prophet (peace be upon him) and the Muslims contributed to the outcome of the Battle of Badr, their contribution alone could never have brought them the kind of victory they achieved at Badr. That recurring comment on Badr, by the Qur'ān, was necessary, lest the Muslims succumb to human arrogance, and the illusion that it was they, their cleverness and courage, which won the day at Badr. By contrast, the Qur'ānic comment on Uḥud, is so elaborate and comprehensive in nature, that no small detail, no turn or twist of the battle was spared. Altogether, there are sixty verses of the Qur'ānic comment on Badr and Uḥud, from verse 121 to verse 180 of *Sūrah Āl ʿĪmrān.* At the outset, the Qur'ān draws a brief comparison between Badr and Uḥud. Badr is a symbol of victory, but since everything about Badr was of God's making, the message is clear: that victory is exclusively from God (assuredly all victory is from God). Since Uḥud is a symbol of defeat, and since defeat at Uḥud was caused by dissension and disagreement among the Muslims, brought about by the Satan, the lesson is also clear: that defeat is from *nafs* (or ego) of the Muslims, as it is also from Satan – an allusion to Satan's role in tempting the Muslims into rebellion, dissent and disagreement. The Qur'ān tells the Muslims that God had fulfilled his eternal promise of making them victorious and so they were indeed victorious in the initial phase of the battle at Uḥud.

12.2 The Real Cause of the Defeat

The Qur'ān lays it out clearly, that the prime cause of defeat at Uḥud was the disobedience and dissension of some Muslims, namely ar-Rumāt, i.e. the archers. God warned the Muslims many times that division and dissension are the prime causes of failure and defeat. At Uḥud, that lesson was practically demonstrated: the Muslims were initially victorious, then they disagreed among themselves (the archers) and they disobeyed the Messenger of God, and defeat became their lot. This is one of the prime lessons of the painful drama of Uḥud:

> *God has made good His promise unto you when you routed them by His leave, until your courage failed you, and you quarrelled about the matter, and you were rebellious, after he had shown you that which you love. Some of you want (the good) of this life, and some of you want (the goods) of the Hereafter. Then He swayed you away from them, so as that He might try! Yet now He has pardoned you, and God is bounteous to the believers.* [*Āl ʿĪmrān* 3:152]

The archers were given explicit and very strict orders, by the Prophet himself, not to move from their position, on the top of the hill, under any circumstances. But as soon as they saw the initial defeat of the Quraysh, and saw some of the Muslims collecting booty, they started to leave their position on the top of the mount, and joined in the collection of the spoils. Their own commander, ʿAbdullāh ibn Jubayr, tried very hard to dissuade them from violating the Prophet's orders, but they were unruly and rebellious. It was Satan that was busy at work, exploiting their lust for worldly things and for wealth. Khālid ibn al-Walīd, the commander of the cavalry of the Quraysh, at that time, exploited the situation, and attacked the Muslims from the rear, and easily made defeat to be their lot.

12.3 God's Design in Permitting the Defeat of Muslims

The Qur'ānic verses here at issue, state very clearly why God permitted the defeat of the Muslims at Uḥud:

a. It was a trial for them to examine the extent and the strength of their faith in God and their love for Him.

b. The defeat was essential to sort out (*Tamḥīṣ*) the true believers, those capable of withstanding the trauma of defeat, of being killed and wounded and of seeing their loved ones killed and wounded. Those true believers would be set apart from the hypocrites and those who were feeble-hearted.

c. That God bestows His highest honours of martyrdom to whom He wills from among those Muslims, whom He loves and favours.

d.. That it would become very clear to them what God's universal laws are in connection with victory and defeat.

e. That the road to Paradise is fraught with trial and suffering, only the patient and the forbearing, will be able to endure the march along that road.

f. It was indeed very significant that the traumatic experience of Uḥud did not spare the gracious person of the Prophet (peace be upon him), though he was not in the least responsible for the failure and disobedience of the archers. That he was destined to suffer, as his Companions did, that he sustained grave wounds as they had sustained… and that, in addition, he had witnessed, to his utter sorrow, and horror, the killing and mutilation of his best friend and uncle Ḥamzah, the killing and mutilation of his cousin ʿAbdullāh ibn Jaḥsh, and the killing of his dear companion Muṣʿab ibn ʿUmayr… was meant to impress upon the Muslims that Muḥammad (peace be upon him) is the Messenger at the end of a long chain of Messengers, who had gone before him. As a Messenger, he was human, who could be wounded, who was mortal and human; not of divine nature. So, would the Muslims forsake and abandon their faith should Muḥammad (peace be upon him) die or be killed? This was indeed a strong rebuke to those sincere Muslims, who lost their heart when they heard the cry that Muḥammad (peace be upon him) had died.

g. Uḥud was also a lesson to the Muslims, concerning the reality of *al-Qaḍā' wa'l-Qadar* (divine decree and destiny). God had decreed that the Muslims would be defeated at Uḥud, because of their rebellion and disobedience, and that destiny must be carried out. God does not favour the Muslims if they become rebellious or sinful. Thus the Muslims ought not to be deluded into the error that, no matter what they do, God will allow them to be victorious and prevail over their enemies.

h. The Muslims, who ran for their lives, leaving the Prophet (peace be upon him) alone in the battlefield, were severely rebuked. It was declared that Satan had caused them to behave in that manner, because of their sins. How unbecoming of a true believer to flee in the face of the enemy, and how unbecoming of him, to abandon the Prophet (peace be upon him), when he was calling upon him not to do so.

i. Yet God was quick to declare His pardon for those Muslims who fled the battle. God is Bounteous to His servants. Knowing that, though they were not lacking in their love of God and his Messenger (peace be upon him), yet they were no more than humans, who were liable to suffer from all intrinsically human weaknesses and frailties. God told the Prophet (peace be upon him) that his heart had been rendered lenient and compassionate unto the Muslims, that it was by God's mercy that he was so, and he too, was ordered to pardon the fleeing Muslims, and to pray that God might forgive them.

j. Though the Muslims, especially the young ones, did not heed the Prophet's considered opinion not to go out to meet the enemy, and though some Muslims might have attributed the defeat at Uḥud to the *shūrā* practice which overruled the Prophet's opinion, yet there is nothing inherently wrong about *shūrā* practice. Far from this, the Prophet (peace be upon him) was most emphatically commanded to persist and to continue that *shūrā* practice among the generality of the Muslims. This is very significant, and it says a great deal about the importance of the *shūrā*, and that it is to be taken seriously at all times and circumstances. This is what the Prophet (peace be upon him) did at Uḥud, accepting and acting upon the outcome of the *Shūrā* Council, even though it ran counter to his own considered opinion. Since the context in which the *Shūrā* Council was held at Uḥud was strictly a war atmosphere, this made it all the more incumbent upon Muslim leaders and *Amīrs* to hold *Shūrā* Councils in peace-time when things were more relaxed and normal. The outcome of the *shūrā*, no matter what it turns out to be, must be binding upon the Prophet (peace be upon him) of God, to whom revelation was given, he who was the most learned and the most insightful of all men, then a *fortiori*, it must be viewed as binding on the ordinary Muslim leaders and *Amīrs*.

k. The Qur'ān reminded the Muslims that if they suffered a mishap, so did their adversaries. It is in the very nature of things, that each of the two parties to a war or a fighting will receive its apportioned share of hardships, losses and suffering. So the Muslims ought not to clamour too much about it. They should view the whole matter as a natural development, a logical consequence of their own doing. This is one of the laws of God; that life has its ups and downs. As the Qur'ān put it:

> *If a wound touches you, a like wound had touched the (unbelieving) people. These are the days (of history), we cause to revolve among men, that God may know who are the true believers, so that He would take from amongst you Martyrs, and God does not love the unjust.* [*Āl ʿImrān* 3:140]

12.4 Martydom, the Highest Honour of the Day

The highest honour of the day of Uḥud was the choice of the martyrs: God's greatest honour to the believers. To be a martyr is to be killed fighting in the way of God. So Uḥud was the greatest day where God elected and chose those he loved the most to be His martyrs, ever living in His Paradise, ever present in His audience, enjoying the eternal bliss of the vision of His most beautiful Countenance; happy and rejoicing in the Bounty of their Lord. The following are the Martyrs who are ever living, ever present, never to die again:

- Ḥamzah ibn ʿAbd al-Muṭṭalib.
- The beautiful Muṣʿab ibn ʿUmayr.
- The handsome ʿAbdullāh ibn Jaḥsh, the Hāshimī, cousin of the Prophet.
- Ḥanẓalah, the bridegroom who spent only one night with his bride: He whom the angels had washed.
- Abū Dujānah, the red-banded knight.
- Anas ibn al-Naḍr al-Anṣārī
- Shammās ibn ʿUthmān, whom the Prophet (peace be upon him) likened to the Jinn, because of his agility and speed, as well as the rest of the seventy martyrs of Uḥud.

The total numbers of the Martyrs at Uḥud were more than seventy. The above names are just some of the most prominent, amongst them. They are in eternal bliss, a recompense for giving up their brief lives early, so that the torch of the Islamic faith, the universal faith of God, may shine forever and enlighten with divine guidance, the whole of humanity.

Death is just the abrupt transition from the shadows and suffering of this life, to the full light of eternity, where no injustice or cruelty can be suffered by the righteous, but only compassion and the merciful bounty of God. There is the abode of rejoicing and happiness for the believers, and the doers of good deeds. Since nobody can escape the appointed day of his death, what a victory it is that, when that day comes, the believer is honoured with martyrdom.

Instead of dying like camels – to quote a phrase from the gallant Khālid ibn al-Walīd the – Qur'ān describes the state of the martyrs of Uḥud with their Lord in the following way:

> *Count not those who were slain in the way of God, as dead. Nay, they are ever living with their Lord, (enjoying) being provided for, rejoicing in the boundary that God has given them, quite happy for those who remain behind and have not joined them that on them is no fear, neither shall they sorrow, jubilant in the blessing and bounty from God, and that God does not waste the wage of the believers…* [*Āl ʿImrān* 3:169-171]

The themes and lessons of Uḥud are indeed too many to do them justice in this brief study. They actually represent a complete code of the most noble, God-inspired conduct for the Muslims; a code valid for all times. They give an indication of the Islamic, Qur'ānic calculus of advantage and disadvantage, of succour and defeat, of success and failure. In the Qur'ānic scale of values, even the Muslims' losses and sufferings are pluses in the balance with their Lord. Those who were slain will become martyrs with their Lord, thus enjoying the fruits of the greatest victory of being in Paradise. For this reason, the Prophet (peace be upon him) retained a good and lively memory of Uḥud, despite the wounds he suffered therein. He would say, whenever he chanced to pass by that mountain of Uḥud: 'Uḥud is a mountain which loves us and we love it.'

12.5 The Immediate Aftermath of Uḥud

The aftermath of Uḥud deserves a separate chapter. It was very eventful and very colourful. It depicts the state of the Muslim community in the wake of disaster and calamity. Though the Muslims, like any human beings, grieved at the loss of their loved ones, and the Prophet (peace be upon him) himself grieved above all for his lost Companions, most of all Ḥamzah and Muṣʿab, yet the tempo of the community, and the mood of the masses was not one of despair, or submission to the events, or dismay or apathy. Far from it, the mood of the community was one of anger and a burning desire to avenge their losses. They wanted to meet their enemy at the earliest possible opportunity, to raise the banner of their faith higher then that of the Quraysh. This defiant mood was symbolized by three occurrences in the aftermath of Uḥud.

a. Exchange between ʿUmar and Abū Sufyān:
When the battle cleared: there came Abū Sufyān, mounted arrogantly on his chestnut horse. He called out to the Muslims:

> 'Where is Abū Bakr, son of Abū Quḥāfah? Where is ʿUmar, son of Al-Khaṭṭāb? This day in exchange for Badr. The days revolve. War is a revolving game: one day for you, another against you. Exalt thyself, O Hubal!'[26]
>
> ʿUmar looked to the Prophet (peace be upon him) who dictated to him:
>
> 'God is more High and more superior in Majesty.'
>
> 'We are not equal,' said ʿUmar, 'Our slain are in Paradise, your slain are in Hell.'
>
> Abū Sufyān recognized the voice of ʿUmar.
>
> 'O ʿUmar, I adjure you by God, have we slain Muḥammad?'
>
> 'No, by God, he is here now listening to what you say.'
>
> Abū Sufyān was dismayed at the news that Muḥammad was alive. He turned back to go, but again shouted:
>
> 'Some of your dead have been mutilated. I want you to know that it was not at the orders of our senior command that they were so mutilated. But I do not regret it either!'[27]

The Prophet (peace be upon him) accepted this, and told someone to shout back, 'Let that be a binding appointment between us.'

b. The second incident, which vividly depicts the mood of the Muslims of Madīnah in the immediate afternoon of Uḥud, is that of al-Sumayrā' bint Qays of the Banū al-Najjār of Khazraj (maternal uncles of the Prophet). A messenger brought her this news:

'Your husband, brother and father and two of your sons were all killed, fighting to defend the Prophet (peace be upon him)'
She asked the messenger: 'What did the Messenger of God do? How did he fare?' She enquired in a matter-of-course way, very calm and composed.
'He is well, thanks are due to God, all right as you would no doubt like him to be!' answered the messenger, looking at her intently, no doubt amazed and impressed by her strength and forbearance.

'I want to look at him. Where is he? Just show me where he is. I want to see him,' she insisted.

'He is over there, look!' said the messenger.

The brave woman said:

'Every calamity is trivial now that I know that the Messenger of God is alive…' The Arabic word *jalāl* means trivial or small, it also means great.

She then had her great two martyred sons put on a camel, which she then quietly led herself in the direction of Madīnah, for their burial. On the road to the city, she met 'Ā'ishah.

'What news?' asked 'Ā'ishah.

'As for the Messenger of God, he is alright. He did not die! But God had chosen *shahīds* (Martyrs) from amongst the believers!' She then recited the Qur'ānic verse:

'Assuredly God repulsed the disbelievers in their wrath; they gained no good, and God spared the believers of fighting.'

'Who are the dead men with you?' asked 'Ā'ishah

'They are my two sons,' replied al-Sumayrā', in her matter-of-course way.

'*Hal*! *Hal*!' said she, pulling the rein of her camel, and off she went towards Madīnah, late in the afternoon of that Saturday of the battle of Uḥud.

This is just one example of these thousands of unknown heroes and great personalities which Islam and the Prophet of Islam have produced for mankind.

c. The third incident, depicting the mood of the Muslims in the immediate aftermath of Uḥud, is provided by the Prophet's call to the Muslims on the next day, to the battle, to mobilize in hot pursuit of the Quraysh. Almost all of those, who participated in the battle, responded with cheer and enthusiasm, even the wounded, some of them badly wounded, came along. The swiftness, the courage and the high morale of the Muslims were indeed phenomenal. The Muslims' army followed the tracks of the Quraysh, who had been pondering a renewed attack on the Muslims. When they heard of the advancing army of the Prophet (peace be upon him), they quickened their pace in the direction of Makkah, frightened at the prospect of renewed fighting. This incident tells a great deal about the Prophet's genius as a leader and a military commander. Something must be done to elevate the morale of defeated Muslims, and at the same time frighten the Jewish enemy within Madīnah, and the unruly Bedouins, *munāfiqīn* (hypocrites) in the area around Madīnah. Also, the Arabs of Arabia at large, must know that the military power of the Prophet (peace be upon him) and the Muslims had not been crushed by the defeat at Uḥud. Far from it, it was largely intact, and the evidence for this was provided by their ability to mobilize quickly and go out in pursuit of their Quraysh enemies. The fact that the Quraysh did not encounter them afresh gave further credibility to their military power and valour after the battle of Uḥud. All these factors helped to bring home to the Quraysh and the hypocritical Bedouins around Madīnah and in the Arabian peninsula at large, that the power of the Prophet (peace be upon him) and the Muslims in Madīnah was still very much intact after Uḥud.[28]

12.6 The Burial of Ḥamzah and Other Martyrs of Uḥud

The Prophet lined up the bodies of the martyrs of Uḥud, all seventy-four or five of them and Ḥamzah was placed first at the head of them. Then he stood to pray for Ḥamzah, visibly shaken with grief. He gave seven *takbīrāt* (reciting *Allāhu Akbar*). As he was standing, ready to start the prayers for Ḥamzah, he caught a sight of his aunt, the valiant Ṣafiyyah bint ʿAbd al-Muṭṭalib, Hamzah's full sister, and mother of ʿAbdullāh ibn al-Zubayr. His grief intensified at the sight of her, and he quickly dispatched her son ʿAbdullāh to bar her, lest she should see the mutilated body of Ḥamzah and ʿAbdullāh ibn Jaḥsh, son of Umaymah bint ʿAbd al-Muṭṭalib, Ḥamzah being his maternal uncle. But Ṣafiyyah was informed of the mutilation, and she was bearing the situation patiently. She insisted on witnessing the service and the Prophet (peace be upon him) allowed her to be present.

Then the Prophet (peace be upon him) prayed separately for each martyr, and it was reported that he prayed seventy-two prayers that morning. Some of the dead were buried in one grave, especially those who were known to be close friends. Some of the relatives of the deceased tried to move their dead to Madīnah to bury them there, but the Prophet (peace be upon him) ruled that they must be buried where they fell in the fighting and he was obeyed.

12.7 Good Tiding for the Martyrs

After finishing the burial, the Prophet (peace be upon him) gave a small speech. He said: 'I bear witness on behalf of the martyrs that whosoever is wounded fighting in the way of God, he will be raised on the Day of Resurrection, with his wound bleeding: the colour is the colour of blood, but the smell is the smell of musk.'

Then the Prophet (peace be upon him) ordered the burial be so arranged that those who were known to be memorizers of the Qur'ān were buried first, at the head of his friend or relatives.

As we said before, when the Prophet (peace be upon him) returned to Madīnah, late that afternoon of Saturday, 15 Shawwāl in the second year of Hijrah, he heard the women of Anṣārs weeping and lamenting the loss of their men. Tears again filled his eyes, and he said: 'But Ḥamzah, who would lament Ḥamzah today?'

The leaders of the Anṣār Saʿd ibn Muʿādh, and Usayd ibn Hudayr, overheard him. They hurriedly summoned and gathered some women of the Anṣārs, and sent them over to the Prophet's house to weep for Ḥamzah. The Prophet (peace be upon him) was satisfied, and after a while gave them leave to go. He praised them and said: 'May God reward you, you have amply consoled us on (the death of) Ḥamzah with yourselves.' The Prophet (peace be upon him) then said: 'May God's mercy be upon the Anṣār. They were known for their ability to give comfort and condolence since antiquity.' Then he ordered the Anṣār women to leave, and all weeping to stop.

CHAPTER 4

From Uḥud to al-Khandaq: Times of Hardship and Sorrow

1. THE LONG TERM AFTERMATH OF UḤUD

Although the outcome of the Uḥud Battle was not a complete defeat, it had all the symptoms of a crushing defeat:

a. More than seventy Muslims were killed, including the valiant Ḥamzah, and the veteran *dāʿiyah* and ambassador Muṣʿab ibn ʿUmayr.

b. The Prophet himself was badly wounded.

c. The Muslims took to flight in battle, and were defeated, for the first time in the history of Islam.

d. The Quraysh was jubilant, and the bodies of the dead Muslims were mutilated by the unbelievers, including those of Ḥamzah and Muṣʿab!

e. The Jews and the hypercritic opposition in Madīnah were elated, and the Bedouins around the Prophet's city were beginning to think of seizing what they saw as the weakness of the Muslims' power, and attack them for the purpose of plunder and material gains.

The morale of the Muslims themselves sank very low, and they were becoming apprehensive lest the Quraysh and the unruly Bedouins of the desert would attack them. The Prophet (peace be upon him) had to move fast to offset these traces of what was widely seen as a defeat at Uḥud, and what it led to by way of compromising and lessening the Prophet's authority and prestige. The pursuit, which the Prophet (peace be upon him) carried out the next day to the battle, did have some effect to offset some of these negative consequences of the defeat, but that was not enough. Some more measures had to be taken, to safeguard the state and the Muslim society. In particular, the Prophet (peace be upon him) had to keep a close watch on the movements and the steering of the Arab Bedouins in the desert around. These Bedouins were known for their treachery and unruliness, and for their cruelty and love for material gain. They had no inhibition to kill and raid for the slightest reason. The only way to check them, was to show them force and power and to convince them that they could get no material gains. For this reason, the Prophet (peace be upon him) was wise enough and vigilant enough to keep a close watch over them. He sent 'eyes' amongst them, and those gave detailed information about the Bedouin movements.

2. THE CAMPAIGN AGAINST BANŪ ASAD

Through his agents 'eyes', the Prophet (peace be upon him) got word about the intentions of the tribe of Banū Asad to attack and plunder Madīnah and kill the Prophet (peace be upon him) himself. Immediately, he dispatched an expeditionary force of a hundred and fifty fighters commanded by Abū Salamah ibn ʿAbd al-Asad. He ordered them to take the enemy by complete surprise. He advised them to take un-trodden roads, and to march by night and hide by day. They reached their destination, attacked the enemy before dawn, and took them by complete surprise, as planned. The enemy fled, and dispersed in all directions, leaving their women and property. The Muslim force gathered plenty of booty and returned safely home. This campaign did a lot to restore the prestige and the authority of the Prophet (peace be upon him) and kept the enemy from within (Jews and hypocrites) well checked and well pacified.

3. THE CAMPAIGN OF ʿABDULLĀH IBN UNAYS

Another incident had a positive effect: ʿAbdullāh ibn Unays was directed against the Arabs of Hudhayl, at Nakhlah, south of Makkah. ʿAbdullāh went there, and found the head of the tribe of Hudhayl, one Khālid ibn Sufyān all by himself, amongst his women. ʿAbdullāh pretended that he was an enemy of the Prophet (peace be upon him), who was eager to join hands with Hudhayl, and their Chief, against Muḥammad (peace be upon him). Khālid told him of his plans to attack Madīnah, and ʿAbdullāh showed his eagerness to hear more about it all. As the two men walked and talked, they were separated from the rest of the men of Hudhayl. At that moment, ʿAbdullāh jumped upon Khālid, and killed him by his sword. He returned safely to Madīnah, and told the Prophet (peace be upon him) of the slaying of Khālid, head and Chief of Banū Hudhayl. As news spread about the demise of Khālid, Banū Liḥyān of the tribe of Hudhayl were duly checked, and their plans to invade Madīnah were frustrated, and eventually dropped.

These two incidents, together with the Prophet's advance to Ḥamrā' al-Asad, went a long way to restore the morale of the Muslims, and to keep the enemies of Islam, both from within and without, duly checked and pacified.

4. THE QUR'ĀNIC COMMENTARY ON THE EVENTS OF UḤUD

However, the greatest solace and comfort, came from Qur'ānic verses revealed in the wake of Uḥud. Almost sixty verses in *Sūrah Āl ʿImrān* gave elaborate commentary on the events of Uḥud, and the significance of the defeat, which the Muslims suffered therein.

We are going to give an English translation of these verses of *Sūrah Āl ʿImrān* (from 121 to 179) as follows:

God said in the following very noble and educative verses, in the whole of the battle of Uḥud calamity, starting from verse 121 through to verse 179.

When thou wentest forth at dawn from thy people to lodge the believers in their pitches for the battle – God is All-Hearing, All-Knowing

When two parties of you were about to lose heart, though God was their Protector – and in God let the believers put all their trust

And God most surely helped you at Badr, when you were utterly abject. So fear God, and haply You will be thankful.

When thou saidst to the believers, 'Is it not enough for you that your Lord should reinforce you with three thousand angels sent down upon you?

Yea; if you are patient and godfearing, and the foe come against you instantly, your Lord will reinforce you with five thousand swooping angles. God wrought this not, save as good tiding to you, and that your hearts might be at rest; help comes only from God

The All-Mighty, the All-Wise;

And that He might cut off a part of the unbelievers or frustrate them, so that they turned in their tracks, disappointed.

No part of the matter is thine, whether He turns towards them again, or chastises them; for they are evildoers.

To God belongs all that is in the heavens and earth; He forgives whom He will, and chastises whom He will God is All-Forgiving, All-Compassionate.

O Believers, devour not usury, doubled and redoubled, and fear you God; haply so you will prosper.

And fear the Fire prepared for the unbelievers, and obey God and the Messenger; haply so you will find mercy.

And vie with one another, hastening to forgiveness from your Lord, and to a garden whose breadth is as the heavens and earth, prepared for the Godfearing who expend in prosperity and adversity in almsgiving, and restrain their rage, and pardon the offences of their fellowmen; and God loves the good-doers;

Who, when they commit an indecency or wrong

themselves, remember God, and pray forgiveness for their sins – and who shall forgive sins but God?

And do not persevere in the things they did and that wittingly.

Those – their recompense is forgiveness form their Lord, and gardens beneath which rivers flow, therein dwelling forever;

And how excellent is the wage of those who labour?

Divers institutions have passed away before you; journey in the land, and behold how was the end of those that cried lies.

This is an exposition for mankind, and guidance, and an admonition for such as are godfearing. Faint not, neither sorrow; you shall be the upper ones if you are believers.

If a wound touches you, a like wound already has touched the heathen; such days we deal out in turn among men, and that God may know who are the believers, and that He may take witnesses from among you; and God loves not the evildoers; and that God may prove the believers and blot out the unbelievers.

Or did you suppose you should enter Paradise without God knowing who of you have struggled and who are patient?

You were longing for death before you met it; now you have seen it, while you were beholding.

Muḥammad is naught but a Messenger; Messengers have passed away before him. Why, if he should die or is slain, will you turn about on your heels?

If any man should turn about on his heels, he will not harm God in any way; and God will recompense the thankful.

It is not given to any soul to die, save by the leave of God, at an appointed time. Whoso desires the reward of this world, We will give him of this; and whoso desires the reward of the other world, We will give him of that; and We will recompense the thankful.

Many a Prophet there has been, with whom thousands manifold have fought, and they fainted not for what smote them in God's way, neither weakened, nor did they humble themselves; and God loves the patient.

Nothing else they said but, 'Lord, forgive us our sins, and that we exceeded in our affair, and make firm our feet,

And help us against the people of the unbelievers.

And God gave them the reward of this world and the fairest reward of the world to come; and God loves the Good-doers.

O believers, if you obey the unbelievers they will turn you upon your heels, and you will turn about losers.

No; but God is your Protector, and He is the best of helpers.

We will cast into the hearts of the unbelievers terror, for that they have associated with God that for which He sent down never authority; their lodging shall be the Fire; evil is the lodging of the evildoers.

God has been true in His promise towards you when you blasted them by His leave; until you lost heart, and quarrelled about the matter, and were rebellious, after He had shown you that you longed for.

Some of you there are that desire this world, and some of you there are desire the next world. Then He turned you from them, that He might try you; and He has pardoned you; and God is Bounteous to the believers.

When you were going up, not twisting about for anyone, and the Messenger was calling you in your rear; so He rewarded you with grief on grief that you might not sorrow for what escaped you neither for what smote you; and God is Aware of the things you do.

Then He sent down upon you, after grief, security – a slumber overcoming a party of you; and a party themselves had grieved, thinking of God thoughts that were not true such as the pagans thought, saying, have we any part whatever in the affair? Say:

The affair belongs to God entirely. They were concealing in their hearts that they show not to thee, saying, 'Ah, if we had a part in the affair, never would we have been slain here. Say : 'Even if you had been in your houses, those for whom slaying was appointed would have sallied forth unto their last couches; and that God might try what was in your breasts, and that He might prove what was in your hearts; and God knows the thoughts in the breasts.

Those of you who turned away the day the two hosts

Encountered – Satan made them slip for somewhat they had earned; but God has pardoned them; God is All-Forgiving, All-Clement.

O believers, be not as the unbelievers

Who say to their brothers, when they journey in the land, or are upon expeditions, 'If they had been with us, they would not have died and not been slain' – that God may make that an anguish in their hearts. For God gives life, and He makes to die; and God sees the things you do.

If you are slain or die in God's way, forgiveness and mercy from God are a better thing than that you amass;

Surely if you die or are slain, it is unto God you shall be mustered.

It was by some mercy of God that thou wast gentle to them; hadst thou been harsh and hard of heart, they would have scattered from about thee. So pardon them and pray forgiveness for them and take counsel with them in the affair; and when thou art resolved, put thy trust in God; surely God loves those who put their trust.

If God helps you, none can overcome you; but if He forsakes you, who then can help you after Him? Therefore in God let the believers put all their trust.

It is not for a Prophet to be fraudulent; whoso defrauds shall bring the fruits of his fraud

On the day of Resurrection; then every soul that should shall be paid in full what it has earned, and they shall not be wronged.

What, is he who follows God's good pleasure like him who is laden with the burden of God's anger, whose refuge is Hell? An evil homecoming!

They are in ranks with God; and God sees the things they do. Truly God was gracious to the believers when He raised up among them a Messenger from themselves, to recite to them

The Book and the Wisdom, though before they were in manifest error.

Why, when an affliction visited you, and you had visited twice over the like of it, did you say, 'How is this?' Say: 'This is from your own selves; surely God is powerful over everything.'

And what visited you, the day the two hosts encountered, was by God's leave, and that He might know the believers; and that He might also know the hypocrites when it was said of them, 'Come now fight in the way of God, or repel!' They said, 'If only we know how to fight we would follow you.' They that day were nearer to unbelief than to belief,

Saying with their mouths that which never was in their hearts; and God knows very well the things they hide;

Who said of their brothers (and they themselves held back), 'Had they obeyed us, they would not have been slain.' Say: 'Then avert death from yourselves, if you speak truly.'

Count not those who were slain in God's way as dead, but rather living with their Lord, by Him provided,

Rejoicing in the bounty that God has given them and joyful in those who remain behind and have not joined them, because no fear shall be on them, neither shall they sorrow, joyful in blessing and bounty from God, and that God leaves not to waste the wage of the believers.

And those who answered God and the Messenger after the wound had smitten them – to all those of them who did good and feared God, shall be a mighty wage;

Those to whom the people said, 'The people have gathered against you, therefore fear them;' but it increased them in faith, and they said, 'God is Sufficient for us; and excellent Guardian is He.'

So they returned with blessing and bounty from God, untouched by evil; they followed the good pleasure of God; and God is of bounty abounding.

That is Satan frightening his friends, therefore, do not fear them; but fear you Me, if you are believers.

Let them not grieve thee that vie with one another in unbelief; they will not hurt God; God desires not to appoint for them a portion in the world to come, and there awaits them a mighty chastisement.

Those who buy unbelief at the price of faith, they will nothing hurt God; and there awaits them a painful chastisement.

And let not the unbelievers suppose that the indulgence We grant them is better for them; We grant them indulgence only that they may increase in sin; and there awaits them a humbling chastisement.

God will not leave the believers in the state in which you are, until He shall distinguish the corrupt from the good,

And God will not inform you of the Unseen; but God chooses out of His Messengers whom He will. Believe you then in God and His Messengers; and if you believe and are Godfearing, there shall be for you a mighty wage.

5. LESSONS TO BE DEDUCED FROM THESE VERSES:

1. God assures the Prophet (peace be upon him) that He was, in full cognizance of the grave events of Uḥud, He is All-Hearing and All-Knowing; every detail of the battle, from the start to the finish was witnessed by Him that He was there when the Prophet (peace be upon him) stationed his forces at the bottom of Uḥud, with the archers on the top of the mountain, and of the Prophet's strict orders to them never to leave their station on the top of the mountain, come what may, even if they saw the imminent death of the Prophet (peace be upon him) himself. God was cognizant

of all these details, even the initial controversy whether to fight from inside the city, or from outside, and the initial hesitation to meet the enemy at all.

2. God was there, All-Present when some factions of Anṣār (namely Banū Ḥārithah, and Banū Salamah) almost defected, influenced by the defection of the hypocrites, headed by ʿAbdullāh ibn Ubayy ibn Salūl, and his fetish friends and allies. This verse reminds the Muslims of Uḥud, not to be demoralized by the withdrawal of one third of the army with Ibn Salūl, because they ought to know better, namely that God is their Lord and Protector, and that He is capable of giving them victory and steadfastness as He did on Badr.

3. Then God reminded them how He made them victorious at Badr, when they were weak and helpless! So they ought to fear God alone and be grateful to Him.

4. The prime lesson to be remembered from Badr, is that success and victory proceeds from God alone, either through the instrumentality of the angels or without them. It so happened that the victory achieved at Badr was through the mediation of the angels, but that was not a necessary arrangement.

5. Thus, the initial victory which the Muslims achieved at Uḥud, in the first day, was also from God, and it was limited and with a limited objective; to cut off part of the unbelievers of the Quraysh, in fact the Muslims killed more than twenty of the associators of Makkah, during the first phase of the battle, before things began to turn against them, due to the disobedience of the archers.

6. When the unbelievers achieved some measure of victory in the second phase of battle, due to the disobedience of the archers, that victory was not complete. God, so designed the events that (a) the Muslims were not routed (b) nor was the Prophet (peace be upon him) killed nor (c) the unbelievers managed to invade and enter the Madīnah.

7. So incensed was the Prophet (peace be upon him) at the sight of the mutilated body of his uncle Ḥamzah, and the beloved Muṣʿab ibn ʿUmayr, that he vowed to do the same with the bodies of Qurayshites, should God make him victorious over them in the coming battles. Yet verse 128 of *Sūrah Āl ʿImrān* admonished him not to do so. Rather, he was advised to leave all matters to the wisdom and the judgement of God alone. He may forgive, and guide them to Islam, as was the case with Khālid ibn al-Walīd, who was so disgusted by the deeds and conduct of the Qurayshite at Uḥud, especially their mutilation of bodies of the dead, that as a result, he converted to Islam soon afterwards. So, God may choose to forgive or punish them in the Hereafter. This is God's privilege Alone. On hearing this verse, the Prophet (peace be upon him) recounted his earlier statement to retaliate against the act of mutilation, and forgave the unbelievers for their deeds, and actually prayed for their salvation.

8. Verses 130-134, hint to the primary cause of defeat at Uḥud, namely the excessive love of material things, especially money. It was their love of gathering booty, that lured the archers to disobey the orders of the Prophet (peace be upon him) and to leave their position at the top of the mountain, though they were strongly ordered not to do so, under any circumstances. It is the love of money and material gains that led some Muslims to indulge in usury with the Jews of Makkah and Madīnah, and it was the love of money that made them unwilling to spend of their wealth in good causes at difficult times. The Muslims were enjoined to be of the God-fearing, and restrain their anger at the outcome of the Battle of Uḥud, especially at the mutilation of the corpses of Ḥamzah and Muṣʿab ibn ʿUmayr, and they were also advised to forgive and forget the wounds inflicted upon them during the Battle.

9. Verse 135 of *Sūrah Āl ʿImrān*, indirectly reminded the Muslims of the major sin they had committed at Uḥud, by their flight from

the battle, and by deserting the Prophet (peace be upon him) to the enemy, with a few number of fighters around him, but it also gives the good-tidings that, if they repent their sins, then God would forgive them.

10. Verse numbers 139 and 140 reminded the Muslims of their high standing with God, and that they were advised not to grieve, and not to lose heart, at the defeat at Uḥud, and the sight of the wounds inflicted upon their gracious Prophet (peace be upon him) himself. These wounds do not mean anything, except that God tries and tests the strength of the faith of the believers, and their steadfastness in their religious belief. That if the Muslims suffer defeat, and if wounds were inflicted upon them or if some of their men were killed at Uḥud, so was the case with the unbelievers at Badr.

11. The tragedy at Uḥud was an essential trial for the Muslims, so that God would know, who would be *mujāhidūn* and those who would bear the outcome with good patience. Muslims should not hope to enter Paradise before that examination or trial was completed.

12. The greatest shock at Uḥud was the news, spread by the unbelievers, that Muḥammad (peace be upon him) was killed. The Muslims ran for their lives and ceased fighting, including some Companions of the Prophet (peace be upon him). Verse 144 of *Sūrah Āl ʿImrān* rebuked the Muslims, who stopped fighting at their hearing of the rumour that Muḥammad (peace be upon him) was killed. Muḥammad (peace be upon him) was no more than a Messenger of God. If he was killed, the worship of God should not cease, because God is Ever-Alive, and He alone deserves to be worshipped, and not the Messenger, because He alone is God and Creator.

13. Verse 146, reminds the Muslims, not to over-grieve, at the losses of Uḥud, or even the death of the Prophet (peace be upon him),

if that death did take place. It draws their attention to the facts and lessons of history, that many Prophets and Messengers were killed, together with their disciples, and the fact that this did not cause them to despair or lose heart.

14. Verses 148 and 149, remind the Muslims that if they follow the ways of the unbelievers (Jews as well as the hypocrites), they would reduce themselves to unbelief (back on their heels)! This is the way it is, according to the laws of God (the *sunan* of God). These laws dictate that conflict and even war is inevitable between truth and falsehood. The Muslims must learn that they have got to fight for their rights to be free to worship none but God alone, and they must fight to make His word supreme on earth. The unbelievers, if they have their way, would not allow them to do so. Life is not the mere enjoyment of food and comforts, or the realization of material goods. It has higher ideals of upholding justice and truthfulness and equality, and above all, freedom to worship God All-Mighty alone. In so far as some men are inclined towards tyranny and oppression, and so long as such a thing as aggressiveness is in-built in the nature of some men, then the Muslims must always be ready to suffer the infliction of wounds, and indeed death itself, in the way of God. As a reward for bearing these inflictions, God has promised them one of the two best eventualities: Victory or Martyrdom. The unbelievers have no such prospects or promises!

15. Verses 150, 151 and 152 tell of God's promises to give the Muslim eventual victory over the polytheists of the Quraysh, and that He will do so by installing terror and fear in their hearts. That promise was realized for the Muslims in the initial phase of the Battle of Uḥud. But subsequently, the Muslims disobeyed and rebelled and were indulged in division and disagreement. All the subsequent calamities and disappointments were a result of these misdeeds of the archers and their disobedience! Verse 153, refers to the worst of all of these disasters, namely the flight of

the Muslims and their abandoning of their Prophet (peace be upon him) to be besieged and wounded by the enemy. This verse (153) clearly says that it was God (and not really the enemy) that caused these calamities to befall the Muslims (*viz; fa-athābakum ghamman bi ghammin*), these calamities were as follows:

i. First, the defeat, and then the flight of the Muslims.

ii. The slaying of Ḥamzah, Muṣ ʿab, together with more than seventy of the Muslims.

iii. The wounding of many more Muslims, including the Prophet (peace be upon him) himself!

iv. The cry and the rumour that the Prophet (peace be upon him) had been killed!

v. That the Muslims were surrounded by the enemy from all sides, and the prospects of utter routing!

vi. The abandoning of the Prophet (peace be upon him), despite his repeated calls for them to rally round him!

16. Verse 154 tells of the mercy of God towards the Muslims, despite their misdeeds, that after these calamities and sorrows, they rejoiced when they discovered that the Prophet (peace be upon him) was alive. Some of them experienced some slumber and managed to have a nap, whilst others of the hypocrites amongst them started an argument about the causes of the defeat, some of them attributing it to what they saw as the wrong decision on the part of the Prophet (peace be upon him) and the young Muslims to meet the enemy outside Madīnah. It was their opinion (together with Ibn Salūl, the head of the hypocrites) to fight from inside Madīnah. However, God rejected their argument, saying that it was only a camouflage, a smoke screen, to hide what they conceal in their breasts of disbelief and hypocrisy. 'They say had we been followed (in our opinion to fight within the city) we would not have been killed, and defeated in this spot of the battlefield!' [*Āl ʿImrān* 3:154].

God advises the Prophet (peace be upon him) to tell these hypocrites that if they fought the enemy from within the city, hiding in their homes, the result would have been the same: and those whom God had destined to die that day, would have come forth from inside their homes, and would have been killed anyway. That is the fate of God, and the fate of God, does not change, come what may. God attributes the misgivings of the hypocrites to the traces of the *Jāhiliyyah* ideas and doubts, still rife in their minds and hearts. They were also due to their doubts about God's promises to make the Muslims victorious! God further promised to disclose and expose the real motives, and the real unbelief, hidden in the breasts and hearts of these hypocrites, motives and unbelief which God knows too well!

17. In verse 153, God tells the Muslims that He caused them disappointment after disappointment (*fa athābakum ghamman bighammin*) i.e. the defeat was actually a consequence of the Muslims' misdeeds, especially that of the archers. In verse 155, it attributes these calamities to Satan, but it adds that Satan only had his way with them, because of their misdeeds, sins and crimes, especially the crime of disobedience to the Prophet's command for the archers not to leave their positions under any circumstances. But the verse also carries the good news of God's forgiveness for the Muslims.

18. Verses 156, 157 and 158, are very educative and noble verses. They enjoin the Muslims that death is not caused by travel or by battle, one dies only when one's set term of life is completed. The morale of this is that Muslims should not fear fighting or travelling or taking any reasonable risks in life, for fear of death. That fear is the characteristic of the thinking modes of the unbelievers, but it is not befitting of the Muslims. That if Muslims were actually killed in battle, when fighting in the cause of God, that is even better for them. They die as Martyrs, and are assured of God's forgiveness and mercy for them in the Hereafter.

It is indeed much better for them than what they collect of the material goods and benefits of this life. That if Muslims die in the battle for the cause of God, their sacrifices would not be in vain. They will be brought unto God, and be gathered in front of Him, when He will amply reward them for the sacrificing of their lives in the cause of God.

19. Verse 159 is again a very noble and educative verse and is fraught with very noble ideas and norms. The Prophet (peace be upon him) is told, that it was due to God's mercy on him, that his nature was so constituted by God that he was actually compassionate and lenient upon Muslims. Had it not been for this compassionate and lenient temperament, and if his temperament was rough and harsh they would have dispersed from around him. So the Prophet was enjoined to invoke this lenient temperament, and forgive the disobedience of the archers, and the ill arguments of the hypocrites, who ascribed the defeat to the Prophet's acting on the outcome of the *Shūrā* Council.

Despite the ensuing, and on-going controversy about the *shūrā*, and hypocrites' charge that the defeat on Uḥud was a direct result of the Prophet's acting on the outcome of the youth-dominated *Shūrā* Council, which decided that the Muslim army move outside the city to meet the enemy, still the Qur'ān, in this noble verse, re-affirmed the importance of the *shūrā* practice, and actually enjoined the Prophet (peace be upon him) to pursue it, just as he pursued the two cordial religious duties of performing *ṣalāt* and paying of *zakāt*. This is meant to give a clear signal, that the practice of *shūrā* is as much obligatory as *ṣalāt* and *zakāt*. Thus *shūrā* here is accorded the very high significance and obligatoriness of the two cardinal pillars of Islam. The impression is here created, by this verse, that the practice and implementation of the *shūrā* outcomes is to be carried out in peace and war times. Moreover, that practice must be all-embracing and most comprehensive in that it should include all Muslim citizens, be they old or young, rich or poor, learned or of the generality of Muslims. Of course there are occasions when only learned and experienced Muslims should be consulted. If the topic of a *Shūrā* Council is a technical one, it makes no sense to insist on consulting the generality of Muslims. But when the issue is a general one, like the one debated by the Prophet (peace be upon him) and the Muslims concerning how best to defend Madīnah, it was anybody's guess. Thus *shūrā* position in Islam is quite an entrenched one. It is at the very core of the political theory of Islam. The way the Prophet (peace be upon him) practiced *shūrā* during the course of events, either leading to Uḥud or ensuing it, and the fact that the gracious Prophet (peace be upon him) followed the outcome of the *Shūrā* Councils is quite significant despite the fact that (1) it was against his own well-considered personal opinion, and (2) despite the fact that the resolution adopted was backed by the youthful Muslims, and opposed by the elderly and the veterans, still the Prophet (peace be upon him) adopted it. All of this goes a long way to prove conclusively, that the outcome of the *shūrā* is obligatory, on both the members of the *Shūrā* Council, and the executive authority. None of the two parties would be allowed to go back upon their resolutions, once they have clearly voted for it. This is borne out by the trial of the youthful Muslims to reverse their earlier resolution to fight the enemy from outside Madīnah, when they realized that their resolutions ran counter to the personal opinion of the Prophet (peace be upon him). However, the Prophet (peace be upon him) rejected that later move, saying that 'no Prophet will change his mind about going out to the battlefield, once he has put on his armour, until God decides between him and his enemy in the battlefield'. *Shūrā* is only a means of reaching the best and the most correct human opinion or resolution. However, it does not guarantee success or achieve victory. This is the privilege of God alone, to give victory or succour. For these reasons, Muslims must strive to reach the most correct or wise course of action. After that they have to put their trust in God alone, because God loves those who put their trust and reliance upon Him alone! Verse 160, again reiterates and confirms the idea that victory and succour are guaranteed by God alone. It is not hampered by any other consideration, except the earning of the Muslims, the quality of their deeds, and the laws of God, which sometimes are meant to test the resolve, the loyalty and dedication of the Muslims to their Lord and to the cause of His religion.

20. Verse 161, praises the Prophet (peace be upon him) and pronounces his innocence from the charge, which must have been made by the hypocrites and those weak of heart and faith, that he would be unjust in his division of the booty of the Battle of Uḥud. It is quite possible that some of the weak-hearted Muslims from amongst the archers, had used this argument to persuade their fellow archers to leave their station, and indulge in the collection of the booty, in the initial phase of the battle, when the Muslims were in fact victorious. Verse 161 questions the proposition that the Prophet (peace be upon him) would be unjust in distributing the booty, asking how would one, like the Prophet (peace be upon him), who was phenomenal in God-fearing, and in his efforts to please his Lord, be like those materialists, who clamour for the rewards and benefits of this world? Prophets as a whole, of whom Muḥammad is the last and the seal, and the Most beloved in the sight of his Lord, are enjoying high rank and positions of esteem and honour in the sight of their Lord, because He knows their strive and *jihād* in His way, and for the sake of conveying His call and commandments. It is the hypocrites and the unbelievers who are of very low rank in the Hell Fire, in the Hereafter.

21. Verse 164, is especially addressed to the early Muslims, most of whom were in fact of Arab stock, saying that what a privilege and honour was bestowed upon them by God. That He should send such a noble Prophet, i.e. Muḥammad (peace be upon him)

from their own kith and kin, an Arab from amongst them, that he would recite the noble verses of the Qur'ān on them, that he would purify and cleanse them from sins and disobedience, and that he would teach them what is contained in the Book of the Qur'ān. Moreover, he would teach them Prophetic wisdom, and the practical implementation of the teachings of the Book, though they were in manifest error and ignorance in their *jāhiliyyah* days.

22. Verses [165-168], reiterate themes, mentioned before, that:
    - i. The calamity that had befallen them in Uḥud, is due to their deeds, yet why should they be vexed that calamity may overtake them? Had they not inflicted a worse disaster and defeat upon the unbelievers at Badr? These are the revolving fates of God and His laws, that whoever does a misdeed, be he Muslim or unbeliever, is punished!
    - ii. Even so, Muslims must know that what had happened to them in Uḥud, was by permission of God; and so that God would know the true believers from amongst them.
    - ii. Also, those events were a trial so that God would also know the hypocrites, who are unwilling to fight in the way of God, and to expose their real stance: being nearest to unbelief rather than faith, they said by their mouths what was not in their hearts.
    - iv. They spread false rumours that, if their position at the *Shūrā* Council was adopted, defeat would not have befallen them at Uḥud. And they stayed behind in Madīnah, and failed to come forth to battle. The verse is obviously an allusion to ʿAbdullāh ibn Ubayy ibn Salūl and his faction, who deflected at the critical hour, and did not take part in the fighting. Ibn Salūl was allied

to the Khazraj, whom he called: 'our brothers', and was saying, if these brothers obeyed him and supported his position that the city must be defended from within, they would not have been killed and defeated.

God rejects such a false argument, and challenges the hypocrites to propel and avert death, if they are truthful in what they say.

v. These verses (121-180) of *Sūrah Āl ʿImrān*, especially the verses of 169, 170, 171 now approach the climax of their themes, when they state the position and the honour of the martyrs unto their Lord.

This magnificant Qur'ānic verse may be translated as follows:

> *Count not those who were slain in God's way as dead, Nay, they are alive with their Lord, receiving their sustenance (as usual) rejoicing in the bounty that God has given them, and joyful in (the prospects of) those who remain behind and have not yet joined them, because no fear shall befall them, neither shall they grieve. Joyful in blessing and bounty from God, and that God does not leave, to waste the wage of the believers.* [*Āl ʿImrān* 3:169-171]

23. This noble Qur'ānic verse, I bear witness to this, as I have seen it in my own personal experience, has changed the lives of many thousands of Muslims, not only in history but in contemporary times; young men who march to meet death, as if they are marching in their wedding ceremony. I have seen young men refusing to marry and take human wives, because they wanted to die martyrs, and be wedded to the maidens of Paradise. I have seen men, predicting the day they would die martyrs and enter Paradise. I have seen men emerge from battle crying because they had emerged alive and did not die martyrs, as they wished to die. I have seen men, predicting the day they would die as martyrs,

and they actually did die as predicted. I have seen some of those who were so sure that they would die on a specific date, to the extent that they gave a farewell party to their friends and loved ones, and then they really died as predicted. And I have heard of men, who saw their martyrdom in their dreams, and it came true like the dawn of a summer day. I have heard of men who had seen the landscape, the place where they would fall martyrs, some fifteen or twenty years ago, and they lived until they came to the actual spot they had seen in their dreams, and they recognized it at once when they saw it, and then they were chosen by God as martyrs in that same spot. I met one of these would-be martyrs and he was constantly carrying a bottle of perfume in his pocket, I asked him:

> 'Ibn 'Umar,' for that was his name, 'I heard that you constantly carry a bottle of perfume in your pocket?' I asked.
> 'Yes, I do,' he replied, and he immediately put his hand in his pocket, and produced the bottle.
> 'Why are you carrying it around,' I asked the young chap, from a very well-to-do family of Khartoum.
> 'Because I hope *Inshā' Allāh* to die a martyr, and I do not want to meet my Lord except cleansed and perfumed.' He replied. About a month later, news reached us in Khartoum that Ibn 'Umar had fallen a martyr in battlefield, and we were told that, on the eve of the day he fell martyr, he gave a party to his best friends, and told them, at the end of the party, which lasted far in the night, that he would definitely die a martyr the next day, and that was exactly what had happened. A friend of his told me that he had fought very gallantly chanting, as did Bilāl ibn Rabāḥ, the Abyssinian Companion and muezzin of the Prophet (peace be upon him).
> 'Today I will meet the beloved ones, Muḥammad and his Companions!"

No doubt, these Qur'ānic Verses (3:169-171) were a major spiritual power that helped to reshape the world's history since the inception of Islam; and no doubt, they will continue to reshape it until God inherits the Earth and those who live on its surface. These verses were also, no doubt, among the dynamic forces behind Islamic conquests, of the early Islamic history, that swept across the globe. Those conquests could only be interpreted in the light of Qur'ānic verses, such as the above mentioned verses, numbers 154 and 169-171 of *Sūrah Āl ʿImrān.*

24. Verses 172, 173, 174 and 175 tell of how the Muslims, the next day after their return from Uḥud, were mobilized again to go out to meet the Qurayshite enemy, still hovering in the vicinity of Madīnah, and how these gallant and dedicated Muslims responded to the call, though many were seriously wounded. They were led by the Prophet (peace be upon him) himself, who was still suffering from the wounds inflicted on his head and face the previous day. The Muslims army marched until they reached a place called Ḥamrā' al-Asad, about eight miles from Madīnah to the South, on the road to Makkah. That was on the 16th of Shawwāl, of the second year of the Hijrah. The Prophet (peace be upon him) and the Muslim army stayed there for three days and nights, terrifying the enemy, and proving the military might and valour of his Muslim army. Some of the companions, who were badly wounded at Uḥud, vowed to accompany the Prophet (peace be upon him), and never to stay behind him. Ibn Hishām, mentioned the example of two men, brothers of the Asʿad Banū al-Ashhal, maternal cousins of the Prophet (peace be upon him). Both of them had been seriously wounded at the Battle of Uḥud. When they heard the call for battle, they vowed to go forth with the Prophet (peace be upon him). One of them, who was less seriously wounded used to carry his brother, who was too weak to walk. It is upon these and other Muslims, including the Prophet (peace be upon him) himself, that God has revealed the Qur'ānic verse 172.

25. Verse 173, is well-known to have a definite spiritual value, it protects the combatants, who recite it during battle; it has been

tried many times over. The Prophet (peace be upon him), as he was encamping at Ḥamrā' al-Asad, met a travelling band of Banū Abd al-Qays; the Prophet (peace be upon him) asked about Abū Sufyān and his intentions. They told him that he gave them a message saying that he was coming back to Madīnah to exterminate the Muslims. At that point, the Prophet (peace be upon him) said: The Qur'ān alludes to this incident and this encounter in verse 173-175. Said God in these verses:

> *Those who responded to the call of God and Messenger, after wounds have hit them, to those who did well and feared (God) is a great reward. Those to whom people said that the people have massed against you, therefore fear them, but it increased them in faith, and they said 'God is Sufficient onto us, and He is an excellent Guardian.' So they returned with blessing and bounty from God, untouched by evil, and they followed the good pleasure of God and God is indeed of bounty abounding. That is the Satan frightening his friends, therefore do not fear them, but fear you Me if you are (true) believers…* [*Āl ʿImrān* 172-175]

26. Verse 176, consoled the Prophet (peace be upon him) and sought to comfort him, concerning the withdrawal of the hypocrites from the battlefield, headed by Ibn Salūl. God told the Prophet (peace be upon him) not to grieve over their behaviour. God desired not to appoint for the hypocrites any portion of rewards in the world to come. Verse 177, still commenting on the behaviour of the hypocrites, and their withdrawing from fighting, said that they would make no difference to God, Who did not need their good deeds, nor did He need their fighting in the way of Him. They will only harm themselves, as they will be severely punished in the Hereafter. Thus, this verse continued to comfort the Prophet (peace be upon him) and the Muslims, on the sad and sorrowful events of the day of Uḥud. In the same vein, verse 178 warns the hypocrites that the fact that God did not cause them to suffer any immediate punishment for their betrayal of the Muslims, and the betrayal of God and his religion, does not mean that it was good

for them. It is only that God gave them a respite, so that they may grow in unbelief and hypocrisy and commit more sins, and consequently suffer more punishment in the Hereafter.

27. Verse 179 is a very significant verse, it spells out God's grand purpose of enacting wars and suffering, such as the Prophet (peace be upon him) and the Muslims suffered at Uḥud. It was meant as a test and trial for them so that God will sort out the bad and the good from amongst them. The true believers will be separated from the hypocrites, as a result of these traumatic experiences, such as that of the Battle of Uḥud. And because it was a trial, the outcome of the trial will not be disclosed to the true believers, whether in this world, (such as the outcome of the war) or in the Hereafter, (as to the destiny of the good and bad factions especially). But God will elect some of His Prophets as He wills, so that Muslims are commanded to believe in them (and follow them!) because if Muslims do believe and fear God, they will indeed be assured of a great reward.

28. Verse 180, comments on the stance of the Jews of Madīnah. According to their covenant with the Prophet (peace be upon him) [spelt out and documented in the *Ṣaḥīfah of Madīnah*], they were obliged to contribute towards the costs of any war that the Prophet (peace be upon him) had to fight in defence of Madīnah. After all, they were accorded full citizenship of the city-state of Madīnah, and they enjoyed all rights and privileges of citizenship of the city. And since they chose not to participate in the defence of the city, by fighting alongside the Prophet (peace be upon him) and the Muslims, the least they could do was to contribute towards the war expenses. But they wanted to do neither, despite the fact that they were rich, and God bestowed upon them of His bounty. This noble verse reminded the Jews of Madīnah, who were niggardly, with the bounty God had bestowed upon them, that they should not suppose that it was better for them, nay it was in fact worse for them. What they were unwilling to spend

in the way of God, and were niggardly with, will be hung around their necks on the day of Resurrection, and to God belongs the inheritance of the Heavens and Earth, and God is indeed aware of all the things these Jews of Madīnah were doing.

Thus we arrive at the end of these sixty verses of *Āl ʿImrān* (from 121-180) which give an elaborate commentary on the lasting significance of those very painful events of the day of Uḥud. They educated and consoled the Prophet (peace be upon him), and the believers, and they unravelled the laws and cannons of God that rule supreme over the social as well as the natural events.

6. TWO OTHER SAD DEVELOPMENTS

Hardly had the wounds caused by the traumatic experience of the Battle of Uḥud healed, than two other very unfortunate events took place with sad and sorrowful consequences for the Muslims. These were the events:

a The Well of al-Rajī[1] (625 C.E.) in which six prominent Companions of the Prophet were treacherously killed, and;

b. The Battle of the Well of Maʿūnah, in which some forty of the best Companions of the Prophet who were quite versed in the Qur'ān, were killed, also in a very mean and treacherous way. These Qur'ānic Scholars were commanded by the Companion of the Prophet, al-Mundhir ibn ʿAmr, of the Anṣār of Banū Sāʿidah. The details of these two events are given by Ibn Hishām, in a very elaborate and detailed way. What we will do here, is just to sketch the main lines of these two sad events, which caused the gracious Prophet (peace be upon him) and the Muslims to grieve profoundly, at a time when the sad memories of Uḥud were still very much fresh in their memories.[2]

7. THE EVENTS OF THE WELL OF AL-RAJĪ'

God chided the Bedouins around Madīnah as being quite confirmed in unbelief and hypocrisy:

> *The Bedouins are more confirmed in unbelief and hypocrisy, and after not to know the bounds of what God has sent down on His messenger and God is All-Wise.* [*al-Tawbah* 9: 97]

God also said of these Bedouins:

> *Some of the Bedouins take what they expend for a fine, and await the turns of fortune to go against you. Theirs shall be the evil turn; God is All-Hearing, All-Knowing.* [*al-Tawbah* 9: 98]

God also condemns the Bedouins of Madīnah, in very clear and harsh words, in another verse, says God:

> *And some of the Bedouins, who dwell around you, are hypocrites, and some of the people of Madīnah are grown bold in hypocrisy, you know them not, but We know them, and We shall chastise them twice.* [*al-Tawbah* 9:101]

Names of Companions killed at al-Rajī' and afterwards are:

1. Marthad ibn Abī Marthad al-Ghanawī, the ally of Ḥamzah ibn ʿAbd al-Muṭṭalib. It is to be remembered that Marthad was sharing the same camel with the Prophet (peace be upon him) on the road to the Battle of Badr.
2. Khālid ibn al-Bakīr, the ally of ʿAdiyy ibn Kaʿb.
3. ʿĀṣim ibn Thābit, from the Aws (Anṣār).
4. Khubayb ibn ʿAdiyy, from the Anṣār.
5. Zayd ibn al-Dathinnah, from Khazraj.
6. ʿAbdullāh ibn Ṭāriq, from the Aws.

All of them were quite versed in the Qur'ān, and some of them memorized it by heart. They were demanded by the clans of *Adhal wa'l-Qarah* of the tribe of al-Hawn of Khuzaymah, to come to their places to teach them Islam. They begged and entreated the Prophet (peace be upon him) to send these learned men to them, so that they might teach them the Qur'ān. But when they were so sent, they attacked them, killing three of them immediately, and taking three others as captives. One of those captives managed to set himself free, and tried to escape. But they killed him by having him surrounded and stoning him. That was ʿAbdullāh ibn Ṭāriq. The other two, namely Khubayb ibn ʿAdiyy and Zayd ibn al-Dathinnah were sold as slaves in Makkah, and eventually killed in the most cruel way.

8. THE EVENTS OF THE WELL OF MA'ŪNAH

The Events of the Well of Ma'ūnah were even harsher and bloodier than those of the Well of al-Rajīʿ. Almost all the forty Muslims, all of the best and more learned, were treacherously killed. They were invited by Abū'l-Barā' ibn ʿAmr, to teach the Bedouin tribe of Banū ʿĀmir of Najd, as most of them were memorizers of the Qur'ān by heart. The Chief of Banū ʿĀmir of Najd was one ʿĀmir ibn al-Ṭufayl, well known for his enmity of the Prophet (peace be upon him) and the Muslims.

The Muslims party set out for Najd, as Abū'l-Barā' gave the Prophet (peace be upon him) very strong assurances that the Muslims were in his protection. They were stopping at the Well of Ma'ūnah, mid-way between the land of Banū ʿĀmir, and the Ḥārah of Banū Salīm, another Bedouin tribe, hostile to the Muslims. The Bedouins attacked them, incited by Ibn Ṭufayl. The men of Banū ʿĀmir refused to obey their chief, Ibn Ṭufayl, as they knew of the protection accorded to the Muslims, by Abū'l-Barā', also a well respected chieftain of the Banū ʿĀmir. But then ʿĀmir Ibn Ṭufayl, mobilized his allies from the Bedouins of Banū Salīm, who obeyed him and suddenly surrounded the Muslims, and overwhelmed them in numbers. The Muslims fought quite gallantly, and did not try to run away, until they were all killed in the fighting, excepting Harim ibn Milḥān, who was sent as an ambassador to ʿĀmir Ibn Ṭufayl, who killed him instantly, before even delivering his message. Another Muslim by the name of Kaʿb ibn Zayd, from Banū Dīnār of the Banū al-Najjār of the Anṣār, was badly wounded, and was abandoned by the unbelivers as dead, but he lived on and made his way to Madīnah, only to die a martyr on the Battle of al-Khandaq. Two members of the group were left with the horses of the Muslim party. They were (a) ʿĀmir ibn Umayyah al-Ḍamarī (b) al-Mundhir ibn Muḥammad (from the Anṣār). The Anṣārī, al-Mundhir ibn Muḥammad, went forth and fought the Bedouins of Salīm and was killed. The other Muslim, namely ʿAmr ibn Umayyah was taken captive, but later set free. It was ʿAmr ibn Umayyah, who broke the sad news of the killing of forty *Qurrā'* (or *Ḥuffāẓ*) to the Prophet (peace be upon him). ʿĀmir ibn al-Ṭufayl was later smitten by Rabīʿah ibn abī al-Barā' ibn Mālik. But the wound was not fatal, and ibn Ṭufayl lived on.

9. TWO MIRACLES FOR TWO OF THESE ḤUFFĀẒ

It was narrated by Ibn Hishām that Ibn al-Ṭufayl (ʿĀmir), when he killed one of those Muslim *ḥāfiẓ*, saw him raised so high that he was above the clouds. He asked who that man was, and was told he was ʿĀmir ibn Fuhayrah, the ally of Abū Bakr.

The second miracle was narrated by Jabar ibn Salamah ibn Mālik. This Jabar was fighting the Muslim *Ḥuffāẓ* with ʿĀmir ibn al-Ṭufayl. He said he plunged his spear between the two shoulders of a Muslim. As he was withdrawing his spear, he over heard the wounded Muslim saying 'I have won, I have won,' Jabar said he was vexed by the Muslim remark, while being killed, and still saying that he had won. Later, Jabar was told of the significance of *shahādah*, and became a Muslim himself.

10. THE JEWISH PLOT TO KILL THE PROPHET!

The sole survivor of the *Ḥuffāẓ*, who were exterminated at the Well of Maʿūnah, by the name of ʿAmr ibn Umayyah, killed two men of the Banū ʿĀmir, the tribe of the treacherous ʿĀmir ibn al-Ṭufayl, no doubt in vengeance for the killing of the Muslim *Ḥuffāẓ* at the Well of Maʿūnah. ʿAmr ibn Umayyah did not know at the time, that the Banū ʿĀmir were under covenant with the Prophet (peace be upon him). When he told the Prophet (peace be upon him) about the killing of the two men of Banū ʿĀmir, the Prophet (peace be upon him) said:

> 'I have an obligation, under the treaty with Banū ʿĀmir, to pay their blood money. I have to ask our confederates from the Jews of Banū al-Naḍīr to help towards that payment, as they are quite rich, and required to do so by the terms of the Agreement of *Ṣaḥīfah of Madīnah*.'

The Prophet (peace be upon him) went to the quarters of Banū al-Naḍīr to ask them to pay their share in the blood money of the two ʿAmirites, killed by ʿAmr ibn Umayyah. He led a big delegation of Muslims, including his three top aides: Abū Bakr, ʿUmar and ʿAlī. The Jews did not receive them well, and they were grumbling about paying the prescribed money. They also showed their resentment of the killing of Kaʿb ibn al-Ashraf, one of the Jews assassinated by the Muslims, because of his role in inciting the Qurayshites and the Bedouins, as well as the Jews to fight the Muslims and invade Madīnah. Then the Jews, as the Prophet (peace be upon him) was standing against the wall of the yard, plotted to kill him. They even commissioned one of them, by the name of ʿAmr ibn Jaḥsh ibn Kaʿb, to climb the wall, against which the Prophet (peace be upon him) was sitting, and drop a rock on his head. But then Jibrīl, the Arch-Angel, informed the Prophet (peace be upon him) of the plot the Jews of Banū al-Naḍīr were about to execute. The Prophet (peace be upon him) rose and took permission, pretending to answer the call of nature; but never to return to his place of meeting with the Jews. When a longer interval than usual lapsed, the Companions left as well.

The Jews tried their best to look friendly and hospitable, lest their plot would be discovered. But, alas, everything was then set for military confrontation between the two former confederates and allies.

The Prophet Muḥammad (peace be upon him) called for the siege of Banū al-Naḍīr. The siege continued for six days and nights. That was in Rabīʿ al-Awwal (the fourth year of the Hijrah, the events of the Wells of al-Rajīʿ and Maʿūnah were in the third year of Hijrah). The Jews of Banū al-Naḍīr withdrew to their strong fortress, and whenever the Muslims approached them, they fired at them with arrows and stones and other weapons. Seeing that the situation was stalemate, the Prophet (peace be upon him) ordered the Muslims to cut down any date trees and destroy their crops. When the Jews saw that, they offered to surrender, provided the Prophet (peace be upon him) gave them save conduct outside the city. The Prophet (peace be upon him) agreed that each of them could carry whatever his camel(s) could carry from his household items, but no weapons would be allowed outside Madīnah. They then moved out of Madīnah in a great show of festival and celebration, as if victory was on their side, with their women singing and sounding the drums. The Prophet (peace be upon him) and the Muslims gained a great deal of booty and weapons, as a result of the eviction of Banū al-Naḍīr.

The great portion of *Sūrah al-Ḥashr* was revealed on the occasion of the conflict between the Prophet (peace be upon him), and the Jews of Banū al-Naḍīr. Verses 2-20 talked about God's design to evacuate the Jews of Banū al-Naḍīr, because of their treachery and plotting to kill the Prophet (peace be upon him), despite the covenants between them and the Muslims. The verses described the typical way in which the Jews characteristically fought their enemy, from behind walls, in fortified townships and from behind fortifications. These verses sanctioned the Prophet's trick of cutting the fruit trees of the Jews to force them out of these fortifications. It also sanctioned the way the Prophet (peace be upon him) had distributed the booty among the poor Muhājirīn, giving the Anṣār a lesser portion, because the Anṣār were relatively richer. The verse enjoining the greatest distribution of the wealth among the greatest numbers, in Muslim society, and which became a permanent rule of the economy in Islam, has been revealed here, and it commended a greater distribution of wealth: says God, in the Holy Qur'ān:

> *Whatsoever spoils of war God has given to His Messenger, from the people of the cities, belongs to God and His Messenger, and the near kinsman, to orphans, the needy, and the traveller, so that it (wealth) be not a thing taken in turns (Revolve) among the rich of you alone. Whatever the Messenger gives you take it, and whatever he forbids you, give it over, and fear God, surely God is Severe in retribution!* [*al-Ḥashr* 59:7]

11. TOTAL BAN ON WINE

It is during the siege of Banū al-Naḍīr, that the total ban on wine was enacted by the Qur'ān, i.e. in Rabīʿ al-Awwal, the fourth year of Hijrah. Before that, the Muslims were only ordered not to pray when drunk, until they knew what they were saying. They were told that the drinking of wine is a big sin, but that it has some benefits, but that its harm was, in fact, greater than its benefit. Then the final ban was effected when a verse was revealed declaring that wine, gambling, sacrificing to idols and divining arrows, as abominations of Satan work, and commanded the Muslims to avoid them happily and they would prosper:

God Says in the Qur'ān:

> *O believers! Wine, gambling, sacrificing to idols and the divining arrows are an abomination of the work of Satan, so avoid it, happily so you will prosper. Satan only desires to precipitate enmity and hatred between you, in regard to wine and arrow shuffling, and to bar you from the remembrance of God and from prayer. Will you then desist?* [*al-Mā'idah* 5:90-91]

It is quite significant that the philosophy of social change advocated in this verse is not a revolutionary one, rather it is a gradual one, even in matters crucially touching the basic issues of conduct and ethics. Although wine drinking, and gambling are serious moral ills, with profounding adverse effect on society, yet the Qur'ān allowed their perpetuation in the Muslim community until the fourth year of Hijrah. This reflects the Qur'ānic preoccupation with changing people's ideas, and winning their emotional alliance first. In so far as conduct is conditioned by convictions, then it is both rational and wise to work to change people's minds and hearts first.

12. THE CONFLICT WITH BANŪ AL-NAḌĪR, AND A BIG RIFT WITH JEWS

The Battle against Banū al-Naḍīr marked a very big and significant rift in Muslim-Jew relations. It was reported that up to the conflict with the Jews of Banū al-Naḍīr, and their subsequent eviction from Madīnah, the Prophet (peace be upon him) used to have a Jewish personal secretary, reported to be very good in writing, and well-versed in the Scriptures, and knew ancient languages, like Hebrew, Syriac, in addition to Arabic. That Jewish Secretary was replaced by Zayd ibn Thābit al-Anṣārī, who was appointed as confident and personal secretary to the Prophet (peace be upon him), after the conflict with the Jews of Banū al-Naḍīr.

13. THE PLEDGED SECOND ENCOUNTER AT BADR

When the annual memory of Uḥud came round in the 4th year of *Hijrah*, the Prophet (peace be upon him) remembered that he had pledged to meet Abū Sufyān and the Makkan unbelievers at Badr after a year. He, therefore, summoned the Muslims to take up their arms, but some feeble-hearted from amongst them, remembered the traumatic experience of Uḥud, and they expressed their wish that they preferred to fight their enemies from within the city of Madīnah. But the Prophet (peace be upon him) was indignant and castigated these Muslims for their weakness and hesitation, and told them that he was going out to Badr, even if had to go it alone. That decisive stance on the part of the Prophet (peace be upon him), sealed the issue, and all hesitation was gone. The Muslims marched to Badr, stayed there for eight full days and nights. However, Abū Sufyān and his army failed to show up. It was reported that, after he started some distance towards Badr, he returned to Makkah, saying that the rainy season was good, and his army was not well prepared. He promised to go out to attack the Muslims the next year, same time. The Muslim army, led by the Prophet (peace be upon him), learned about the retreat of Abū Sufyān. They were jubilant, and they stayed there, in good cheer and high spirit. They even conducted some profitable trades with Bedouin tribes. Their prestige and authority over Arabia, were greatly enhanced, to the disadvantage of the Quraysh, who failed to take the field against the Prophet (peace be upon him), although the initial challenge came from their part, the Prophet (peace be upon him) only responding.

Thus, events began to move in the direction of a major and final battle between the Muslims and the Qurayshites. To Abū Sufyān, the Prophet's military show in Badr in the fourth year of *Hijrah*, and his own failure to show up was most disquieting. So he started to mobilize early in the fifth year, for a major show-down with the Muslims. Before we discuss the Battle of al-Khandaq, and the major events leading to it, let us take a last glance at the epic of Uḥud and its aftermath.

14. SOME HIGHLIGHTS OF UḤUD

The Prophet (peace be upon him) managed to keep his ground, to rally the Muslims back, and to complete an orderly withdrawal towards the bottom of the mountain. Although bleeding and utterly exhausted, he maintained his coolness, mental alertness and his good cheer. When the Prophet (peace be upon him) reached the bottom of the mountain, Khālid ibn al-Walīd and his horsemen were still there, having routed the disobedient archers. At their sight, the Prophet (peace be upon him) gave a very loud and great shout of anger, resolve and indignation.Which means: 'They have no right to be stationed above us!'[3] repeating it a number of times, referring to the Qurayshite soldiers led by Khālid ibn al-Walīd.

Hearing that indignant cry, a Muslim force gathered at once, commanded by ʿUmar ibn al-Khaṭṭāb. They swiftly climbed to the top of the mountain and engaged Khālid ibn al-Walīd (at that time still an unbeliever) and his company and managed to remove them off that position and push them back quite a distance. Thus, it was due to the courage and firmness of the Prophet (peace be upon him) and his military acumen, that the fortunes of the Battle of Uḥud were reversed. The major move in all of this was the hot pursuit which he undertook the next day to Ḥamrā' al-Asad. The unbelievers were assembled to consider whether they ought to attack the Muslims again, so as to rout them. But when they learned about the new march of the Muslims they hurried back to Makkah.

15. THE MARTYRDOM OF MUKHAYRIQ, THE JEW

It is to be remembered that Mukhayriq had converted to Islam, in the early days of the Prophet's arrival in Madīnah. When the Prophet (peace be upon him) learned about his conversion to Islam, he said: 'Mukhayriq is the best of the Jews.' On the day of the Battle of Uḥud, Mukhayriq went to the Jews and said:

'You know very well that is obligatory upon you (according to the precepts of the document of Madīnah *Ṣaḥīfat al-Madīnah* to support Muḥammad against the attack of Quraysh.' But the Jews replied that it was Saturday, and they could not fight or do any work on Saturdays.

'This is only an excuse; but I am going to fight along side with him, and if I am killed all my money and property must go to Muḥammad.' Then Mukhayriq joined the battle, and fought gallantly until he was killed a martyr.

Thus the events that came in the wake of the Battle of Uḥud were closing. The initial shock and grief of defeat were gradually giving way to optimism and more self-confidence, especially after the defeat and eviction of the Jews of Banū al-Naḍīr. The Prophet's outing first to Ḥamrā' al-Asad, and then second to Badr in the fifth year, duly scared the Quraysh, and deterred the aggressive, war-pruned desert Bedouins and greatly enhanced his power and prestige in Madīnah. The sad memories of the Uḥud, and the killing of the *ḥuffāẓ* at al-Rajī' and Ma'ūnah were largely forgotten. Yet the war against the Quraysh was far from being over, and the Arab desert Bedouins had still to be watched closely, and Muslims at Madīnah had still to worry about the enemy from within, namely the hypocrites, headed by Ibn Salūl. It was this Ibn Salūl who incited the Jews of Banū al-Naḍīr to break their covenant with the Prophet (peace be upon him), and promised to come to their help, should hostilities break out. He even promised to go out with them, should it come to that. But he miserably failed to honour any of these two promises. Thus Ibn Salūl used the Jews of Banū al-Naḍīr to fan his own opposition to the Prophet (peace be upon him). But in the crucial hour, he failed to act. These misdeeds of Ibn Salūl were alluded to in *Sūrah al-Ḥashr*, we mentioned earlier.

Two small expeditions which the Prophet (peace be upon him) directed against the Bedouins around Madīnah, and which were successfully carried out, greatly enhanced the security of the city, and further strengthened the position of the Prophet (peace be upon him) and the Muslims therein. Thus the Prophet (peace be upon him) enjoyed a brief period of peace and stability, and was able to take care of some of the home and family problems, which were left pending during these tremulous years of war and conflict. One of these was the question of Zaynab bint Jahsh and her unstable marriage to his former adopted son, Zayd ibn Ḥārithah. The Prophet's cousin Zaynab bint Jaḥsh, was a Hashimite, and her family was not approving her marriage to Zayd, a former slave, but accepted the marriage out of reverence to the Prophet (peace be upon him). However, life between the young couple became more and more untenable. Zayd used to complain to the Prophet (peace be upon him), who loved Zayd as much as a father would love his dear son. But every time Zayd complained, the Prophet (peace be upon him) would advise him against divorce, and would tell him to fear God and keep his wife.

16. THE CHARACTER OF ZAYNAB

Zaynab was a quiet, good and devout Muslim, and was known to have great compassion for the poor, the needy and the orphans. Yet there was no social and emotional compatibility between her and Zayd, whom she respected quite well. In particular, her family, especially ʿAbdullāh ibn Jaḥsh was against the marriage on the grounds set by the Arab's aristocratic customs, that mitigated against mixed marriages, especially to former slaves or even Arabs of non-Qurayshite stock. But, as said before, the Prophet (peace be upon him) had to force the marriage to destroy Arab racism and false feeling of superiority. Indeed the Prophet (peace be upon him) was seeking to establish the new egalitarian and non-discriminatory values of Islam, that sought to rank persons only by their worth and piety, and not by their ethnicity or colours. The Qur'ān denounced racism, and sentiment of ethnical superiority, in the most harsh words. Said God in the Qur'ān:

> *O mankind, we have created you from male and female, and appointed you races and tribes, that you may know each other, surely the noblest among you (the most honoured) in the sight of God are the most God-fearing of you, God is All-Knowing, All-Aware.* [*al-Ḥujurāt* 49:13]

Customs and traditions of nations and races do not change easily, or in a short span of time. Although the Qur'ān rejected all racial biases, and the Prophet (peace be upon him) condemned racialism and ethnicity in the strongest terms, and did all he could to combat these social ills, rife in the pre-Islamic society, yet they persisted on, as the Zayd-Zaynab marriage amply demonstrated. Even today, racialism and ethnicity is not dead in Muslim society, which is a fact to be derided, given that the Qur'ān and the *sunnah* had abrogated it almost fourteen centuries ago. It is of course true that racialism exists in a mild form in the Muslim countries, compared with non-Muslim countries, especially in the West. But almost all Western countries are now quite timid to acknowledge that racial discrimination is practised in their countries, and they are doing all they can to combat it, especially in France, Germany and Scandinavian Countries.

Although orientalists have tried to make a scandal out of the marriage of the Prophet (peace be upon him) to Zaynab, after her divorce from Zayd, a divorce which the Prophet (peace be upon him) tried hard to avert (advising Zayd many times to 'hold to your wife and fear God'), yet the question was actually quite natural and ordinary in traditional Arab society. Even today, if a women is divorced, or if widowed the next of kin would marry her as to protect and provide for her. Zaynab (may God be pleased with her), might have been beautiful, but that was not the overriding reason why the Prophet (peace be upon him) married her, after her divorce from Zayd. At any rate, Zaynab was his cousin, who was under his eyes since she was a child. Had it being a question of love or lust, as the orientalist conjectured, he could have married her earlier on, and would not have been instrumental, as he really was, in arranging her marriage to Zayd, so as to break an old Arabian custom that fathers by adoption could not marry the ex-wives of their adopted sons. Thus, the Prophet's marriage to Zaynab was actually commanded by the Qur'ān, for very objective considerations. It might be true that the Qur'ānic command concurred with the Prophet's own personal wish to solve the problem of the unsuccessful marriage of his adopted son, Zayd, and his cousin Zaynab. It might even be true that he liked the idea of marrying the compassionate and beautiful Zaynab and to bring her some happiness, as she had earlier agreed to marry Zayd, merely out of respect and reverence for the Prophet (peace be upon him), though she had no feelings for him. Be that as it may, the Qur'ān commended the marriage in clear and unequivocal terms.

> *When you said to him whom God has blessed, and you had favoured; keep your wife to yourself and fear God; and you were concealing, within you, what God would reveal, fearing other men but God has better right for you to fear Him! So when Zayd had accomplished what he would of her; we gave her in marriage to you, so that there should not be any fault in the believers marrying the ex-wives of their*

adopted sons, when they have accomplished what they would of them, and God's commandments must be performed... [*Al-Aḥzāb* 33:37]

God said, quite explicitly, in the above quoted Qur'ānic verse that 'so when Zayd had accomplished what he would of her. We gave her in marriage to you (O Muḥammad)...' and further more, God explained the rationale behind this was to abolish the habits that it was taboo, in the eyes of those Arabs, for one to marry the ex-wife of one's adopted son. Be that as it may, the Prophet (peace be upon him) married Zaynab who was quite happy, as expected, to have him as husband and Prophet, a relative and the most sweet of all men. The Prophet (peace be upon him) himself had some moments of peace and tranquillity after the turbulent days of Uḥud, the Well of al-Rajīʿ, the Well of Maʿūnah, where some of the best of his Companions were killed by the crude and blood-thirsty Arabs of the desert Bedouins. At the same time, he also got married to other ladies. But these other marriages were for political reasons and other human motives, as most of them were women advanced in age, and without much of what men normally desire for in marriage, i.e. beauty, wealth, or noble birth. The orientalists made a lot of fuss, concerning these marriages, accusing the Prophet (peace be upon him) of having excessive desire and lust for women. Nothing was further from the truth than these accusations. For a more detailed account of the orientalists' position, the reader can consult Sir William Muir, Dermenghem, Washington Irving, Lammens and others. The reader can also consult Haykal, 'The Life of Muḥammad', translated by Ismail al-Faruqi, who gave quite a comprehensive summary of the views of these orientalists. Events now started to build towards an imminent confrontation with the Quraysh. Just before the Battle of al-Khandaq (The Trench), the Prophet (peace be upon him) waged two more attacks at the Bedouins of the desert. These were excursions of (a) the expedition of Dhāt ar-Riqāʿ and (b) the second expedition was directed to Dūmat al-Jandal. Both of these expeditions were quite successful, and dealt considerable blows to those unruly Bedouins of the desert. The stage was now towards a final showdown with the Quraysh. The Muslims' position was much better than it was in the immediate aftermath of Uḥud. The Bedouins were checked and the Jewish opposition from within was greatly reduced, though not exterminated completely, as the formidable Jews of Banū Qurayẓah were still a resident inside hazard. They kept a low profile, but when the combined forces of the Quraysh and the desert Bedouins invaded Madīnah, the Jewish enmity and plotting surfaced again in full vogue.[4]

The remaining Jewish tribe of Banū Qurayẓah started mobilizing for war, and hopes of avenging the expulsion of the Jews of Qaynuqā' and those of Banū al-Naḍīr were raised quite high. Some of the Jews of Qurayẓah were quite sure that the Muslims could never make it that time, seeing many thousands of soldiers of the combined forces of the allied Quraysh, the Bedouins desert Arabs, and the Jews of Banū al-Naḍīr and Khaybar. The army of so-called *al-Aḥzāb* (or the confederates) was quite big.

The Jews of al-Naḍīr and those of Khaybar played a tremendous role in convincing the Quraysh to attack the Prophet (peace be upon him) and the Muslims at Madīnah. They promised to fight alongside them, and assured the Qurayshites, that the defeat of the Muslims was an absolute certainty. Those Jews also contacted the Jews of Banū Qurayẓah and incited them to break their covenant with Muḥammad, and join the Confederates' Expedition. Thus the stage was set for the biggest battle yet between Muslims and the Qurayshites.[5]

CHAPTER 5

The Battle of al-Khandaq: Muslims Under Siege

1. THE JEWISH DELEGATION TO MAKKAH

The following reasons may be said to have precipitated the battle of al-Khandaq:

a. The inconclusive outcome of Uḥud, and the Quraysh failure to confront the Prophet (peace be upon him), as they had boasted they would do at Badr, a year from the day of Uḥud, left the Makkans unsatisfied with their military effort to exterminate the Prophet (peace be upon him) and Muslims. Therefore the agitation for war against the Prophet (peace be upon him) was very much alive. The Jewish activists in Makkah continued to incite decisive action against the Prophet (peace be upon him).

b. The second cause of waging the al-Khandaq campaign was the spite, the grudge and the enmity of the Jews who had been expelled from Madīnah, especially the Banu al-Naḍīr. Seeing that the Quraysh seemed in no haste to mount a campaign after Uḥud, they sent a big delegation of their notables to Makkah.

These included: Ḥuyayy ibn Akhṭab, their foremost leader, Sallām ibn Abī al-Ḥuqayq; Kinānah ibn Abī Ḥuqayq; Ḥawdhah ibn Qays, of the tribe of Wā'il and Abū ʿAmmār of the tribe of Wā'il.

The Jewish mission was to convince the Quraysh that the time was right to attack Muḥammad (peace be upon him), and exterminate the

Muslims once and for all. The Quraysh were hesitant, knowing from previous experience, that to wage war against Muḥammad (peace be upon him) was no light undertaking. They wanted assurances from the Jews, which they keenly provided:

a. They told them that Banū al-Naḍīr were quite ready to attack Madīnah; they were stationed not far away on the road between Madīnah and Khaybar, armed and ready.

b. The Jews of Banū Qurayẓah were quite prepared for war. Since they feared the same fate as Qaynuqāʿ and al-Naḍīr before them, they were ready to attack the Muslims from within Madīnah.

2. THE JEWS FAVOUR PAGANISM TO MONOTHEISM

Then the Quraysh wanted to further test the position of the Jews. They asked them whether the worship of idols was better than the religion of Muḥammad (peace be upon him). The Jews did not hesitate to say that the paganism of the Quraysh and Ghaṭafān was better than the monotheism of Muḥammad (peace be upon him). Now this position of the Jews was dictated by sheer expediency. By giving this false testimony, they were actually undermining themselves and their religion, more than they were undermining Islam. The gracious Qur'ān chided them for this false testimony. Referring to it, God says in the Qur'ān:

> *Would you not consider those who were given a share of the Book, believing in demons and idols, and saying to the unbelievers that they are better guided to the way than the believers. Those are they whom Allah has cursed, and he whom Allah has cursed, you would not find for him any helper.* [*al-Nisā'* 4:51-52]

So desperate in their enmity of the Muslims were the Jews, that they were prepared to compromise their own religious creed, although they were resisting Islam and fighting the Muslims on the ground that they would not abandon their religion of Abraham and monotheism.[1]

3. THE CONFEDERATION FORCES

When the Muslims heard news of the armies advancing towards them, they were naturally apprehensive. They assembled to consider the situation and evaluate the extent of the threat against them. They knew that it was such a huge gathering of forces of the confederates; these included:

a. The Quraysh with approximately six thousand fighters – four thousand on foot, camel corps of one thousand five hundred and the rest were horsemen.

b. Ghaṭafān, clans of Sulaym, Ashjaʿ and Murrah supplied a combined force of one thousand five hundred (700+400+ 400).

c. Banū Fazārah sent a force of camel corps of one thousand; and a large number of infantry.

d. Banū Asad and Saʿd (clans of Ghaṭafān) also contributed a large number of fighters.

Altogether, the combined forces of the Quraysh and their Bedouin allies exceeded ten thousand soldiers well armed and quite determined to crush and exterminate the Muslims and the Prophet (peace be upon him) in Madīnah. The situation was indeed very grave, and the very existence of the Muslims as a community was in peril. The only way for them to defend themselves and their territory was to fortify and defend the city from within.

4. THE DIGGING OF THE KHANDAQ (THE TRENCH)

It was Salmān, the Persian, who suggested the digging of a *Khandaq* (trench or dry moat) around the city. The idea was quite new, but the Prophet (peace be upon him) accepted it and work to dig the trench was undertaken with all speed, as it had to be ready before the advancing army reached Madīnah. It was reported that the Muslims undertook the work with such zeal and enthusiasm, that the project was completed in just six days. Seeing that the Prophet (peace be upon him) himself took part in the actual digging, no Muslim spared any effort to complete the work before the arrival of the enemy. In any case, the danger that hung over them, was more than a sufficient incentive for all to do their utmost, and all the necessary preparations were completed before the enemy arrived.[2] Large quantities of stones were place on the inside of the *Khandaq* on the roofs of the houses, inside Madīnah and next to the *Khandaq*, so that children might help the Muslims by throwing them at the enemy.

5. AN UNPLEASANT SURPRISE FOR THE QURAYSH

When the forces of the Quraysh arrived, they were confronted by the trench, the most unpleasant surprise that they might have expected. In view of their large numbers they hoped to overwhelm and storm the city of Madīnah with ease. The obstacle of the trench was quite perplexing to them, as the Arabs knew only open combat in open space. True, the Jews of Arabia used to fight from behind walls and fortifications, as the Qur'ān reports in *Sūrah al-Ḥashr*, but they had never seen anything like a trench. The moat itself was so wide that only once, after many trials, the knights of the Quraysh were able to jump over it, at a point where it was rather narrow; only four knights made the jump. A fifth was not so lucky, and his horse fell in the moat and was instantly killed. Quraysh were so exasperated at the construction of the barrier, that they shouted, 'Cowards, Cowards,' at the Muslims. The Quraysh knights who managed to cross the trench to the Muslim side were:

a. ʿAmr ibn ʿAbd Wudd, a formidable and well-known knight of the Quraysh, much feared and hated by the Muslims.

b. ʿIkrimah ibn Abī Jahl, the son of the well known leader of Banū Makhzūm of Quraysh, killed at Badr.

c. Hubayrah ibn Wahb (from Banū Makhzūm).

Those knights charged forward to mount Salaʿ, and challenged the Muslims to come out for single combat. The chivalrous ʿAlī ibn Abī Ṭālib accepted, and ibn ʿAbd al-Wudd said: 'But why for Goodness sake, do you want to fight with me, my cousin, for I do not like to kill you, son of my brother.'

'But, by God I want to kill you,' said ʿAlī. At this reply, the Ibn ʿAbd al-Wudd became very worked up, and charged at ʿAlī furiously. But ʿAlī managed to kill him. When that formidable Quraysh knight fell dead, the other three knights were frightened and dismayed and fled back, across the trench to their own side. That incident disheartened the Quraysh, who made another failed attempt to cross over to the Muslims, before accepting the only course of action open to them: to encamp and lay siege to Madīnah. They dismounted, and put up their tents. The siege proved a long, tedious and expensive affair. Only sporadic exchanges of arrows, and stone throwing, was attempted from time to time. The siege continued for almost a month, without any positive results. The *Khandaq* proved a very effective device, and the Muslims were not short of provisions, so long as Banū Qurayẓah were pacified, and were prepared to sell food and other provisions to Muslim allies. But Ḥuyayy ibn Akhṭab was quick to see the importance of depriving the Muslims of that logistical advantage. So he made his way to the quarters of Banū Qurayẓah.

6. ḤUYAYY IBN AL-AKHṬAB'S SEDITION OF QURAYẒAH

When the leader of Banū Qurayẓah Kaʿb ibn Asad saw Ḥuyayy at his doors, he first refused to admit him. The following dramatic exchange passed between them.[3]

'O Kaʿb please open the door, you cannot shut it in my face, for Goodness sake.'

'But O Ḥuyayy, you are indeed a sinister visitor, don't you know that there is a pact between me and Muḥammad, which I have no intention of violating, since I have known nothing from him, except trust, credence and faithfulness.'

'Just open the door, for I have something very important to tell you,' cried Ḥuyayy.

'I am not going to open it to you,' replied Ka'b.

'I bet you do not want to open the door, so that I shall not share your dinner,' said Ḥuyayy.

At this last remark, Ka'b offended and embarrassed, opened the door, he did not want to give the impression that he was niggardly to his guests. When allowed in, Ḥuyyay proceeded at once to persuade his host:

'Dear Ka'b I have come to you with the prospect of the honour of the age, and with an up-roaring sea, I have come to you with the whole of Quraysh, army and leaders, and with the whole of Ghaṭafān, leaders and army. They have told me most emphatically and given a very strong pledge, that they are not going to turn back to their homes this time, until they destroy Muḥammad and the Muslims completely.'

'Have you finished Ḥuyayy?' began Ka'b, still unconvinced, and still greatly disturbed by the mission of Ḥuyayy; 'by God, you have indeed brought me the indignity and shame of eternity, and an empty cloud which he already shed its water while it still thunders and shows lightening, with nothing in its wake, Woe to you, Ḥuyayy, leave me as I am with Muḥammad, for I have always found him loyal and faithful.' But Ḥuyayy would not budge and did not leave Ka'b alone. He continued wheedling, until Ka'b gave in to his persuasion, and agreed to violate his pledge with the Prophet (peace be upon him). Ḥuyayy succeeded in assuring Ka'b, that he could always count on his support, and that of his Arab friends. He even pledged that, should the Arabs depart without defeating Muḥammad, he would stay behind to defend Qurayẓah, and share with them whatever consequences that might lead to. By that assurance, Ka'b was duly swayed to what would lead to a disaster, for him personally, and for his whole tribe, as we shall see in the sequel.

7. MUSLIMS PANIC AT THE PROSPECT OF ATTACKS

Despite the Prophet's effort to conceal it, news reached the Muslims of the betrayal of their former allies, the Jews of Banū Qurayẓah. That news caused a great deal of panic and fear in their ranks. If the news proved to be true, that meant that another war front would be opened against them. Moreover, their sole source of food and other provisions would be lost. They were already exhausted, cold (for the season was exceptionally cold and wet) and hungry. The siege had by that time gone on for about a month approximately, and their money and supplies were very low indeed. Their army of just over three thousand men was greatly out-numbered and out-matched by the combined armies of the Quraysh and the Bedouins of over ten thousand soldiers armed to the teeth. The prospect now, of attacks from the south by the Arabs and from the inside (from underneath) by the Jews of Qurayẓah was more than some could bear. The Gracious Qur'ān portrays the situation, and panic of the Muslims most vividly; God said in the Qur'ān:

> *When they came against you from above and below you, and when your eyes swerved and your hearts reached your throats, while you entertained (evil) thoughts about God.*
> *There it was, when the believers were tried and shaken most mightily, and when the hypocrites and those in whose hearts is sickness, said God and His Messenger promised us only delusion? And when a party of them said:*
> *'O People of Yathrib, there is no abiding here for you, therefore return,' and a party of them were asking leave of the Prophet, saying 'our houses are exposed' Yet they were not exposed, they desired only to flee...* [*al-Aḥzāb* 33:10-13]

8. THE PROPHET RESORTS TO STRATEGIC TACTICS

It is well-known that ruses feature very largely in the Prophet's strategy of waging war. To him is attributed the famous Hadith. 'Assuredly, quite often war is won by tricks.'

Even pre-Islamic Arabs, who were well known for their love of war, valued highly the role played by good judgement, and by clever ruses in winning battles. During the Battle of Badr, as we saw, the strategic positioning of the Muslims, by the side of the wells, was a major, decisive factor in gaining a huge military advantage over the enemy.

An Arab poet stressed the importance of good judgement in winning wars: 'Sound opinion is more important (in winning wars) than the courage of the bravest knights. It is the basic requirement and bravery comes second,' he said.

As the Muslims faced overwhelming odds, and their situation worsened because of the treachery of the Jews of Qurayẓah, the Prophet (peace be upon him) began to use intrigue against his enemies, as they, especially the Jews, did against the Muslims.

His first aim was to divide the confederates, to attack and destroy their apparent unity. He turned his attention first upon the most powerful ally of the Quraysh, namely the tribe of Banū Ghaṭafān, and their minor allies. He sent an envoy to them, with a message:

'Go home, and quit this affair in which you have no stake, because this is only the Quraysh trying to avenge their defeats at Badr and Uḥud. Go home, and I will give you one third of next year's date harvest in Madīnah,' offered the Prophet's messenger to Ghaṭafān.

The offer was very tempting and Banū Ghaṭafān began to discuss it amongst themselves. Their zeal and enthusiasm for the fighting began to wane and, as many of them became inclined to accept this offer, it considerably weakened their morale.

9. THE WONDERFUL TRICK OF NUʿAYM IBN MASʿŪD[4]

However, the most brilliant trick, resorted to by the Prophet (peace be upon him) in that difficult and fearful situation, was to instruct Nuʿaym ibn Musʿūd who was a recent convert to Islam, but his conversion was at that time kept a secret to confuse the enemy. The Prophet (peace be upon him) commissioned him to 'go and weaken the enemy's resolve and will to fight with us....' the Prophet (peace be upon him) instructed Nu ʿaym ibn Mus ʿūd.

Nu ʿaym ibn Mas ʿūd was a friend of Qurayẓah, and had been a frequent visitor of their quarters. In particular, he used to visit them to buy and drink wine in their cafés before his conversion to Islam. He decided to exploit his friendship with Qurayẓah. He went to the fortifications of Qurayẓah, and asked to speak to Ka ʿb ibn al-Asad, their leader. He reminded him of his affection for them, and of the special tie that was between them. When Banū Qurayẓah assured Nu ʿaym that they did not suspected him, he said: "O Qurayẓah, you know very well that the situation of Quraysh and that of Ghaṭafān are not like your situation. The land is your land ; your property, your wives and children are on it, you cannot leave and go elsewhere, should it come to that. Now Quraysh and Ghaṭafān came to fight Muḥammad and his companions and you have aided them against him. However, their lands their property and their wives are not here. So they are not like you. If they see an opportunity, they will make the most of it. But should things go badly, they will go back to their own land, and leave you to face the man in your country. However, you will not be able to do this, if you are left alone. So I advise you not to fight with these people, until they give you some of their chiefs as hostages, to remain in your hands, as security that they will fight Muḥammad with you, until you eradicate him and his Muslim followers.' argued Nu ʿaym.

The view and counsel of Nu ʿaym were appealing to Qurayẓah, and they waited for the right moment to confront the Quraysh with their new demands for hostages.

Meanwhile, the wily Nu ʿaym went to the camp of the Quraysh with a different proposition: 'You know my affection for you, and that I have left Muḥammad. I have heard something very important, and I think it is my duty to convey it to you by way of warning, which you must keep very confidential.' When they promised to do so, he began: 'You must know, and mark my words, that the Jews of Qurayẓah have regretted their action opposing Muḥammad, and they have actually sent to tell him so, saying:

"Would you like us to get hold of some chiefs of the two tribes, Quraysh and Ghaṭafān, and hand them over to you, so that you can cut their heads off? Then we can join you in exterminating them." Muḥammad has sent word back to them accepting their offer, so if the Jews ask you demanding hostages, do not send them a single man.' Nu'aym told the Quraysh.

Nu'aym went to his own tribe, Ghaṭafān, and had no difficulty in convincing them of his sincerity and his counsel, as he did with the Quraysh.

This plan worked quite well. The Quraysh wanted to test the alliance of Qurayẓah in the light of what they heard, they sent one envoy, by the name of 'Ikrimah ibn Abī Jahl on the eve of the Sabbath of Shawwāl, the fifth year of *Hijrah*. 'Ikrimah told Banū Qurayẓah that it was not feasible for them, to prolong their siege of Madīnah any longer. Their horses and camels were dying and indeed the morale of their army was generally sinking very low; that now it was the time to attack the Muslims, and deal with them once and for all; that they were looking forward to, indeed demanding Banū Qurayẓah to participate in this final, and decisive battle against Muḥammad (peace be upon him). However, the response from Qurayẓah was quite disappointing. They said, as it was Sabbath, they could do nothing, their religion very strictly forbade them to do anything on Sabbath, lest a severe chastisement should befall them. Moreover, they demanded that the Quraysh and Ghaṭafān should give them some of their chiefs to be held with them, as a security that should Qurayẓah engage in fighting Muḥammad, those two tribes would fight alongside them to the finish. Qurayẓah expressed their fears that should the battle turn against them, their allies (Quraysh, Ghaṭafān) would leave for their homes, abandoning Qurayẓah to face Muḥammad alone. But this was an eventuality they did not wish for, because Qurayẓah alone could not successfully engage Muḥammad and his Muslim army.

Quite exasperated and angry, 'Ikrimah quickly withdrew and returned directly to the Quraysh, telling them what Qurayẓah had said in reply to their demands. The Quraysh said that Nu'aym had indeed been right. They sent word to Qurayẓah that they could expect no hostages from them. When that reply reached Qurayẓah, they in return said what Nu ͑aym had told them was indeed correct, and thus a wedge was driven between the two allies of the confederates that laid siege to Madīnah, during the Battle of al-Khandaq (or the Battle of Aḥzāb).

This is how God's design worked, and how the Prophet (peace be upon him), by the will of God, managed to sow distrust, and dissension, amongst the enemies of Islam.

10. THE RAIN AND THE COLD WIND[5]

The refusal of Qurayẓah to join in the battle against Muḥammad (peace be upon him), until Quraysh and Ghaṭafān agree to give hostages, meant that the besieging forces and their already low morale sank even lower. As if this was not enough, that night a bitterly cold wind blew across the plain, accompanied by torrential rain, so heavy and so cold that every soldier was shivering from cold, fatigue and hunger. The wind moreover, uprooted the confederates' tents, and extinguished their fires, and their food was spilled over as their food pots were overturned by the wind. The rain was accompanied with thunder and strong dazzling lightning. The Quraysh were struck by a frightening thought that Muḥammad might take advantage of the unfavourable climate and attack them.

11. THE PROPHET SENT ḤUDHAYFAH IBN AL-YAMĀN TO RECONNOITRE QURAYSH CAMP[6]

When the Prophet (peace be upon him) heard about the dissension between the Quraysh and Jews, and when the rain and the cold wind struck their encampments, he called among Muslims for a volunteer to go to their encampment, and bring him news about their situation. The Prophet (peace be upon him) said that whoever volunteered, would be assured of Paradise. But the Muslims were so exhausted with cold and hunger, and so afraid that none of them volunteered to go, despite the fact that the Prophet (peace be upon him) repeated his demand more than once, and despite the promise of Paradise extended by him. Seeing that no one was willing to volunteer, the Prophet (peace be upon him) called upon Ḥudhayfah ibn al-Yamān to go. Ḥudhayfah said that he had only complied out of respect for the Prophet (peace be upon him).

Ḥudhayfah managed to penetrate deep into the enemy's army and camp. It was so dark and so cold and noisy that nobody was paying any attention to anything except his own safety and survival. Ḥudhayfah drew very near to where Abū Sufyān was standing, about to deliver a decisive speech. Had he been authorized, Ḥudhayfah said, it would have been easy for him to kill Abū Sufyān, from where he had been sitting.

Then Abū Sufyān stood up and gave a speech; but at first warned against the possibility of Muslim espionage and infiltration, asking that everyone of them should check who was sitting next to him. Ḥudhayfah proved very vigilant and quick minded, because he promptly asked the man sitting next to him about his identity. In this way he avoided the possibility that his neighbour would take the initiative, with the prospect that he might be discovered.

The address of Abū Sufyān was quite clear that the army had no other option but to withdraw; Abū Sufyān furthermore, made it very clear that he himself was withdrawing without delay. Said Abū Sufyān:

> 'O Quraysh, we are not in a permanent camp, the horses and the camels are dying. The Banū Qurayẓah have broken their word to us, and we have heard disquieting reports of them. You can see the violence of the wind, which leaves neither cooking pots, nor fire and tents to count on. Be off, for I am going.'

Ḥudhayfah said that: Abū Sufyān was in such a hurry that he rode on his camel without undoing its tackle, forgetting to do this in his haste, fear and confusion. Ḥudhayfah said he was near enough to

Abū Sufyān that he could have easily killed him but, he remembered the Prophet's instruction not to do such a thing.

Thus the Aḥzāb forces (the confederates), departed that night, in such haste and confusion that they left their things, and some of their weapons behind. When next morning dawned, there was no sign of them. The Muslims came out to look; the space across the *Khandaq* was quite empty. They could not believe their eyes! There, they beheld yet another sign of God's great mercy and favour upon them. The Aḥzāb, who just one day before, posed the greatest ever danger for them and Islam had by then been vanquished, almost without any fighting being carried out. Just as in Badr, God managed the war almost exclusively by Himself, on behalf of the Prophet (peace be upon him) and Muslims. The only effort carried out by the Muslims was to dig the *Khandaq* and put up patiently with the month-long siege of Madīnah. They also bore the perilous news of the treachery of Qurayẓah, and their cutting off the food supplies. ʿAlī ibn Abī Ṭālib and his company managed to guard the *Khandaq* well and prevent any attempts to cross it by the horse-men of Quraysh. The Qur'ān refers to these dramatic events in very vivid terms:

> *O believers, remember Allah's blessing upon you, when soldiers came against you, and We sent against them a wind (hurricane) and soldiers you saw not, and Allah sees what you do. When they came upon you from above and below, and when your eyes we swerved and your hearts reached your throats, and you entertained evil thoughts, about Allah. There it was, that the believers were tried and shaken most mightily.* [*al-Aḥzāb* 33:9-11]

12. THE BATTLE OF AḤZĀB WAS THE GREATEST TRIAL

No doubt, the Battle of Aḥzāb (al-Khandaq) represents the climax of trial and suffering in the history of the Prophet (peace be upon him) and his Companions. Compared with al-Aḥzāb, Uḥud was just a single set-back, a single battle that was lost, after an initial victory. Although the Prophet (peace be upon him) himself sustained serious wounds, his uncle Ḥamzah was killed, and his body mutilated, and seventy of his best and most gallant companions were killed, yet the adverse consequences for the Muslims were not very great, and they managed to offset them the very next day, by setting out in pursuit of Abū Sufyān and his forces. Moreover, the Quraysh victory was far from being conclusive, and achieved no decisive results for them. Although it was a psychological boost for them, avenging their slain at Badr, they were unable to achieve any strategic advantage over the Muslims. They did not manage to kill the Prophet (peace be upon him), nor did they manage to enter Madīnah or destroy the military strength of the Muslims. By contrast the Battle of al-Khandaq threatened the very existence of the Muslim community. Never before had the Quraysh and their Jewish allies managed to gather such a mighty army, and never before had they been able to lay siege to Madīnah for almost a whole month. Lastly, never before had the alliance against the Muslims been so extensive and great, drawing together all the adversaries of the Muslims for the first time, whereas the Prophet (peace be upon him) was not able to call upon his traditional allies of Banū Khuzāʿah, because of the suddenness and completeness of the siege; the alliance brought together for the first time. The following forces comprised the army of the Quraysh and allies:

a. The Quraysh and their immediate allies from the Bedouins of the deserts of Makkah (Banū Ghaṭafān, Sulaym, Ashjaʿ, Murrah, Fazārah, etc.).

b. All the clans of tribes of the Ḥijāz.

c The combined forces of the confederates reached above twelve thousand, together with an uncounted number of Bedouins from immediate outskirts of Madīnah, who joined the advancing Aḥzāb army.

In addition to their number, they had the best equipment and armaments of the time in Arabia. It is to be remembered that the main objective of the Jews of Banū al-Naḍīr, who urged the war, was the complete annihilation of Muḥammad (peace be upon him) and the Muslims. Similarly, the leaders of the Quraysh, when they set out towards Madīnah surrounded by their confederate army of the Bedouins, had as their main objective to uproot the Muslim presence in Arabia, once and for all. Qurayẓah also, when they agreed to join in the Aḥzāb Battle, put as their main condition that they be assured that the objective of the expedition was the complete destruction of the Muslim authority, before the war would end and Quraysh and Ghaṭafān would depart. For all of these reasons, the Battle of al-Aḥzāb was truly the most trying and most dangerous confrontation that the early Muslims yet had to face. It was far more perilous than Uḥud. The only other battle that may exceed al-Aḥzāb in significance was the battle of Badr, because then also the very existence of the Muslims was under threat. It is for this reason, that the Qur'ān refers to Al-Aḥzāb as the occasion when the Muslims were most severely tried and shaken most mightily.

It is the only occasion in the Qur'ān when God describes and exposes the great panic and fear that the Muslims experienced:

> *When the eyes (of the Muslims) swerved, and their hearts reached to their throats, and you entertained unseeing evil doubts about Allah.* [*al-Aḥzāb* 33:10]

I know of no better description of the situation of the psychological state of the combatants, when facing the real possibility of death, than the description given in the above verse. Even the bravest of men, when they experience that kind of situation for the first time and for a brief moment, when the prospects of death and defeat loom very large, experience the same symptoms, referred to in the above Qur'ānic verse i.e. their eyes swerve and their hearts seem to reach their throats (from its violent beats).

The Qur'ān also describes the Muslims' military situation as very desperate indeed, as they were surrounded and attached from all directions 'from above you and from below you!' This encirclement was also experienced in other respects, as they were hungry, cold and without any of their traditional allies. Also they faced really overwhelming odds: in the number of men, in armaments and carriers such as horses and camels.

Indeed so great was God's power and favour to the Muslims that in a single night, all of that had totally changed. The Battle of al-Aḥzāb was very similar to Badr, in that everything had been planned, arranged and managed by God alone. What the Muslims contributed was nothing compared to God's Divine and most perfect determination of things.

13. THE MARCH AGAINST QURAYẒAH

Once the Confederate Forces had departed, the Jewish threat of Banū Qurayẓah was very much in the minds of everyone. The Prophet (peace be upon him) called for general mobilization against the treachery of Qurayẓah, when they had been given no cause to betray the Prophet (peace be upon him). By the admission of their leader, Kaʿb ibn al-Asad, that they have always found him loyal and faithful.

Except for the treasury and sedition of Ḥuyayy ibn al-Akhṭab, Banū Qurayẓah might have been content to stick to their pledge with the Prophet (peace be upon him) and Muslims. The Prophet (peace be upon him) himself observed the useful working relations with the Jews of Madīnah in his early days of arrival there. Not only did he pray towards the Aqṣā' Mosque, but he used to observe the Day of Atonement and fast the Day of *Āshūrā'*. He also used to visit the Jews in their homes, and religious schools, and even engaged them in religious and theological discussions. Politically, and according to the provisions of the Document of Madīnah (*Ṣaḥīfat al-Madīnah*) the Jews were accorded full citizenship of the City State of Madīnah, and even the first private secretary of the Prophet (peace be upon him) was a Jew. Then Qurayẓah violated their covenant with him, and he could no longer, for security reasons, have a Jewish secretary. According to the provisions of the *Ṣaḥīfah*, which envisaged a kind of federation, the Jews enjoyed a considerable degree of freedom to run their own affairs. They were fully integrated in the commercial life of the city with Muslims, buying and selling with them. It is quite significant that, though the three Jewish settlements in Madīnah were originally comprised of immigrants from al-Shām and Palestine, the Prophet (peace be upon him) never hinted that they should depart on the grounds that they were Jewish or of foreign origin. The Prophet (peace be upon him) welcomed all people, and reached out to the foreigners, and the destitute, Muslims and non-Muslims, for he was profoundly generous and tolerant. But of course, it was not easy for the Jews of Madīnah to see prophethood departing from the house of Jacob (Israel). They became very envious and spiteful of the Prophet (peace be upon him). Their betrayal of the Prophet (peace be upon him), and their violation of the covenant with him, left him no other course of action than to take punitive military action against them. As the events of the Battle of the Aḥzāb had shown, it was clear beyond doubt, that they constituted a security hazard, which he could no longer afford to ignore.

The Prophet (peace be upon him) therefore, soon after the Confederates had departed, gave the general order:

> 'Whoever believed in God and the Hereafter, let him not pray the ʿ*Aṣr* prayer of that day, of the departure of the Aḥzāb, except in the quarters of Banū Qurayẓah.'[7]

As a result, there was a massive exodus of Muslim soldiers of Madīnah towards the quarters of Quraysh some miles outside Madīnah. The flag was given to ʿAlī ibn Abī Ṭālib, and he advanced towards their fortifications to which they had retreated, closing the doors behind them. As ʿAlī came near, he heard the Jews voicing insults about the Prophet (peace be upon him). When ʿAlī saw the Prophet (peace be upon him) approaching the fortifications, he hurried to him, hoping to hold him back so that he would not hear them speaking ill of him.

This was a rare moment when the Prophet (peace be upon him) allowed himself to express anger at the outrageous conduct of

Qurayẓah: 'You brothers of the monkeys, has not God disgraced you, and brought His vengeance upon you?' The Jews replied 'O Abū al-Qāsim, you are not a barbarous person.' The Jews then realized that they had pushed the Prophet (peace be upon him) beyond what he could take. After all, the Prophet was still human, i.e. a Prophet of human nature. Contrary to some religions, in Islam Muḥammad has never been regarded as a divine being. Quite often, the Qur'ān had to correct him, blame him or even rebuke him. This is one of the miraculous aspects of the Qur'ān. Had Muḥammad (peace be upon him) been the author of the Qur'ān, he would never declare himself to be wrong, or rebuke-worthy, as he was in fact so many times declared to be in the Qur'ān.

14. THE SIEGE AND DEFEAT OF QURAYẒAH

Having arrived at the fortification of Qurayẓah, and seeing that they were quite entrenched in these fortresses, the Prophet (peace be upon him) ordered that they would be besieged. It is narrated, by Ibn Hishām, that Gabriel not only told the Prophet (peace be upon him) to lay siege to Qurayẓah, but himself participated in the siege, appearing in the form of the handsome Companion of the Prophet, Diḥyah al-Kalbī, with an embroidered white turban, riding a white mule. The siege lasted for twenty-five days and nights, until the Jews were very hard pressed, and God cast terror in their hearts.

Ḥuyayy ibn al-Akhṭab made good his promise, and joined Qurayẓah in their fortress after the Confederates departed. When Kaʿb ibn al-Asad the leader of Qurayẓah saw that the Qurayẓah could no longer bear the siege, he advised them to convert to Islam, if only to avert the terrible consequences of surrender. He knew very well, what they had done to the Prophet (peace be upon him), and the Muslims, and he was sure that the Prophet (peace be upon him) was so infuriated by their uncalled for treachery that it was unreasonable to expect anything from him but a severe judgement. However, the rank and file of Qurayẓah refused to leave the religion of their forefathers, or to abandon the Torah, their holy book. Despairing to persuade his people to convert to Islam, Kaʿb Ibn al-Asad turned to the Prophet (peace be upon him), and asked him to be lenient and to treat them, as he had treated Banū al-Naḍīr before them, namely to allow them to leave the city, and move northward towards al-Shām. They asked their former Arab ally of the Aws, by the name of Abū Lubābah ibn al-Mundhir, to negotiate for them the terms of their surrender.

15. THE EPITHET OF ABŪ LUBĀBAH[8]

When Abū Lubābah came through the gate of the fortress, he met a women from Qurayẓah, crying and lamenting. He was moved by compassion for their plight. When she asked what the Prophet (peace be upon him) would do if they surrendered, he moved his hand across his throat, meaning that he would kill them all. Then he realized that he had betrayed the Prophet (peace be upon him), by disclosing his intentions towards Qurayẓah. When he came back to the city, he made it straight to the Prophet's mosque, and tied himself to its main column, and vowed not to untie himself, until God had forgiven him. When the Prophet (peace be upon him) learned of what Abū Lubābah had done, he only said: 'I would have forgiven him, had he come to me first but now, I am afraid he will have to stay there until God makes His judgement concerning him.'

God's forgiveness of Abū Lubābah came at the dawn of the next day, in the house of Umm Salamah. The Prophet (peace be upon him) woke up laughing:

'What are you laughing about O Messenger of God?' asked Umm Salamah, the Prophet's wife.

'God has forgiven Abū Lubābah,' answered the Prophet (peace be upon him).

'Am I free to tell the news to Abū Lubābah,' asked the Prophet's wife.

'I see no reason why not,' said Muḥammad.

Umm Salamah stood at the door of her apartment which opened on the Prophet's Mosque, as did many of the Prophet's private apartments, and shouted:

'Rejoice Abū Lubābah, for God has forgiven you.' At that time, the Prophet's wives and indeed Muslim women at large, used to mingle rather freely with men. This was before segregation (or *ḥijāb*) was prescribed. After the *ḥijāb* was prescribed, such intermingling was prohibited. This did not happen until well after the Aḥzāb Battle, which took place in the fifth year of the *Hijrah*.

16. QURAYẒAH VIOLATE THEIR AGREEMENT WITH THE PROPHET[9]

No doubt, the Qurayẓah's action in violating their covenant with the Prophet (peace be upon him), for no other reason but the irrational envying of him, and their vengeful desire of seeing him destroyed, was a very unfortunate development in Muslim-Jewish relations. However, their alliance with the Quraysh and Ghaṭafān, and their pledge to utterly destroy and exterminate the Prophet (peace be upon him) was the most unfortunate thing to do, given the Prophet's good treatment of Qurayẓah, and the fact that he kept his pledge to them in the most perfect manner. The Prophet (peace be upon him) might have felt some compassion for their plight, being the kind man he was known to be, but he was Prophet (peace be upon him) and statesman and as a statesman, he was obliged to see to it that justice had been done. This course of action was endorsed by revelation as well.

God Himself, as the Qur'ān tells us, disapproved of the action of Abū Lubābah and called it, 'treachery to Allah and His Messenger.' '*O believers, betray not Allah and His Messenger and betray not your trust and that wittingly.*" [*al-Anfāl* 8:27]

Gabriel himself had ordered the Prophet (peace be upon him) to take immediate action against Qurayẓah, on the very day of the departure of the Aḥzāb. He addressed the Prophet (peace be upon him) 'why have you put down your arms? The Angels have not put down their arms yet. So march toward Qurayẓah, because I am marching there,' advised Gabriel.

So, clearly the whole affair of Qurayẓah was divinely ordained. The Prophet (peace be upon him) himself did not appear in the front line of events. He did not arrange to meet Qurayẓah, after their treachery, nor did they ask to meet him. They knew they had no face to meet him. They had not only violated their covenant, but they actually spoke ill of him publicly, they had plotted to exterminate him and his followers. Moreover as he approached their fortifications, they had loudly vilified him, in the worst foul and profane language.

17. SAʿD IBN MUʿĀDH APPOINTED AS JUDGE

When Qurayẓah declared that they would abide by whatever verdict the Prophet (peace be upon him) made the Prophet (peace be upon him) accepted their surrender. The Aws demanded that, since the Jews of Qurayẓah were their friends and allies, the judge who would rule in their case be from them. Saʿd ibn Muʿādh was suggested. The Prophet (peace be upon him) immediately agreed, as Saʿd was known to the Prophet (peace be upon him) to be a fair decisive and a noble man. The Aws then surrounded Saʿd who was badly wounded by an arrow when defending the *Khandaq* and said, 'Have clemency on our friends and allies, Qurayẓah, for the Prophet made you judge over them, knowing that you were their friend and ally, so that you might show mercy and compassion upon them,' but Saʿd was unmoved by these pleas.

He retorted 'it is high time that Saʿd did not compromise in the cause of God, nor care for the censure of anyone any more.'

When Saʿd reached the place where the Prophet (peace be upon him) was sitting, the Prophet (peace be upon him) said; 'O Muslims stand up and greet your leader.' Again the Anṣār pleaded for clemency, while the Muhājirīn kept silent. Saʿd demanded assurance that his verdict would be final, and that everybody would abide by it, including the Prophet (peace be upon him), whom he did not mention by name, out of respect. When the Prophet (peace be upon him) and the Muslims said they would abide by whatever verdict Saʿd would pass on Qurayẓah, he said, 'Then I give the verdict that men of combatant age be killed, their property divided among the Muslims and their women and children taken captives.'

That judgement was carried out. It was indeed a very severe judgement, but in the light of the intention of Qurayẓah to exterminate each and every Muslim, including women and children, it was not unexpected that the verdict against them would likewise be a hard one.

The episode of Qurayẓah ended the epoch of friendly relations between Muslims and Jews, an epoch which was recorded by the Qur'ān itself.

What the Qur'ān said, in this respect, can be rendered in English as follows: '*There you are; you love them, and they love you not, and you believe in the whole of the Scripture.*' [*Āl ʿImrān* 3:119]

With the vanquishing of Qurayẓah, the city was emptied of its Jewish population; the three Jewish settlements were brought to an end.

The Jews of Qurayẓah, were utterly routed, only four men were saved, three of whom converted to Islam; the fourth ʿĀmir ibn Suʿdah did not convert to Islam, but as he had objected to the violation of the covenant with the Prophet (peace be upon him), was allowed to go freely unimpeded. He departed in the direction of the north. A Muslim commander, by the name of Muḥammad the Muslim had set him free, without even consulting the Prophet (peace be upon him), saying, as he released him: '*O God, do not deprive me of the honour of accepting the excuse of the noble.*'

Sūrah al-Aḥzāb commends the patience of the Muslims:
Sūrah al-Aḥzāb has given a vivid account of the state of the Muslims during the Battle of al-Khandaq. The *sūrah* earlier on had depicted, without any ambiguity, the fear and panic of the Muslims, when they were encircled by the Confederate Forces from above and the Jews from below.

It later commended their patience and forbearance, and their unwavering trust in their Lord:

> *When the believers saw the confederates; they said; this is what God and His Messenger promised us, and God and His Messenger have spoken truly, and it only increased them in faith and surrender to Allah. Among the believers are men who were true to their covenant with Allah, some of them have fulfilled their vow by death and some are still awaiting, and have not changed in the least. That Allah may recompense the truthful ones for their truthfulness, and chastise the hypocrites, if He will, or turn to them in mercy! Surely Allah is All-Forgiving, All-Compassionate.* [*al-Aḥzāb* 33:22-24]

After the defeat of the Aḥzāb, and the vanquishing of Qurayẓah, the Prophet (peace be upon him) and the Muslims enjoyed a brief period of peace and tranquillity. Then the unruly and hypocritical Bedouins around Madīnah started to stir again, and the Prophet (peace be upon him) had to carry arms, and move against them, always taking great care not to await the first blow from the enemy, but to deal with them first if he could. In the aftermath of the Battle of Al-Aḥzāb, the Prophet launched expeditions against the Bedouins of Banū Liḥyān, Banū Fazārah, and Banū al-Muṣṭaliq.

In addition to these raids on the Bedouins, the brief period of peace that the Prophet (peace be upon him) and the Muslims enjoyed, was soon to give way to some very sad and traumatic experiences; these included:

a. The death of Saʿd ibn Muʿādh.

b. The *Ifk* Affair (the Lie Affair).

Another major event in the wake of al-Khandaq was: the conversion to Islam of some very prominent persons, including ʿAmr ibn al-ʿĀṣ and Khālid ibn al-Walīd, which actually boosted the Muslims' morale, raised their depressed spirits, and allowed them to look ahead, and hope for better days and more victories for Islam.

CHAPTER 6

The Aftermath of the Battle of al-Khandaq

1. THE QURAYSH WILL NEVER AGAIN INVADE MADĪNAH

When the Quraysh and the Confederates left Madīnah, after having been hit by a terrible hurricane, it is reported that the Prophet (peace be upon him) made a prophecy:

'The Quraysh will never again invade Madīnah. We will invade them, but they will not be able to invade us,'[1] said the Prophet in a jubilant tone of voice, and very high spirits.

This prophecy was borne out by subsequent events. The Quraysh never again was able to invade Madīnah. On the contrary, the Prophet (peace be upon him) and the Muslims first made the unarmed expedition of al-Ḥudaybīyah, and then the armed expedition that resulted in the conquest or 'opening' of Makkah.

2. THE DEATH OF SAʿD IBN MUʿĀDH

Meanwhile, the Prophet (peace be upon him) and the Muslims had had to endure the grief of the passing away of the chief of the Aws, the gallant Saʿd bin Muʿādh, who was badly wounded by a flying arrow, while defending the Moat of al-Khandaq. He was nursed by his sister Rufaydah, in a tent near the Prophet's Mosque, on the orders of the Prophet (peace be upon him) himself who, no doubt, wanted to keep a close watch on his health. When called to sit as a judge on Qurayẓah,

Saʿd came leaning on two men. Saʿd was immensely liked by the Prophet and the Muslims at large. He was handsome, courageous, wise, and very generous. Sometime after the trial of Qurayẓah, his wound burst open again, and he died.

It is narrated that Gabriel woke Muḥammad in the middle of the night to inform him of the death of Saʿd ibn Muʿādh.

'Who is it, do you know, O Muḥammad, that has died tonight, and for whom the doors of Heaven were flung open, and the Throne of Allah shook?' asked Gabriel.

The Prophet rose quickly and went out, dragging his garments, straight to where Saʿd was lying, in the tent of his sister Rufaydah. He found Saʿd already dead.

The Prophet (peace be upon him) and his household grieved profoundly. ʿĀ'ishah met Usayd ibn Ḥuḍayr, who just came from Makkah, to find that one of his wives had died. He showed considerable grief for her, for which he was rebuked by ʿĀ'ishah: 'May Allah forgive you, O Abū Yaḥyā, you grieve for a woman, when you have lost the son of your uncle, for whom the Throne shook!'

Some of the hypocrites, who intensively disliked Saʿd, said they found his bier very light, even though in old age, he had became quite corpulent.

'Saʿd has other carriers [meaning Angles]. By Him who holds my life, and in His hand is my soul, the angels rejoiced at receiving his soul, and the Throne shook for him,' said the Prophet.[2]

3. THE BURIAL OF SAʿD IBN MUʿĀDH

The Prophet prayed for Saʿd and buried him. As he was sitting behind his tomb, he exclaimed loudly: '*Subḥān Allāh! Subḥān Allāh! Subḥān Allāh*,' then he exclaimed again '*Allāhu Akbar*!' When the Prophet became quite again, the Companions asked him about his exclamations:

The Prophet (peace be upon him) said: 'The grave was constrained on this good man, until God eased him from it.' Meaning that, as the grave was being constrained the Prophet (peace be upon him) exclaimed *Subḥān Allāh!*, then when it was eased he exclaimed: *Allāhu Akbar*!

ʿĀ'ishah narrated that the Messenger of Allah said: 'Every grave is constrained; if anyone could have escaped that it would have been Saʿd ibn Muʿādh.'[3]

One of the Anṣār said:

'We have never heard of the Throne of God shaking for any dead man, but for Saʿd ibn Muʿādh.'

'Every wailing woman lies except the one who lamented Saʿd ibn Muʿādh,' said the Prophet!'[4]

4. THE ASSASSINATION OF SALLĀM IBN AL-ḤUQAYQ

Sallām ibn al-Ḥuqayq, from the Jews of Khaybar, played a major role in inciting the Quraysh to wage the Battle of Khandaq. The Khazraj after the defeat of the Quraysh, asked permission of the Prophet to assassinate him, for his enmity to the Prophet and the Muslims, and his uncalled for provocation of the Quraysh and Ghaṭafān to attack Madīnah in order to exterminate the Muslims. The Aws and Khazraj used to vie with one another, so as to please the Prophet (peace be upon him). But it was the Aws who had carried out the plot that killed Kaʿb ibn al-Ashraf. So, the Khazraj wanted to undertake the plot against Sallām. It is difficult now to understand the extremity of the conflict between the Muslims and their Jewish adversaries, in that remote historical time. But it would appear that the two groups were locked in struggle for survival. In general, the Qur'ān has enjoined and encouraged peaceful coexistence between Muslims and the People of the Book, as is well known from many verses of the Qur'ān, and as was practised in the history of Islamic civilization. Be that as it may, a group of Muslims from the Khazraj managed to penetrate the Jewish castle of Khaybar, to the north of Madīnah city. They made their way to the home of Sallām ibn al-Ḥuqayq, found and killed him. The hostilities between Muslims and Jews intensified, and the campaign to conquer Khaybar became inevitable.

ʿAmr ibn al-ʿĀṣ converted to Islam whilst in Abyssinia. He had originally been sent to the Negus (ruler) of Abyssinia, as an ambassador of the Quraysh. He demanded the extradition of a group of Muslims who went to Abyssinia seeking political asylum therein. Whilst he was in the court of the Negus, the Prophet (peace be upon him) sent ʿAmr ibn Umayyah al-Ḍamrī to look for Jaʿfar ibn Abī Ṭālib and his group. ʿAmr then demanded that the Negus should hand over ʿAmr ibn Umayyah al-Ḍamṛī. The Negus was so furious at this request that ʿAmr ibn al-ʿĀṣ was quite taken aback. So much so that he wished the earth might open up, so that he could escape the embarrassment of the situation. He apologized to the Negus, saying that had he known that his request would encourage the Negus in that way, he could never have made it. The Negus then expressed conversion to Islam, and the deep respect he felt to the Prophet of Islam:

'It is Muḥammad to whom the great Nāmūs came, as it used to come to Moses. This and what Jesus has brought have some from the same niche.'[5] ʿAmr ibn al-ʿĀṣ then asked:

'Is he really so great?'

'Definitely so' replied the Negus. 'So obey me, O ʿAmr and follow him, for by Allah he is right and he will triumph, over his adversaries, as Moses triumphed over the Pharaoh and his armies.'

Then ʿAmr decided to return to Arabia and declare his Islam. On the way to Madīnah, he met Khālid ibn al-Walīd who was heading north of Makkah, also to declare his conversion to Islam. It must then have been evident to anyone who reflected clearly on the situation that Islam was destined for total victory in Arabia. the Quraysh's resistance was effectively broken, and the Jews of Arabia were vanquished. As for the desert Bedouins, the Prophet (peace be upon him) struck terror in their hearts. Be that as it may, the struggle for Islam was far from being over.

5. MORE RAIDS AGAINST THE BEDOUINS

Many tribes and factions among the Bedouins continued to conspire and fight against the Muslims. Therefore, further raids had to be directed against them.

5.1 The Raid against Banū Liḥyān

Six months after the defeat of Qurayẓah, the Prophet (peace be upon him) was again on the march, this time against the Bedouins of Banu Liḥyān, to avenge the killings of his Companions, Khubayb ibn ʿAdiyy and his band, at the well of al-Rajīʿ. He made it appear as if heading to al-Shām to the north, so as to take the enemy by surprise. He appointed Ibn Umm Maktūm as his deputy at Madīnah. However, when he arrived in the place of Liḥyān, he found that the enemy had been alerted and entrenched themselves at the top of the mountains. He did not attempt to launch an attack against that position as that would have been counterproductive. Instead, he moved in the direction of Makkah, in order to threaten the Quraysh, though in fact he had no plans to attack them. Then he returned to Madīnah saying: 'Returning repentant, God-Willing, giving thanks to our Lord, I take refuge in Allah from the difficulties of the journey, and its unhappy ending; and from unpleasant sight, and from bad homecoming and from losses in money and family,' a supplication which later became standard for travellers when returning home from a long trip.

5.2 The Raid on Dhū'l-Qarad

A few nights after his return to Madīnah, a certain ʿUyaynah ibn al-Ḥiṣn al-Fazārī, raided the outskirts of Madīnah, where the Prophet's milk-camels were grazing. They killed the shepherd and carried off his wife together with the camels.

The Prophet (peace be upon him) ordered immediate hot pursuit of the raiders. A group of knights, under the command al-Miqdād ibn ʿAmr (nicknamed al-Miqdād ibn al-Aswad), set off after the kidnappers. They overtook the rear of the raiding force and succeeded in freeing some of the stolen milk-camels as well as the kidnapped wife of the shepherd who had been killed. However the chief of the raiding party, ʿUyaynah ibn al-Ḥiṣn escaped, with some of the camels. When the Muslims' main force, led by the Prophet (peace be upon him) himself, arrived on the scene, the raiders had already reached their destination. Some of the Muslims wanted to continue the raid, but the Prophet (peace be upon him) advised against it, as the immediate objective was the limited one of recovering the kidnapped woman and camels, and teaching the raiders a lesson. It was not part of Prophet's aims to attack Ghaṭafān at large. The rescued woman, who was very elated by her escape, told the Prophet (peace be upon him) that she had vowed to slaughter the camel she was riding if she lived. The Prophet (peace be upon him) responded jubilant and light-hearted.

'What a terrible reward you are proposing for her (the she-camel)! Allah carried you on her, and delivered you to safety on her, and now you want to slaughter her! Moreover, no vow is valid in disobedience of Allah, nor is the camel your own property… she is one of my own camels,'[6] explained the Prophet (peace be upon him), joyfully, and in good humour.

5.3 The Raid on Banū al-Muṣṭaliq

By far, the most important raid which the Prophet (peace be upon him) carried out after al-Khandaq was the raid on Banū al-Muṣṭaliq. It was the largest, and with far reaching consequences. It was also the raid that was associated with the Affair of the *Ifk*, (The Affair of the Lie) in which ʿĀ'ishah, wife of the Prophet and Mother of Faithful, was unjustly accused of misconduct. It was also important for the petty quarrel that arose between an Anṣārī and a Muhājir during the march incident which threatened to cause a major rift between the Muslims for the first time in their history. However, the Prophet (peace be upon him) managed to contain it.

5.4 The Cause of the Raid

In Shaʿbān of the 6th year of the *Hijrah*, some two months after the raid on Dhū'l-Qarad, news reached the Prophet (peace be upon him) that the Bedouins of Banū al-Muṣṭaliq were preparing to attack him. At once he put together a large force, and set out to reach them. He appointed Abū Dharr al-Ghifārī, as governor of Madīnah. The Banū al-Muṣṭaliq were commanded by al-Ḥārith ibn Abī Ḍirār, the father of Juwayriyyah, whom the Prophet (peace be upon him) married later on. The two armies met at a well called al-Murays', on the way to Qudayd towards the sea-shore. There was some fighting, and the Banū al-Muṣṭaliq were utterly defeated, and fled in all directions, leaving their women, children and property behind. Only one Muslim was killed in that battle.

6. THE FIGHT BETWEEN JAHJAH (MUHĀJIR) AND SINĀN (ANṢĀRĪ)

After this good, decisive victory, a nasty incident marred the day, and threatened a rift among the Muslims. Two men, Jahjah (of the Muhājirīn) and Sinān (of the Anṣār) fought each other at the well, and each one called out for his faction. The conflict was averted, but the head of the hypocrites, Ibn Salūl, was angry because a number of his people, including a young boy, Ibn Arqam, were hurt in the quarrel. Ibn Salūl said in exasperation: 'Have they actually done this? If they have disputed our priority in this well, they have also outnumbered us in our own homes! Nothing so fits us and those vagabonds of Quraysh, as the ancient proverb: "Fatten your dog and it devours you". By Allah, when we return to Madīnah (the stronger the more empowered) will drive out the weaker."' (The powerless).[7]

Then Ibn Salūl addressed the Anṣār: 'You have done this to yourselves, you have let them occupy your homes, and you have divided your property among them, had it not been for that they would have gone elsewhere!'

Later on, after the dispute died down, Zayd ibn al-Arqam, went to the Prophet and told him about the unbecoming and insulting remarks of Ibn Salūl. But Ibn Salūl denied having said those remarks, and took a strong oath to that effect. Of course, he was lying; and the

Qur'ānic revelation exposed his real stance, and nobody believed him afterwards. Says God in the Qur'ān, commenting on this incident:

> *They say: If we return to the city the mightier ones of it will expel the more abased. Yet glory belongs unto Allah, and unto His Messenger and the believers, but the hypocrites do not know it."* [*al-Munāfiqūn* 63:8]

7. ʿUMAR IBN AL-KHAṬṬĀB ADVISES THE KILLING OF IBN SALŪL

When the above Qur'ānic verse was revealed, exposing the betrayal and hypocrisy of Ibn Salūl, ʿUmar ibn al-Khaṭṭāb advised the Prophet (peace be upon him) to kill him. But the Prophet (peace be upon him) rejected ʿUmar's proposal, saying: 'But what if the Arabs should say that Muḥammad kills his own companions? No, I will not do it.'[8]

The Prophet's decision was indeed a wise one. Ibn Salūl was only technically a Companion of the Prophet (peace be upon him). In reality, he was not a companion. Actually, he was the head of the hypocrite movement, which was set against the Prophet (peace be upon him) and opposed his authority. However, as far as external appearances mattered, in the eyes of the Bedouins, he was indeed one of the community of the Muslims. Furthermore, Ibn Salūl used to have many friends and allies among the Khazraj in particular, and the Anṣār in general. That fact was underscored by Usayd ibn Ḥuḍayr, who advised the Prophet (peace be upon him) to treat Ibn Salūl well, because he was almost made king before the advent of the Prophet (peace be upon him) in Madīnah. The Prophet (peace be upon him) concurred with the views of Usayd ibn Ḥuḍayr, and said he would deal kindly with Ibn Salūl, and make much of his companionship, so long as he remained with the Prophet (peace be upon him) and the Muslims. The Prophet (peace be upon him), in this way, gave an excellent example of how a Muslim political power should treat its political opposition, with tolerance and accommodation. Islam is inclusive, in its political system, not exclusive. It is pluralistic and not monolithic. It allows, indeed it encourages, non-Muslims to freely express their separate identity, so long as their political alliance, as citizens, is to the state, and they carry out their obligations and duties as loyal citizens. It was this line of thinking, that allowed the Prophet (peace be upon him) to accord the Jews of Madīnah full rights of citizenship in the commonwealth of Madīnah. But, alas, the Jews turned that offer down, and violated their covenant with the Prophet (peace be upon him), a covenant duly documented in the *Ṣaḥīfah of Madīnah*.

The son of Ibn Salūl, who was a Muslim, volunteered to kill his father, should the Prophet (peace be upon him) choose that course. But again the Prophet (peace be upon him) declared that he had forgiven him. Later on, all the Muslims learnt of the affair of Ibn Salūl and he was ill-treated by them all.

8. THE PROPHET (PEACE BE UPON HIM) ORDERED THE ARMY TO MARCH ON FOR TWO DAYS

The Prophet (peace be upon him) ordered the army to march on at noon time. It was not his habit to do this, but he wanted to avert any exacerbation of the quarrel between Anṣār and Muhājir. He made them march the whole of that afternoon, all the night as well as the next morning. When he halted again, they were too exhausted to engage in controversy. As soon as their bodies touched the ground, they fell asleep. It proved a most effective way to avert a potential split among the Muslims.

9. THE PROPHET'S MARRIAGE TO JUWAYRIYYAH[9]

Juwayriyyah was the daughter of al-Ḥārith, the chief of Banū al-Muṣṭaliq. She fell captive in the hands of a Muslim soldier. Not wishing to remain in captivity, she sought to ransom herself and be free. She came to the door of Prophet (peace be upon him), seeking his help toward the payment of her ransom, no doubt because of the Prophet's reputation for magnanimity and generosity. 'Ā'ishah reported that she tried to turn her away, lest the Prophet (peace be upon him) should see her, and be impressed by her exceptional beauty. Ibn Hishām described Juwayriyyah as being sweet and very attractive. But the Prophet overheard the exchange between the two women and came out of his room, to find Juwayriyyah standing there on the doorstep.

'Who is this woman, O 'Ā'ishah?' asked the Prophet.

'I am Juwayriyyah bint al-Ḥārith, chief of Banū al-Muṣṭaliq, Messenger of Allah,' responded Juwayriyyah, at once.

'What do you want?' asked the Prophet.

'I have fallen captive to the hands of Thābit ibn Qays al-Shammās, and I have written an agreement with him to ransom myself. I come to you to help me in paying that ransom, O Messenger of Allah.'

'How is it if I give you a better offer?' said the Prophet.

'What is it, O Messenger of Allah?' asked Juwayriyyah.

'I pay your ransom, and marry you,' said the Prophet. 'Yes, O Messenger of Allah.' said Juwayriyyah, well pleased with the offer.

The Prophet said 'It is done!'

When the Muslims learnt that the gracious Prophet (peace be upon him) had married Juwayriyyah bint al-Ḥārith, daughter of the chief of Banū al-Muṣṭaliq, they set their captives free, saying that they had become the relatives of the Prophet (peace be upon him) by marriage. More than a hundred captives were released that afternoon, as news spread of the Prophet's marriage to Juwayriyyah. Thus, Juwayriyyah proved a great blessing to her people, by her wits as well as by her good looks.

10. THE AFFAIR OF THE LIE AND THE HONOUR OF THE PROPHET

Hardly had the celebrations of that marriage concluded, when dishonourable rumours became rife in the city of the vicious lie, concerning 'Ā'ishah and the Prophet's Companion, Ṣafwān ibn al-Muʿaṭṭal. The notorious gossip was about the delayed return to Madīnah of ʿĀ'ishah, riding the camel of Ṣafwān ibn al-Muʿaṭṭal, a handsome young Companion of the Prophet (peace be upon him), after the raid of the Banū al-Muṣṭaliq. The perpetrators of that lie were Muslims, close to the Prophet's family:

1. The Prophet's poet and friend: Ḥassān ibn Thābit.
2. Ḥamnah bint Jaḥsh, a cousin of the Prophet, and sister of Zaynab Bint Jaḥsh, wife of the Prophet.
3. Misṭaḥ ibn Uthāthah, poor relative of Abū Bakr, who depended on his allowances.
4. Ibn Salūl, the head of the hypocrites, and some of his friends, and supporters from the Khazraj, spread the lie across the city far and wide.

The matter was so grave, and the Prophet (peace be upon him) and the Muslims were so hurt, that life was totally disrupted in the city. The Prophet (peace be upon him) could not longer carry on his usual business of delivering God's call (*daʿwah*), nor of managing the state. Always brave and open and totally transparent, the Prophet (peace be upon him) could not hide from the vicious rumours, and decided to bring the matter into the open. A public meeting was called in the Mosque, and the Prophet (peace be upon him), sad and pale, addressed the hushed and apprehensive gathering. After thanking God and praising Him he said: 'Why are some men hurting me, by staining the honour of my family, saying false and indecent rumours about them? By Allah, I know only good about them; and they say these things about a man of whom I know naught but good, who never enters my house but in my company…' argued the Prophet (peace be upon him).[10]

When the Prophet (peace be upon him) made that moving speech and the Muslims noticed that he was deeply hurt, they were naturally very disturbed and dismayed. Usayd ibn Ḥuḍayr, paramount leader of the Aws, after the martyrdom of Sa ʿd ibn Mu ʿādh, sprang to his feet and said: 'If the men you alluded to are of the Aws, we will rid you of them, but if they are from our brothers, the Khazraj, give us your orders, for they ought to have their heads cut off…' said Usayd ibn Ḥuḍayr.

Having heard the words of the leader of Aws, about the Khazraj, Sa ʿd ibn ʿUbādah, their leader, was hurt. Quite annoyed, he got up and said: 'By Allah, you lie! They shall not be beheaded. You would not have said this had you known that they were of the Aws. Had they been of your own people, you would not have said it.' 'Liar yourself, by Allah,' responded Usayd ibn Ḥuḍayr. 'You are but a hypocrite, arguing on behalf of the hypocrites?'[11]

Feelings ran so high, that the two Muslim factions of the Anṣār almost came to blows, and a full scale conflict among the Muslims was a very real possibility. But the Prophet (peace be upon him), using his exceptional wisdom, managed to avert it with some difficulty. In his bewilderment and dismay, the Prophet (peace be upon him) retired to his own private apartment. He sent for ʿAlī ibn Abī Ṭālib, and Usāmah ibn Zayd. It was his habit and custom to consult with Abū Bakr and ʿUmar, ibn al-Khaṭṭāb, his two senior aides. But the issue was an exceptional one. He could not consult Abū Bakr, because he was the father of ʿĀ'isha, and he could not consult ʿUmar because he was known to be severe on women. As for Usāmah, he spoke quite well of ʿĀ'ishah, strongly condemning the rumours as false and unjust. But as for ʿAlī, his greater concern was for the personal well-being of the Prophet (peace be upon him), as well as the welfare of the *Ummah* at large. He was very concerned lest the crisis should affect the Prophet's noble and sensitive nature, knowing his great affection and love for ʿĀ'ishah, and at the same time he was very mindful, lest the whole affair should adversely affect the society at large. So he sought to dismiss the whole thing, and lessen its importance, bearing in mind the dangers and challenges of the mission that still lay ahead. It is regrettable that many writers on this topic have tended to over-simplify what was, in fact, a very complex situation. I also dare say that our mother ʿĀ'ishah, in her anguish and grief, also misread the thinking of our master ʿAlī, may Allah be pleased with him, as he said: 'O Messenger of Allah, women other than she, are plentiful, and you can always change one for another.'[12]

It is reported that ʿĀ'ishah never forgave ʿAlī for that remark. Some historians even suggested that the remark made by ʿAlī, left a permanent scar and bitterness in the personality of ʿĀ'ishah, which was a major factor in shaping Ā'ishah's negative position, towards the succession of ʿAlī to the Caliphate, after ʿUthmān, may Allah be pleased with both of them.

11. ʿĀ'ISHAH'S PERSONAL ACCOUNT OF THE LIE AFFAIR[13]

Be that as it may, we must now give a brief statement of ʿĀ'ishah's own version of the unfortunate affair of the *ifk*:

ʿĀ'ishah used to sit in the *hawdah* with curtains drawn, as was the women's custom after the *ḥijāb* (women's seclusion or segregation) was ordained in the fifth year, after the Battle of al-Khandaq. Because she was very light in weight, the carriers of the *hawdah* had difficulty determining whether or not she was inside.

ʿĀ'ishah giving her version of the story said:

> 'As the Prophet was about to move on, after spending part of the night encamping, I slipped away to relieve myself, wearing a necklace of Zafar beads around my neck. When I had finished, the necklace fell without my noticing. On returning to the camp, I discovered that I had lost it. At that time some of the men started to move. But I went back to look for the necklace, until I found it, thinking that there was still time to catch up with the caravan. When I got back, the place was totally deserted! Obviously, the carriers of my *hawdah* did not realize my absence, no doubt because of my very light weight. So I wrapped myself in my smock and then lay down where I was, knowing that if I were missed, they would come back for me and by Allah I had just laid down, when Ṣafwān ibn Muʿaṭṭal passed me. He had fallen behind the main body for some purpose, and had not spent the night with

the troops. He saw my form and obviously recognized me. So he came and stood by me. He used to see me before the veil (the *ḥijāb*) was prescribed for us, so when he saw me he exclaimed in astonishment '*Inna lillāh wa innā ilayhi' rāji'ūn*, the Messenger's wife,' while I was wrapped in my garments. He asked me what had kept me behind, but I did not speak to him. Then he brought up his camel and told me to ride it, while he stood behind. So I rode it, and he took the camel's lead, going forward quickly in search of the army, and by Allah, we did not overtake them, and I was not missed until the following morning. The men had halted, and when they were resting, up came the man leading me, and the liars spread their reports and the army was much disturbed. But, by Allah I knew nothing about it.

'Then we came to Madīnah and I fell ill, and so I heard nothing of the matter. The story had reached the Messenger of Allah, and my parents, yet they told me nothing of it all, though I missed the Messenger's accustomed kindness to me. When I was ill, he used to show compassion and tenderness towards me, but in this illness, he did not, and I missed his attention. When he came in to see me, in the presence of my mother who came in to nurse me, all he said was "How is she?"

I was immensely hurt, so I asked him to let me go to my mother's house, so that she could nurse me.

"Do what you like," he said, and I was taken to my mother's home, still knowing nothing of what had happened, until I recovered from my illness some twenty days later. Now, we were Arab people; we did not have those privies which non-Arab people had in their houses; we loathe and detest them. Our practice was to go out to relieve ourselves in the open space outside Madīnah. The women used to go out every night, and one night I went out with the mother of Misṭaḥ. As she was walking with me, she stumbled over her gown, and exclaimed, "May Misṭaḥ stumble!"

What a bad thing to stay about one of the Muhājirīn, who fought with the Prophet at Badr! said.

'She replied "haven't you heard the news, daughter of Abū Bakr?"'

'When I told her that I had heard nothing, she told me what the liars had said about me. By Allah, I could not relieve myself, and

> I broke down crying, until I thought that my liver would burst. I continued to cry for almost two days. I said to my mother: "God forgive you, O mother. Men have spoken ill of me all this time, and you told me nothing about it!"
>
> 'She replied: "My little daughter, don't let the matter weigh on you. Seldom is there a beautiful woman, married to a man who loves her, but the rival wives of her husband gossip about her, and men also do the same!"'

However, ʿĀ'ishah was not to be consoled. She withdrew into herself, and in her seclusion, sinking into despondency and dejection. She knew that it was her cousin, Ḥamnah, and her other cousin, the poor Misṭaḥ, who was living on the charity of her father, together with Ḥassān ibn Thābit, the Prophet's poet, who were promulgating the false rumours about her and Ṣafwān. The Prophet (peace be upon him), for his part, did not know what to think and what to believe. In his desperate search for the enlightening truth, he found himself eventually in ʿĀ'ishah's room. She was sitting at a corner with a woman-friend from the Anṣār, both of them crying. In another corner, ʿĀ'ishah's parents were sitting, speechless, their gaze fixed to the ground, in their deeply troubled thoughts. When the Prophet (peace be upon him) broke into the room, everybody looked up. ʿĀ'ishah's tears dried out suddenly, and blood rushed to her cheeks, as she looked into the face of the man whom she loved and venerated so much, and who had suddenly, become cool towards her, and stayed away from her for more than a month. The Prophet (peace be upon him), looking intently into ʿĀ'ishah's face, eventually put the question directly to her:

> 'O ʿĀ'ishah! You know what people say about you: Fear Allah, and if you have done wrong, as men say, then repent towards Him for He accepts repentance from His servants,' said the Prophet (peace be upon him).[14]
>
> ʿĀ'ishah said"
>
> 'As the Prophet said these words, my tears totally ceased. I waited for my parents to answer on my behalf, but they said nothing. By Allah, I thought myself too insignificant for Allah to send down

a chapter of the Qur'ān about me, which would be recited in the Mosques. But only hoped that the Prophet would see my innocence in a dream or something of that sort".

Presently she turned to her parents;

'Won't you answer for me?'

Despondently, they said they had nothing to say. Again 'Ā'ishah burst into tears. Then she sprang to her feet and, drying her tears, addressed the Prophet (peace be upon him) with fire of anger and determination in her face and eyes.

'By Allah, I will never repent to Him of what you mention! By Allah, I know that if I were to confess to what men say of me, Allah knowing that I am innocent of it, I should admit what did not happen; and if I denied what they said, you would not believe me.' 'Ā'ishah said that she then racked her memory for the name of Jacob but could not retrieve it, so she said:

'But I will say what the father of Joseph said "My duty is to show plenty of patience and Allah's help is to be asked against what you describe."'[15]

Having said those words, to the Prophet (peace be upon him), she quietly laid down on her bed.

Hardly any time passed than the Prophet (peace be upon him), standing where he was, was seized by the trance that used to take him, whenever revelations came to him. He lay on the floor, wrapped in his clothes, with a leather cushion under his head. Although it was a winter day, the Prophet (peace be upon him) sweated profusely, drops of sweat on his forehead were like pearls. When he came back to his normal state, he shouted with excitement and happiness: 'Good news, O 'Ā'ishah good news! Allah has just revealed to me your innocence!'[16] 'Ā'ishah said her parents were looking gustily, as they feared that the notorious rumour would be confirmed. However, 'Ā'ishah herself feared nothing, as she knew that she was totally innocent. When 'Ā'ishah heard the news of Allah's revelation of her innocence, she said: 'Praise be to Allah Alone!'

The Prophet (peace be upon him) went out at once, and addressed the Muslims at the Mosque. He recited the Qur'ānic revelation, he had received concerning the innocence of ʿĀ'ishah, for whom now at last, the ordeal was over.

12. QUR'ĀNIC VERSES ABOUT ʿĀ'ISHAH'S INNOCENCE

The ordeal was not only over for ʿĀ'ishah, and her immediate family, but it was indeed over for the Prophet (peace be upon him) and the entire Muslim community.

The Qur'ānic Verses affirming ʿĀ'ishah's innocence run as follows:

> *Those who came with the slander are a band of you; do not reckon it evil for you; rather it is good for you. Every man of them shall have the sin that he has earned charged to him, and whosoever of them took upon himself the greater part of it, for him there awaits a mighty chastisement. Why, when you heard it, did the believing men and women not think good thoughts of each other, and say; 'this is a manifest lie!'*
>
> *Why do they not (demand of the accusers that they) produce four witnesses to prove their allegations? For if they do not produce such witnesses, it is they (accusers) who, in the sight of Allah, are liars indeed.*
>
> *And were it not for Allah's Favour upon you, and His Grace in this world and in the life to come, awesome suffering would indeed have afflicted you, in consequence of all that in which you indulged; when you took it up with your tongues, uttering with your mouths something of which you have no knowledge, and deeming it a light matter, whereas in the Sight of Allah, is a grave matter indeed.*
>
> *And [once again] why do you not say: whenever you hear such [a rumour]: it does not behove us to speak of this, O You Who are limitless in Your Glory, this is a manifest falsehood! Allah admonishes you (hereby) lest you ever again revert to the like of this (sin), if you are (truly) believers. For Allah makes (His) signs clear unto you, and Allah is All-Knowing, All-Wise.* [*al-Nūr* 24:11-18].

God says to the Muslims: 'Do not consider the lie affair a setback; it is a good and positive thing.' One of the beneficial results of the lie affair are those elaborate laws and regulations revealed in relation to it. Some of these laws and regulations are given in the Qur'ānic verses quoted and translated into English above. But the full compass of those laws and regulations is very wide: They are given in *Sūrah al-Nūr* and are further explained in the *sunnah* of the Prophet (peace be upon him). They deal with false rumours, allegations, slant and slander. They also deal with dressing and costumes of a Muslim woman, and the mingling and separation of the two sexes in Islam (*ḥijāb*). Severe punishment of eighty lashes is prescribed against those who indulge in spreading false rumours and allegations. The Companions of the Prophet, who were known to have been involved in the rumour were flogged, including the famous poet of the Prophet, Ḥassān ibn Thābit; so too Misṭaḥ, relative of ʿĀ'ishah, was flogged. The punishment was carried out in public. Concerning this punishment of spreading false rumours, God says in the Qur'ān:

> *Those who falsely accuse chaste women of adultery, and do not bring forth four witnesses to this effect, shall be flogged with eighty stripes, and their testimony shall never be admitted as evidence in any matter! Those are the indecent, the immoral.* [*al-Nūr* 24:4]

13. THE STORY OF ABŪ AYYŪB AND HIS WIFE

The Qur'ān alludes to the story of Abū Ayyūb (Khālid ibn Zayd) and his wife, from the Anṣār.

Wife of Abū Ayyūb: 'Did you not hear what the men are saying about ʿĀ'ishah. O Abū Ayyūb?'

Abū Ayyūb: 'Yes, I heard. These are damn lies! Would you, Mother of Ayyūb do it?'

Wife of Ayyūb: 'Most emphatically no!'

Abū Ayyūb: 'By Allah ʿĀ'ishah is a better woman than you!'

Alluding to common sense, good will and piety of that Muslim couple of Anṣār, Allah revealed the following Qur'ānic verse:

Why, when you heard it, did the believing men and women not think good thoughts of each other and say: this is a manifest lie? [*al-Nūr* 24:12]

14. THE CHARACTER OF ʿĀ'ISHAH

The way in which ʿĀ'ishah, the young Mother of the Faithful, conducted herself during the trying ordeal of the ʿ*Ifk* Affair', tells a great deal about the character of that beloved wife of the Prophet. Although still quite young, either 15 or 17, the manner in which she put up with the scandal, showed that she had been of immense moral and spiritual strength. Not only that, but she possessed a rare gift of analytical thinking, and judgement, together with an excellent command of the language. The strength of her character, and her immense sense of pride and dignity, not only her beauty or fairness, go a long way towards explaining why the Prophet (peace be upon him) found her company so fascinating and compelling. Also, the generality of the Muslims were very fond of her, first of all, not only because they knew her favoured place with their beloved Prophet (peace be upon him), but also because of her extra-ordinary gift for memorizing the Qur'ān, for her excellent knowledge of jurisprudence and law, and also history of poetry. As the Prophet (peace be upon him) once remarked: 'She is truly the daughter of Abū Bakr.'

All the beloved character traits of Abū Bakr, ʿĀ'ishah inherited, especially his moral courage and nobility of soul. Abū Bakr was an accomplished scholar of Arab history as well as poetry. He had a rare gift for eloquence, and so too had ʿĀ'ishah. It was for these qualities, and not just her fairness and beauty, that the Prophet held ʿĀ'ishah in such a high esteem, and likewise the community of the faithful.

The account ʿĀ'ishah gave of the '*Ifk* Affair' was very consistent and wholesome. To the Muslim mind, the whole matter was settled once and for all by the Qur'ānic revelation of the *sūrah* of the Light, quoted above. But for any objective enquirer, the account left not the least shadow of a doubt, that Ā'ishah was innocent, and that she was the victim of a very vicious accusation. After God revealed her innocence in the Qur'ān, her parents said to her, 'Get up and thank the Messenger of Allah.' She said 'By Allah, I am not going to thank him, or anyone else, for that matter, but I only thank Allah alone!'

As God said in the Qur'ān, the '*Ifk* Affair' was not evil or harmful to the Muslim society of Madīnah. Rather, much benefit and good resulted from it.

The Muslim society was severely tested and tried. They knew thereafter how harmful gossiping and false accusations are. They were given a new and very effective penal code to combat slander and slant false accusations, and to reinforce the values of chastity and good conduct. Moreover, a whole code of how the relationship between the sexes should be arranged in Islam, was revealed in the wake of the '*Ifk* Affair'.

Ḥassān ibn Thābit, the Prophet's poet, repented and was forgiven by the Prophet (peace be upon him), by 'Ā'ishah and the Muslims at large. The Companion Misṭaḥ (who fought at Badr) was likewise forgiven by the Prophet (peace be upon him), Abū Bakr and the generality of the Muslims. He even continued to enjoy the charitable stipend which he used to receive from Abū Bakr, following the directive of the Qur'ān itself, which told the Muslims that Allah had forgiven the whole affair. The Prophet's name and honour were cleared, whereas the hypocrites were given a harsh lesson in moral behaviour, and their position in Madīnah was further tainted and weakened.

The Prophet (peace be upon him) was now entitled to some rest, peace and tranquillity, and indeed peace and happiness descended again on that blessed household. 'Ā'ishah's position vis-à-vis the Prophet (peace be upon him) and his other wives, and vis-à-vis the whole Muslim community, was never challenged again. She gradually emerged as a leading authority on the Qur'ān, Islamic jurisprudence and *ḥadīth* [sayings and practices of the Prophet (peace be upon him)]. She is said to have became the third-ranking authority on Islam, in the whole of the Muslim community, and was recognized as such by the leading Muslim jurists, in her own right, and not because she was the favourite wife of the Prophet (may Allah be pleased with Mother ʿĀ'ishah!).

Once the storm of the '*Ifk* Affair' subsided in Madīnah, the Prophet (peace be upon him) started to think and plan for the great events that still lay ahead. The thinking of the Prophet (peace be upon him) at that crucial juncture of Islamic history was preoccupied with finding a final solution to the question of Makkah and the Quraysh. Despite the great suffering inflicted on the Prophet (peace be upon him) by the Quraysh, he never ceased hoping for their eventual conversion to Islam. He knew very well the role which the Quraysh Arabs could play in the history and civilization of Islam. He also knew of the crucial and most central position that Makkah and its ancient sanctuary, the *Ḥaram*, would occupy, in the religion of Islam. So his thoughts now were all centred on finding a peaceful solution to the conflict with the Quraysh. He knew also that the Quraysh would never again be able to invade Madīnah, that, at least from the military point of view, the Quraysh was a spent force that posed no strategic threat to his authority. But the Quraysh were the honoured chiefs and leaders of all Arabia. So if the Prophet (peace be upon him) could only win them over to Islam peacefully, the position of Islam in Arabia would be secure forever or at least greatly enhanced. Also, should any hostilities break out between the state of Madīnah and the powerful empires to the north, the Arabs of Quraysh, if converted to Islam, would be a valuable support and resource. Later on, ʿUmar ibn al-Khaṭṭab, the second Righteously Guided Caliph of the Prophet, used to say: 'The Arabs are the mainstay of the power of Islam,' in other words 'the Arabs are the main factor in the strength of Islam: (The substance of Islam).'

It was in the wake of the '*Ifk* Affair' that the Prophet (peace be upon him) saw the dream which precipitated the events that eventually led to the conclusion of the Ḥudaybīyah Pact or Armistice in the following year. That was followed by the Great Victory or the Opening of Makkah and the peaceful winning over of all the Arabs to the cause of Islam. The Ḥudaybīyah Pact was actually the prelude to the eventual, and final victory of Islam over its adversaries, and the much-awaited signal that peace was at last coming to that war-torn land of Arabia.

If it was true that the Prophet (peace be upon him) was war-oriented in the greater part of his career at Madīnah, yet the deep yearning of his heart was always for peace, for harmonious living in the service of God and pursuit of justice. Peace is a central theme in Islam, since the very essence of Islam is to achieve peace and tranquillity through total submission to God. So it is peace, rather than war, which is the 'highest good' in Islamic society. But alas, such is the nature of man that he more often than not inclines to aggression and injustice. Because of this, and because the Prophet (peace be upon him) himself and his followers were subjected to uncalled for and unnecessary oppression, the Muslims were obliged to fight wars against the idol-worshippers and the belligerent Jews of Arabia.

In the coming chapter, we are going to tell the most extraordinary story of how hard the Prophet (peace be upon him) had to fight in the cause of achieving peaceful reconciliation with the Quraysh and their supporters. It was quite clear, in the mind of the Prophet (peace be upon him), that what he needed was peace rather than war, to fulfil his mission of bringing the light of Islam to humanity at large, as he was commanded by his Lord! It is unfortunate that Western orientalists of old as well as of today, have insisted on a false image of the Prophet (peace be upon him) as war-monger. Some of them have even compared him to Hitler! Nothing is further from the truth. The truth is that he followed the course of peaceful resistance to the tyranny of the Quraysh, and the ignorant Bedouins for the whole of the Makkan period of thirteen years, until God gave him and the Muslims the permission to fight back: God said in the Qur'ān:

> *Leave is given to those who fight, because they were wronged – surely Allah is able to make them victorious. Those who were expelled from their homes without right, except that they say: Allah is our*

Lord. And had Allah not driven back the people; some by the means of others, cloisters and churches, oratories and mosques would have been destroyed, wherein Allah's name is much mentioned. Assuredly Allah will make victorious those who uphold His cause! [*al-Ḥajj* 22:39-40]

The Prophet's attitude towards war and peace was without doubt wholly dictated by the provisions of the Qur'ān. In the Qur'ān, war is always portrayed as an evil, except when waged in a just cause. Muslims are in many verses are commanded not to initiate hostilities. However, it is legitimate for them to do so in self-defence, or when it is deemed necessary and essential to fight off injustice and oppression. People have a basic right to freedom of worship, be they Muslims, Christians or Jews, or indeed any other religious dominion, especially if they have a Revealed Scripture. So here, Muslims are commanded even to fight in the general cause of religious freedom for themselves and for others, as is amply demonstrated by the verses quoted above. But when Muslims resort to war, they are expected, as commanded by the Qur'ān, to fight with absolute firmness and commitment, so that war would be won for the cause of Islam, and human freedom and dignity, so that human beings can freely worship God alone, be they Muslims or non-Muslims.

If an enemy proposes an armistice, then it is the religious duty of Muslims to respond at once by accepting it: This is commended by God in the Qur'ān itself:

And if they become inclined towards peace then you must be so inclined, and put all your trust in Allah, He is All-Hearing, All-Knowing!

And if they desire to trick you, then Allah is sufficient unto you. He has strengthened you with his victory and the believers, and brought their hearts together! Had you expended all that is on earth, (of wealth) you could not have brought their hearts together, but Allah brought their hearts together.
Surely, He is All-Mighty, All-Wise. [*al-Anfāl* 8:61-63]

As the above Qur'ānic verses amply demonstrate, peace is strongly urged and collaborated in the Qur'ān. For the sake of attaining peace, worthwhile risks and initiatives must be taken. If the enemy shows any signs of being inclined towards peace, then the Muslims must respond, even at the risk of their enemy being insincere in the gesture. God holds all the strings of power, and would not allow deceit and falsehood to triumph over Islam.

Thus, throughout his career, the Prophet's primary search was for peace, and the most profound desire of his heart was for just and durable peace. He was always honourable and magnanimous with his enemies, and indeed very charitable and accommodating. The one exception in the whole history of the Prophet's career, was the harsh judgement on the Jewish Tribe of Qurayẓah . But that must be viewed as an extreme and exceptional measure, taken in extreme and exceptional circumstances against a uniquely exceptional enemy, as Qurayẓah were bent on exterminating the Prophet (peace be upon him) and his community, totally and completely, if they were victorious.

The Prophet's trip to Ḥudaybīyah, and his subsequent attempt to strike a peaceful accord with the Quraysh, was a hallmark, and a corner-stone, in his search for peace. Ḥudaybīyah marks a turning-point, because it marks the beginning of the peaceful era in the Prophet's life, and the beginning of the great drive towards peace that was to prove so instrumental in the lasting and eventual victory of Islam. Without that peace, Islam could not have had the chance to spread so far, so quickly, and establish the most brilliant civilization in history.

That the treatment which the Prophet meted to the Jews of Qurayẓah was in fact exceptional, can be further demonstrated from the fact that anti-Semitism did not exist in Islam, neither as a state nor civilization. As a faith, Islam recognizes Judaism and Christianity as religions based on Revealed Scriptures, and recognizes the Jews as People of the Book. Moreover, far from being anti-Semitic, the Muslims, Arabs and non-Arabs alike, regard Abraham as their spiritual father, the one who gave them their name as 'Muslims'. They also recognize the Jewish or Israelite Prophets, as their own Prophets. The Arabs, in particular, regard themselves as Semitic, being the descendents of Ishmael, son of Abraham, despite the present-day habits of some Jews who call the Arabs the Hagarities or sons of the Egyptian slave-girl of Abraham, Hagar, and being as such, not authentic Semites, but only half-cast or hybrids.

Moreover, the Jews of later times were not affected by the episode of Qurayẓah. They continued to enjoy a respectable place in Islamic civilization, and occupied high offices of state as well as a high place in the commercial life of many Muslim societies, beginning with the Umayyad Dynasty. Throughout Muslim Spain, and the Ottoman Empire, the Jews never experienced anything like the Inquisition Courts or the Nazi Holocaust. On the contrary, they enjoyed full rights as citizens, and were employed as physicians, and even ministers, and government advisors. During the Abbāsid Dynasty, they participated fully in the cultural as well the scientific life of the society. For examples Maimonid (Mūsā ibn Maymūn al-Qurṭubī) the great Jewish philosopher, studied under Ibn Rushd and other philosophers and scientists of Muslim Spain. It is even said that Ibn Rushd, in fact, acted as his personal supervisor and mentor, even lodged him (i.e. Maimonid) in his own house, when he was a student in his academy.

CHAPTER 7

The Search for Peace at Ḥudaybīyah

1. THE SIGNIFICANCE OF THE ḤUDAYBĪYAH PACT

The significance of the Ḥudaybīyah Pact cannot be over estimated. During the first two years after the Pact, more people embraced Islam than in the whole of its previous history of nineteen years. When the Prophet (peace be upon him) called for the march to Makkah for the pilgrimage, which ended in the Ḥudaybīyah episode, not more than one thousand four hundred Muslims responded to the call. Some versions put the number of the men who accompanied the Prophet to Ḥudaybīyah at no more than seven hundred. But when he called for the conquest of Makkah, more than ten thousand responded. The Quraysh were compelled, for the first time in their history, to openly and publicly admit the political reality of Islam as a religion and state. Prophet Muḥammad (peace be upon him) was at last recognized as head of the greatest and most powerful political entity in Arabia as a whole. The Bedouins of Arabia were quick to see the shift in the balance of power, and started to deal with the Prophet's authority at Madīnah. They were no longer swayed by the Quraysh, which was then seen as a force in decline. All of these considerations weighed heavily in the direction of the final victory of Islam in Arabia, and the final downfall of the Quraysh and paganism.

2. THE PROPHET'S EFFORTS TO WIN PEACE AT ḤUDAYBĪYAH

The events that led to the conclusion of the Ḥudaybīyah Pact show very clearly that the Prophet (peace be upon him) spared no effort in his quest for peace. The way he patiently put up with the Quraysh's insolence and arrogance, and the extraordinary flexibility and forbearance with which he dealt with the successive delegations sent by the Quraysh, testified to his insight and unshakable determination to reach a negotiated peace with the Quraysh. No doubt, it was Divine guidance that was steering his course. It was shown to him, in a dream, that he would enter Makkah peacefully, and without fear or bloodshed, with his head shaven, a mark of the pilgrim. He believed in that dream, and worked hard to realize it.

3. CONFRONTATION WITH THE QURAYSH AVERTED

As the Prophet's unarmed and peaceful procession was drawing nearer to Makkah, with about seventy sacrificial camels, well-decorated, driven in front of them, it was met by a certain Bashīr ibn Sufyān. He told the Prophet (peace be upon him) of the Quraysh's elaborate preparations for war, that the bulk of their army was at Dhū Ṭuwā, and that Khālid ibn al-Walīd, not yet a Muslim, since his conversion to Islam took place after the Ḥudaybīyah Pact was concluded, was commanding their Cavalry at a place called Kurāʿ al-Ghamīm. The Prophet (peace be upon him) was saddened by this news, and said:

> Woe be to the Quraysh; war has devoured them! What harm would it be to them, if they had left me and the rest of the Arabs? If they should kill me that is what they want; and if God gives me victory over them, they would enter Islam, with dignity in large numbers. And if they do not like any of these opinions, they could fight me while they have enough strength. For what are the Quraysh thinking of? For by God, I will not cease fighting for the mission with which God has entrusted me until He makes me victorious, or I have my neck cut off in this trial.[1]

The Prophet (peace be upon him) then took a difficult and mountainous road, in order to avoid meeting the armies of the Quraysh. The march along that rocky and rugged road was very hard the Muslims. As they emerged on to the plain of the valley of Ḥudaybīyah, the Prophet (peace be upon him) asked the Muslims to say: 'We ask God's forgiveness and we repent of Him.'

The Muslims complied and said those words, at which point the Prophet (peace be upon him) told them that, in a similar situation, the Israelites were asked to say these words and they refused, God's anger then descended upon them!

4. THE KNEELING OF AL-QAṢWĀ'

When the Prophet's pilgrimage procession reached the valley of al-Ḥudaybīyah, his she-camel, named al-Qaṣwā', suddenly knelt down, and wouldn't get up. People said that al-Qaṣwā' had become stubborn and difficult, and was refusing to get up. The Prophet (peace be upon him) denied that, and said that al-Qaṣwā' did not refuse nor was that her nature. Rather, the animal had been banned from entering Makkah, by the same power that had banned the elephants of the Abyssinian army, that attempted destruction of the Kaʿbah, the year the Prophet (peace be upon him) was born.

The Prophet (peace be upon him) took the kneeling of al-Qaṣwā' and its unwillingness to move forward, as a signal from God to make peace with the Quraysh. He declared that he was stopping there, and that he would agree to any peace proposals by the Quraysh. When the Companions protested that there was no source of water in the vicinity, the Prophet (peace be upon him) called upon one Companion, gave him an arrow, and told him to shoot into one of the dry waterholes. On doing this, the water gushed forth, and it was so plentiful that the whole army and its animals drank, without affecting the water level, which constantly remained high, a sure miracle of the gracious Prophet (peace be upon him).

5. DIFFICULT NEGOTIATIONS WITH QURAYSH

Hardly had the Prophet (peace be upon him) rested in the valley of Ḥudaybīyah, than delegations from Makkah started to arrive, one after the other.

5.1 The arrival of Budayl ibn Waraqah al-Khuzāʿī

First came a delegation from the tribe of Khuzāʿa, who were long time allies of the Prophet (peace be upon him), even though most of them remained non-Muslims, Khuzāʿah were ancient enemies of the Quraysh, so it was natural that they felt inclined to the Prophet (peace be upon him) from the start. The Prophet (peace be upon him) told them that he came as a pilgrim, and showed them the proof of the sacrificial animals. They were convinced, and their leader Budayl hurried to the Quraysh, and told them of what he saw, and that the intentions of the Prophet (peace be upon him) were peaceful. But the Quraysh were adamant. They wouldn't budge from their position. They told the chief of Khuzāʿah that even if they accepted that the Prophet's intentions were peaceful, he would not be allowed to enter Makkah against the will of the Quraysh. They did not want the Arabs to say: that Muḥammad had entered Makkah and performed pilgrimage against the will of the Quraysh.

5.2 The Delegation of Al-Ḥulays ibn Ḥafṣ

Quraysh then sent al-Ḥulays ibn ʿAlqamah, head of the powerful troops of the Aḥābīsh, said to be troops who were originally from Abyssinia. Al-Ḥulays personally was a Qurayshite (of Banū ʿAbd Manāt ibn Kinānah). When the Prophet (peace be upon him) saw al-Ḥulays coming, he told his Companions that he was from a religious group known to be devout. He ordered them to send the sacrificial camels to meet him, so that he would take notice of them. When al-Ḥulays saw the sacrificial animals, duly decorated, he was very impressed. He even went back without meeting the Prophet (peace be upon him), as he was totally convinced of his peaceful intentions, and that he came solely for the purpose of pilgrimage.

When al-Ḥulays conferred with the Quraysh, and told them of what he saw, they rebuffed him unkindly, saying that he was merely an ignorant, inexperienced Bedouin of the desert, who knew nothing about politics. When they saw that he was angered by their response, they told him to wait and be quiet until they obtained acceptable terms from Muḥammad (peace be upon him), apparently to assure him that they would ultimately allow Muḥammad (peace be upon him) to enter Makkah, but on their own terms. That assurance did the trick, and al-Ḥulays was pacified, and did not take any action against the Quraysh, as he had initially vowed to do.

5.3 The Coming of the Insolent ʿUrwah in Masʿūd

Then Quraysh sent ʿUrwah ibn Masʿūd al-Thaqafī to the Prophet (peace be upon him). ʿUrwah was known for his insolence. He addressed the Prophet (peace be upon him) disrespectfully; he even dared to rebuke the Prophet, by telling him that he had gathered the scum of the earth, a mixed people, and brought them out in order to destroy his own people. He told the Prophet (peace be upon him) that the Quraysh had gathered a mighty army, and that his mixed army and people would soon desert him, if it came to military confrontation. Abū Bakr was standing by, obviously incensed by the insolent remarks of ʿUrwah, because he directed some severe words at him. But ʿUrwah took them lightly, saying that he owed Abū Bakr some previous favours. Then ʿUrwah started touching the Prophet's beard, slightly pulling it, as was the custom of Bedouin Arabs, when talking in a friendly way to a senior chief. A Companion of the Prophet, al-Mughīrah ibn Shuʿbah, who was standing behind the Prophet (peace be upon him), would strike ʿUrwah's hand, each time he pulled at the Prophet's beard.

The Prophet (peace be upon him) told ʿUrwah what he had told the previous ambassadors, and ʿUrwah was very much impressed. On returning to the Quraysh, he told them how much the Muslims loved, venerated and obeyed the Prophet (peace be upon him). Comparing the Prophet (peace be upon him) to Caesar and Chosroe, ʿUrwah said, he was even more loved and obeyed than the latter were, and that Muḥammad (peace be upon him)'s people would not give him up for anything in the world.

6. THE PROPHET'S AMBASSADORS TO QURAYSH

Then the Prophet (peace be upon him) sent Khirāsh ibn Umayyah al-Khuzāʿī to the Quraysh. But he was unsuccessful and narrowly escaped death at their hands, had it not been for the Aḥābīsh, who protected him. Then the Prophet (peace be upon him) asked ʿUmar ibn al-Khaṭṭāb to go to the Quraysh, but he excused himself, saying that there were not enough of his own tribe of Banū ʿAdiyy in Makkah to protect him, that he had too much enmity with the Quraysh, and had treated them quite roughly. ʿUmar suggested ʿUthmān ibn ʿAffān, and the Prophet (peace be upon him) agreed. So ʿUthmān was dispatched. Quraysh received ʿUthmān (of Banū Umayyah) quite well, and even offered to let him visit and worship at al-Ka ʿbah, if he so desired. But ʿUthmān declined the offer, saying that it was unbecoming of him to do so, while the Prophet (peace be upon him) was not allowed to do the same. Then Quraysh told ʿUthmān that they could not allow the Prophet to enter Makkah, lest the Arabs would think that he had entered it by force. However, ʿUthmān's return to the Muslims' camp was delayed, and rumours came that he was killed. The Prophet (peace be upon him) was very angry and said, he would never return to Madīnah without engaging the Quraysh in battle.

7. THE PLEDGE OF AR-RIDWAN OR THE PLEDGE OF THE TREE

When ʿUthmān's return was delayed, and rumours came that he had been killed, the Prophet (peace be upon him) summoned the Muslims to give their undertakings. The ensuing Pledge of al-Riḍwān took place under a tree. Most men said that the Prophet (peace be upon him) had taken their pledge that they would fight until they were victorious or die with him as martyrs. However the Prophet's Companion, Jābir ibn ʿAbdullāh, reported that the Prophet only took their pledge not to flee the battle. All the Muslims present gave their pledge, except one Muslim who refused. When the Prophet (peace be upon him) heard the news that ʿUthmān was well and safe, he abandoned his plan to attack the Quraysh, and resumed his peace efforts. ʿUthmān returned and explained the Quraysh's position that:

a. They knew very well that Muḥammad (peace be upon him) came for pilgrimage only, and had no aggressive designs.

b. That they had no right to prevent him or the Muslims from visiting the House of God.

c. That, in spite of that, they could not allow him to enter that year, lest the Arabs should say that he had entered by force.

d. Instead, they hinted that the Prophet would be allowed to enter next year, if he so wished.

8. THE NEGOTIATIONS OF ḤUDAYBĪYAH PACT

Seeing that many of their powerful allies did not approve of denying the Muslims (or for that matter any Arab) the right of visiting the Ancient House of God, especially al-Ḥulays ibn ʿAlqamah, the commander of the Aḥābīsh, the Quraysh agreed, in principle, that the Prophet (peace be upon him) and Muslims would be allowed access to the Kaʿbah; but not that year. It had to be the next year, and they would have to be notified well ahead, so that they would vacate the city, and make other suitable arrangements. They argued that they could not allow him to enter that year, since they had taken their weapons, and made to the roads to prevent him. Should they allow him to enter Makkah, in these circumstances, it would look as if they had allowed him because of fear or weakness. The Bedouins would draw the wrong conclusions, and say that Muḥammad (peace be upon him) had entered Makkah by force.

9. EMISSARY OF SUHAYL IBN ʿAMR

When the Quraysh agreed to negotiate, they sent Suhayl ibn ʿAmr, as their emissary. When the Prophet (peace be upon him) saw Suhayl, he said: 'Quraysh now wants peace, otherwise they would not have sent Suhayl ibn ʿAmr' When Suhayl came, real negotiations got underway for the first time. They were long and difficult negotiations, and Suhayl was tough on a number of points:

a. First, he refused a document which set out the provisions of the pact because it opened with *Bismillāh*, i.e. 'In the name of God, the Most Merciful, Most Compassionate.'

b. Suhayl also objected to the phrase 'Muḥammad, the Messenger of God'. He rejected it, he said, because he was unfamiliar with it, and because, if he recognized Muḥammad (peace be upon him) as the Messenger of God, he would not have fought with him. The Prophet told ʿAlī ibn Abī Ṭālib, who was writing the document of the pact, to make due allowances to both objections (a & b) made by Suhayl. Ultimately the document of the pact was written as follows:

'This is what Muḥammad (peace be upon him) ibn ʿAbdullāh has agreed on with Suhayl ibn ʿAmr;'

a. They have agreed to lay aside war for ten years, during which men shall be safe and refrain from hostilities.

b. If one from the Quraysh side should come to Muḥammad (peace be upon him), without the permission of his guardians, he will be returned to them!

c. But should anyone from the side of Muḥammad come to the Quraysh, they will not return him to the Muslims.

d. None of the signatories to the pact shall show enmity or bad faith, or secret reservations towards one another.

e. Whoever wants to enter into bond and agreement with Muḥammad, may do so, and whoever wants to enter into bond and agreement with Quraysh, may do so. (At this point, Banū Khuzā'ah, leapt up and declared themselves allies of the Prophet (peace be upon him), and Banū Bakr leapt up and declared themselves allies of Quraysh.)

f. Muḥammad has to go back to Madīnah, but he could come next year, when he would be allowed to enter the city, and stay there for three days and nights, carrying no weapons, except the traveller's weapons, namely swords in their sheaths.

10. SHOCK AND DEJECTION AMONG MUSLIMS

When the pact's provisions were completed, the Prophet (peace be upon him) summoned some Muslims and some polytheists to witness its conclusion. There was a profound sense of disappointment and dejection among the Muslims. When they set out from Madīnah, they had no doubts that they would enter Makkah, and carry out their devotional rites of circuiting the Ka'bah, and worshipping God, in peace, in the Ancient House. No doubt some, among the Muhājrīn, were also looking forward to visiting their homes and relatives. Had not the Prophet (peace be upon him) told them what he had seen in his dream that he would enter the Sacred Sanctuary, in peace and security, fearing nothing, and with his head shaven. But now, what happened was just the opposite, they were barred from visiting the City, and the House, when they were standing so near to it, and the polytheists were threatening to attack them. The Prophet (peace be upon him) rose up, slaughtered his sacrificial animals and shaved his head. The Muslims had been passive in their bewilderment and confusion, not knowing what to do, until they saw the Prophet (peace be upon him) act as he did, and heard his prayers for those who followed his example. They were reassured and everybody got up, slaughtered his sacrificial animal and shaved. The Prophet (peace be upon him) told them that God had indeed promised them a dignified and peaceful entry into the Holy City, but had not said it was going to be in that year.

11. ʿUMAR IBN AL-KHAṬṬĀB QUESTIONS THE TERMS OF THE PACT

ʿUmar led the opposition to the conclusion of the Ḥudaybīyah accord. He asked: 'Are they not the polytheists? Are we not the Muslims? Are they not on the path of falsehood, we on the path of truth? Why then are we to suffer the demeaning of our religion?' ʿUmar first talked to Abū Bakr, and when he didn't get a satisfactory answer from him, he went straight to the Prophet (peace be upon him), and put the same questions to him.

The Prophet answered: 'I am God's Servant and His Messenger, and I will not go against His commandments, and He will not make me a loser!'[2] ʿUmar was very sorry for challenging the Prophet's decision. He felt remorse about this for a very long time to come and, in expiation, he fasted much, and gave charity to the poor.

ʿUmar was obviously unhappy at the apparent imbalances in the pact:

a. The Muslims were denied entrance to the Holy City for no good reason.

b. They were not allowed to write the name of God, the Merciful, the Compassionate, and were not allowed to declare the Prophethood of Muḥammad, declarations which were the most fundamental articles of their faith.

c. Their defectors would not be returned to them, whereas they were required to return the defectors from the Quraysh.

d. When they would come next year, they would be allowed to stay only for three days and nights, and would not be allowed to carry their weapons, except for the travellers' weapons. Who would guarantee their safety, and what if the Quraysh turned out to be traitors, just as the Bedouins of the desert at the well of al-Rajīʿ and Maʿūnah?

However, the Prophet (peace be upon him) had been favoured with insights from his Lord, about the benefits of the Pact; benefits that by far outweighed the kinds of misgivings expressed by ʿUmar.

12. DIVINE GLAD-TIDINGS ABOUT THE CONSEQUENCES OF THE PACT

On the return journey, God sent glad-tidings to His Prophet about the consequences of the pact just concluded. The Qur'ān called it a magnificent victory. A whole *sūrah* was revealed to Muḥammad (peace be upon him), which commented on the events of that day, and praised the resolve and dedication of the Companions, who had taken the Pledge of al-Riḍwān under the Tree, with the Prophet (peace be upon him): God said, in the Qur'ān, commenting on those events:.

> *Surely, We have given you a manifest victory, that Allah may forgive you your former and your later sins, and complete His blessing upon you, and guide you on a straight path, and that Allah may give you a mighty victory. It is He Who sent down peace (*Sakīnah*) into the hearts of believers, that they might add faith to their faith. To Allah belong the hosts of heavens and the earth, Allah is All-Knowing, All-Wise.* [*al-Fatḥ* 48:1-4]

The reasons why God, called the Ḥudaybīyah Pact a victory are all given in these opening verses of this *sūrah*.

a. The Prophet's sins, whatever they might have been, were all forgiven, and the ones to come in the future would also be forgiven.

b. God's blessing upon the Prophet (peace be upon him) would be completed, an obvious allusion that the cause of Islam would be victorious, and many people would enter into Islam.

c. The Prophet (peace be upon him) was assured of continuing help and guidance from God.

d. Lastly, another glad-tiding was given that there was a mighty victory in the near future, stored for the Prophet (peace be upon him) and the Muslims, as a consequence of the conclusion of the Pact of Ḥudaybīyah.

e. The verses also told the Prophet (peace be upon him) that a Divine Intervention had taken place, that relieved the shock and dismay, which the Muslims experienced on account of the apparently inequitable terms of the Pact. God sent down the *sakīnah* (i.e. calm and serenity) on the hearts of the believers, and they accepted what the Prophet (peace be upon him) had accepted, in order to make the Pact possible, in the face of the intransigence and arrogance of the Quraysh.

13. THE MEN OF AL-RIḌWĀN PLEDGE ARE PRAISED

In subsequent verses of *Sūrah al-Fatḥ*, God praises the Muslims who took the Riḍwān Pledge with the Prophet (peace be upon him), under the Tree. God said, in this connection:

> *Those who pledge fealty to you pledge fealty in truth to Allah, Allah's hand is over their hands, then, whosoever breaks his oath, breaks it but to his own disadvantage, and who so fulfils his covenant made with Allah, Allah will give him a mighty wage".* [*al-Fatḥ* 48:10]

14. THE CASE OF THE DEFECTORS

Hardly had the ink on the Ḥudaybīyah Pact dried, than the terms of that pact were put to a severe test. The very son of the negotiator, Suhayl ibn ʿAmr, defected to the Muslims, before they had even departed from the valley of Ḥudaybīyah, and whilst the Quraysh signatories to the pact were still there, in the Muslim camp, including Suhayl himself. Suhayl demanded the extradition of his son Abū Jandal. The Prophet (peace be upon him), to the utter dismay and dejection of the Muslims, especially ʿUmar ibn al-Khaṭṭāb, immediately agreed to give up Abū Jandal. On hearing this, Abū Jandal called out loudly: 'Am I to be returned to the polytheists that they may entice me from my religion, O Muslims!' But the Prophet answered:

> 'O Abū Jandal, be patient and control yourself, for God will provide relief and a means of escape for you and those of you who are helpless. We have made peace with them, and we and they have invoked God's name in our agreement, and we cannot deal falsely with them.'[3]

The Prophet (peace be upon him) proved his great capacity to remain cool and calm, in the face of high emotion and provocation. He had given the word of God's message, and must remain true to it. He wanted also to teach them that pacts and treaties are not worthwhile if broken no sooner than made. He must set the example, even to enemies, known for their cruelty and infidelity. If the Prophet (peace be upon him) would break his word, who else could be expected to keep it?

15. THE EPISODE OF ABŪ BAṢĪR

However, the case of the defectors soon developed into a major crisis for the Quraysh. A certain defector, by the name of Abū Baṣīr, came to the Prophet (peace be upon him) in Madīnah, and the Prophet sent him back, with his persecutors, just as he did with Abū Jandal ibn Suhayl ibn ʿAmr, the ambassador of the Quraysh. But, during the journey, Abū Baṣīr managed to free himself from his captives, and took up residence on the trade route of the Quraysh to Syria. There he was joined by other Muslims who had been detained in Makkah, and the whole group developed into a serious and great threat to Quraysh trade to Syria. Altogether, about seventy Muslims gathered around Abū Baṣīr, as their leader, at Al-ʿAshīr on the sea coast. This Muslim force succeeded in disrupting the Makkan trade, and the Quraysh wrote to the Prophet (peace be upon him) requesting him to take them into Madīnah, in spite of the very term of the Ḥudaybīyah Pact that had been so obnoxious to the Muslims, especially ʿUmar ibn al-Khaṭṭāb. Many Muslim women from Makkah managed to reach Madīnah and were not returned to the Quraysh.

In concluding this section on the Pact of Ḥudaybīyah, it is important to re-emphasize the steadfastness with which the Prophet (peace be upon him) persisted in the pursuit of peace. Nothing succeeded in distracting him from his set objective, to achieve some accord with the Makkans:

a. They almost killed his first ambassador, after killing his camel (which actually belonged to the Prophet (peace be upon him) himself).

b. They prevented him from visiting the Ancient House, in flagrant violation of the tradition of Abraham, Quṣayy and Hāshim; and the religious customs of the Quraysh at large. It was an unreasonable thing to do; since every Arab had the right of access to the Holy Sanctuary, why discriminate against Muḥammad (peace be upon him) and the Muslims?

c. They raided the Muslim camp with fifty knights, during the Sacred Month of Dhū'l-Ḥijjah, in violation of the religious code of Banū Abraham.

d. They held ʿUthmān ibn ʿAffān, as a captive for a few days, and only set him free when they learnt that the Muslims vowed to release him of his captivity by force and to avenge his blood, if killed.

e. Last but not least, the Quraysh negotiators were most provocative and impolite during the negotiations, and insisted on the most unjust and unbalanced terms, but the Prophet (peace be upon him) bore all of this, with wonderful patience and magnanimous tolerance. The wisdom of the Prophet (peace be upon him) became manifest, as the consequences of the Pact enabled him to emerge as the paramount spiritual, political and moral force in Arabia. The Quraysh's power and authority further weakened and waned away, never to revive again. Many Makkans, on seeing the imminent downfall of the Quraysh, headed north and joined the Prophet (peace be upon him). Some of those who converted to Islam at this period, in the wake of Ḥudaybīyah, included such prominent names as Khālid ibn al-Walīd; nickname the Sword of God, for his prominent role in the victorious and far reaching Muslim conquests (*al-Futūḥāt al-Islāmiyyah*); while ʿAmr ibn al-ʿĀṣ, who became the celebrated Governor of Egypt, and one of the principal builders of the Umayyad Dynasty, also became a Muslim during that time, in the wake of the Ḥudaybīyah Pact.

16. THE CONQUEST OF KHAYBAR

Students of the life of the Prophet (peace be upon him) may wonder at the extent of his military exploits. His main adversaries were no doubt the Quraysh idolaters, but the desert Bedouins and the Jews proved no lesser adversaries. Those Jews, in particular, surprise the student of Arab history by their aggressive nature, inflated self-image to the exclusion of everybody else, and their martial character. These were hardly the qualities one would expect from a religious minority, living in a predominantly Arab land, peopled moreover by many bellicose and Bedouin tribes. In the three Jewish settlements of Madīnah, the Banū Qaynuqāʿ, the Banū al-Naḍīr and Banū Qurayẓah, the Jews lived in separate quarters that:

a. were exclusively Jewish of the same clan

b. consisted of very elaborate fortifications

c. were almost self-sufficient, and self-contained, with all the necessary amenities such as market-places, carpentry, bakeries, blacksmiths jewelleries, textile and flour-mills and arms' factories. In particular, those Jews were very tough fighters, and they thrived, as warlords, and traders in armaments. No wonder, they perpetuated the notorious war of Buʿāth, between the Aws and Khazraj. The Banū Qurayẓah allied themselves with the Aws. The third Jewish settlement of al-Naḍīr sided with a lesser Arabian tribe. It was the Jews who incited the wars between the Khazraj and Aws, and they also had wars amongst themselves. When the Prophet (peace be upon him) established his state at Madīnah, they found a new role of inciting war and hatred between Muḥammad and his Arab adversaries. Although initially they entered into the *Ṣaḥīfah* Covenant with the Prophet (peace be upon him), they repudiated it one after another. When the Prophet (peace be upon him) agreed to let them leave Madīnah, they went to swell the Jewish settlements in the north of Arabia, Khaybar, Umm al-Qurā, Fadak, and others. They also established new colonies. From there, they continued their new role as inciters of sedition and war against the Prophet (peace be upon him), and the Muslims in Madīnah. The Muslims' initial efforts to gain the friendship and alliance of the Jews (as People of the Book) against idolaters of Makkah were all in vain. Not only that, but the Jews of the north allied themselves totally with the Quraysh and the Arab Bedouins of the desert, and told them that their ancient Arabian religion of idol-worship was a better religion than Islam. Thus the Jews were in the fore-front of hostilities against the Prophet (peace be upon him), and as such he could not ignore their designs. Thus the Prophet (peace be upon him), who had been so enthusiastic about winning the friendship and alliance of the Jews, and who was so assiduously seeking peace and reconciliation with his adversaries at Ḥudaybīyah, was compelled by the intransigence and belligerence of the Jews of Arabia to fight them to the bitter end. On purely religious and ideological grounds, there need not have been such a conflict, for the Qur'ān recognizes Judaism as a revealed religion, and the Jews of Arabia were bound to a legally binding Covenant with the Prophet (peace be upon him). But that was how events developed, with unfortunate consequences for those two great traditions, especially the disastrous consequences for the Jewish community of Arabia. Such was the Jewish threat to the security of the nascent Muslim state of Madīnah, that the Prophet (peace be upon him) had to move against their stronghold at Khaybar, to the north of the city. The struggle against Qurayẓah and the events of al-Khandaq made it absolutely clear that the Prophet (peace be upon him) could not ignore the Jewish threat from Khaybar, given the major role which the Jews of Khaybar played in inciting and mobilizing the Quraysh, and the desert Bedouins, to join forces against the Muslims at al-Khandaq.

17. THE KHAYBAR EXPEDITON (7 AH)

From a purely military point of view, the Ḥudaybīyah Pact was a sort of anticlimax for the Muslims. It had no spectacular results, but of course, its long-term political and moral consequences were tremendous. The Qur'ān, as we have noted, described Ḥudaybīyah as a 'Manifest Victory'. But to the generality of the Muslims, the political and moral consequences were not obvious, and their morale in Madīnah continued at a low ebb in the aftermath of the Ḥudaybīyah Pact. When the Prophet (peace be upon him) gave the order to march against the Jews of Khaybar, there was an enthusiastic response. The expedition was underway, only six weeks after the return of the Muslims from Ḥudaybīyah, i.e. in the month of al-Muḥarram, in the 7th year of *Hijrah.*

Now, the Jews of Khaybar were the strongest, the richest and the bravest of the Jews. They were famous for their elaborate fortifications, which they had built in their rich and fertile valleys at Khaybar, Fadak, Wādī al-Qurā and Taymā'. Contrary to the common impression among some students of Islamic history, Khaybar was not a single fortress, but consisted of a network of elaborate fortifications. The Prophet (peace be upon him) had to overtake them one by one. As was his habit, the Prophet (peace be upon him) did not disclose his exact destination, when he marched towards Khaybar. He knew that the Bedouins of the Ghaṭafān were allies of the Jews of Khaybar, and had he disclosed his intentions of attacking Khaybar, word would have been easily sent to them. So, the Prophet (peace be upon him) marched by night, and it took him three nights' march to reach their fortifications in the small hours of the third night. Early next morning, the Muslims charged against them! The Jews of Khaybar were just opening the doors of their fortresses, and their peasants and workers were setting out for their usual business, when they saw the Muslims' army coming towards their doors.

They shouted and yelled at the top of their voices: 'It is Muḥammad and his army.' They ran back to the doors of their fortresses, entered and quickly slammed the doors after them! The Prophet (peace be upon him) was reported to have shouted back, 'Allāhu Akbar! Khaybar is Doomed! Allāhu Akbar! Khaybar is Destroyed!'[4] Then, he recited part of a Qur'ānic verse, and said: *When it (doom and chastisement) arrived in a people's square it is indeed a bad morning for those who have been warned.* [*al-Ṣāffāt* 37:177]

The Prophet's allusion to 'people being warned' was indeed very significant. Ibn Hishām mentions that when the Prophet (peace be upon him) returned from Ḥudaybīyah, he sent a strong warning to the Jews of Khaybar, though its wording was polite and persuasive. This letter is given by Ibn Hishām, when discussing the general issue of the Qur'ānic dialogue with the Jews in *Sūrah al-Baqarah*. But it is quite clear, that the letter was sent, after Ḥudaybīyah, since it contains verses of *Sūrah al-Fatḥ* which was revealed to the Prophet (peace be upon him) on his way back from Ḥudaybīyah, in the year 6 A.H. The letter reads as follows:

> In the name of God, the Merciful, the Compassionate. From the Messenger of God, friend and brother of Moses:

> *God says in the Qur'ān (God says to you, O people of the Book, and you will find it in your own Book) 'Muḥammad is the Messenger of Allah, and those with him are hard on the unbelievers, compassionate among themselves; you see them bowing and prostrating; seeking grace and acceptance from Allah; the mark of their prostration is on their foreheads, that is their description in the Torah. And their description in the Gospel is like a seed which sends forth its off-shoots and they strengthen it, and it becomes thick, and rises straight upon its stalk, delighting the sowers, that he may cause the unbelievers to burn with rage at (the sight of) them. Allah has promised those who believe, and do good works, forgiveness and a great reward.'* [*al-Fatḥ* 48:29]

Then the Prophet continued his letter to the Jews of Khaybar:

> 'I adjure you by God, and by what He has sent down to you, and by His drying the sea for your fathers, when He delivered them from the Pharaoh and his soldiers, that you tell me, do you find in what He has sent down to you that you believe in Muḥammad (peace be upon him)? If you do not find that in your Book, then there is no compulsion upon you, the right path has become plainly distinguished from error, so I call you to God and His Messenger....'

This letter is a significant proof that the Prophet (peace be upon him) was trying very hard with the Jews of Khaybar, as he had tried with the Qurayẓah, to reach some kind of peaceful accord that would end the hostilities, and open the road for peaceful dialogue. It is of course through peaceful dialogue that ideas spread, and common understanding between people is achieved. As put by Barakat Ahmed, the Prophet (peace be upon him) was trying very hard to find a *modus vivacity* with the Jews of Khaybar, the last Jewish stronghold in Arabia, to break the cycle of violence and counter-violence. But his letter went unanswered, and his efforts came to nothing. The Jews of Khaybar were not lacking in courage or resources, but they were lacking in vision and in leadership. They could not see clearly, that it was fruitless and vein to fight off a far stronger political and military force, that Quraysh and their Bedouin allies had been unable to defeat. They were given to the leadership of the embittered Banū al-Naḍīr who lost their capacity of objective evaluation of things, because the only thing they could ever think about was to avenge their defeat and expulsion from Madīnah by the Prophet (peace be upon him). Moreover, their traditional system of defence was inappropriate, as it was designed primarily to stop the raids of the desert Bedouins, which were small-scale and brief. The Bedouins were not capable of laying siege to the fortress of Khaybar, having neither the patience nor the resources to maintain sieges. It was a different matter with the Prophet (peace be upon him), who understood the device of war, himself suffered it, during the Khandaq battle. The Jews of Khaybar were the strongest, and the most arrogant of the Jews of Arabia. They always held the Prophet (peace be upon him) in contempt, and grossly underestimated his power and his ability to win wars. They failed to see the changing fortunes of the times, and that the days of the domination of north Arabia by the Jews had ended. Even if they saw these changes, they were unable to adjust and adapt to them. Moreover, these fortresses were isolated from each other, no co-ordination or common leadership existed between them. In that way, it was not difficult for the Prophet (peace be upon him) to storm the lesser ones among these fortresses as he gathered the bulk of his army to attack the two main strongholds.

These fell one after the other. The Jews' morale was then very low. Their Arab allies of Banū Ghaṭafān did not come to their help because, apparently, they were discouraged by the sudden surprising appearance of the Muslims' army.

The Prophet (peace be upon him) then marched to the last strongholds of Khaybar, namely Waṭīh and al-Sulālim. These were very well fortified and well-defended. The Jews of Khaybar put up their best fighting men, as well as their best pieces of armour. The Prophet (peace be upon him) laid siege to these forts for more than ten days and nights. When conditions became untenable, and the Jews of Khaybar thought it was imminent destruction, they consented to surrender, and asked the Prophet (peace be upon him) to let them leave safely, and he could have their money and property. The Prophet (peace be upon him) agreed, but later he allowed them to stay as tenants on their land, in return for getting half their agricultural produce, especially the dates. That was a good deal for the Jews of Khaybar, because they were already paying that to the Bedouins of Banū Ghaṭafān. Before the surrender, there were not many casualties, as no open fighting took place, only isolated duels, arrow and stone throwing which claimed few lives. The few duels that took place were initiated by some Jewish knights, who came forward asking for them. These included Marḥaba, a Jew of Yemeni origin, from Banū Ḥimyar. He was a poet as well as a brave and skilful warrior. He was killed by Muḥammad ibn Maslamah, who had lost a brother the day before, as the Muslims were besieging the fortress. Yāsir, brother of Marḥaba, who came forward to avenge the killing of his brother, was killed by al-Zubayr ibn al-ʻAwwām, son of Ṣafiyyah, the aunt of the Prophet (peace be upon him).

After these two duels, no Jews dared to come out, and the Jewish morale sank even lower, leading to their eventual surrender. The example of Marḥab and Yāsir supports our view that the character-traits of Jews of Arabia had undergone significant change. They were no longer city-traders and money-lenders. They had become war-like, and adopted the Arabs' martial customs and characteristics. Many of them were accomplished poets, and used to brag about their bravery and generosity, as did their Arab compatriots.

One of the most famous poets of pre-Islamic Arabia, was a Jew of Khaybar. His name was al-Samaw'al ibn ʻAdiyā. He was a famous knight-cum-poet. He was very rich, too, and had a fortress of his own, called al-Ablaq. He is remembered for two things:

1. His famous pre-Islamic ode . This is a long and very beautiful poem full of wisdom. It starts with the famous verse:

'If a man's honour is not stained by bad conduct then any costume he wears is beautiful!'

2. The second thing was his fidelity. The famous Arab Poet Imra' al-Qays, deposited his armour with him, when he journeyed to the north, to meet the Caesar. Some people came and demanded Imra' al-Qays's armour, whilst he was away, but Samaw'al refused and a fight ensued in which his son was killed.

We have mentioned the incidents of Marḥaba, and his brother Yasir and the knight-poet al-Samaw'al ibn ʿAdiyā to show that the Jews of Khaybar were not lacking in courage or in will and power to fight, but they only lacked vision and leadership. The Jews of Arabia were a self-centred lot; all they cared about was their own privileged status, as the paramount power in Arabia (that was before the advent of Islam) and that they were the chosen sons and beloved friends of God. The Qur'ān quotes them as saying:

> *Say the Jews and the Christians we are the sons of God, and His beloved ones; say: Why then does He chastise you for your sins? No; you are mortals, of His creation. He forgives whom He will, and chastises whom He will, for to God belongs the Kingdom of the heavens and of the earth, and all that is between them. To Him is the eventual return.* [*al-Mā'idah* 5:18]

18. THE PROPHET'S MARRIAGE TO ṢAFIYYAH

Many of the Prophet's marriages had religious and political motives. Such was the case of his marriage to Ṣafiyyah bint Ḥuyayy ibn al-Akhṭab, the Jewish Chief of Banū al-Naḍīr, now defending Khaybar. Her father was killed with Banū Qurayẓah, as he played a major role in persuading them to violate their covenant with the Prophet (peace be upon him), and then stayed with them to the last eventuality, as he promised. Ṣafiyyah was married to a Jewish relative. She saw a strange dream: that the moon fell in her lap. When she told her husband, he hit her hard in the face, so that he blackened her eye, saying: You just dream of the king of Ḥijāz, Muḥammad. The blow left a permanent scar on her face which she afterwards, showed to the Prophet (peace be upon him), when she told him about the dream which had now come true.

Before Ṣafiyyah, the Prophet (peace be upon him) had also taken Rayḥānah, a Jew of Qurayẓah, in his household. It is not certain whether he married her or not, but the act was meant as some consolation for the loss of her family. These two incidents, and the fact that the Jews of Khaybar and Fadak managed to reach peaceful solutions with the Prophet (peace be upon him), by which they were allowed to stay on their lands and property in return for paying half the produce, meant that the expeditions against Qurayẓah and Khaybar did not result in an absolute rift between Jews and Muslims. Jews remained and played a crucial role in the inception of the Islamic civilization afterwards. The treatment the Prophet (peace be upon him) meted out to the Jews of Khaybar and Fadak, which is considered by historians to have been, in the circumstances of total war and confrontation, rather light, suggests that the number of the Jews of Qurayẓah killed in Madīnah may have been exaggerated by later sources. Six hundred men is a very large number to have been killed, and it stands out as very odd, in the struggle between the Prophet (peace be upon him) and the Jews in Arabia.

19. THE PRAYER OF THE PROPHET AS HE ENTERED KHAYBAR

When the Prophet was about to enter Khaybar, he stopped and said:[5]

> 'O God, Lord of heavens and what they over-shadow, Lord of the lands and what they are made to grow, Lord of the devils, and what into error they throw, Lord of the winds and what they winnow, we ask You for the good of this town, and the good of its people, and the good of what is in it, and we take refuge in You from its evil and the evil of its people, and the evil that is in it. Forward, in the name of God!'

The Prophet (peace be upon him) used to regularly repeat these words, whenever he entered a town for the first time.

20. THE SURRENDER OF FADAK

When the Jewish People of the fertile oasis of Fadak heard about the relatively mild way in which the Prophet had treated the people of Khaybar, they asked him to give them similar terms, and he agreed. In this way, the Jews of Fadak proved wiser than those of Qurayẓah, Khaybar or Banū al-Naḍīr. Thus, no siege of Fadak was necessary and the *fay'* (Land-tax) of Fadak was allotted as private property to the household of the Prophet (peace be upon him), and his relatives exclusively. This arrangement was decreed by the Qur'ān itself:

> *And whatever spoils of war Allah has given unto His Messenger from them against which you pricked neither horse nor camel, but Allah gives authority to His Messengers, over whomsoever He will. Allah is Powerful over everything.* [*al-Ḥashr* 59:6]

21. THE YOUNG MAIDEN OF GHIFĀR

Ibn Hishām tells of a group of Ghifārī women (i.e. from the tribe of Banū Ghifār), who came to the Prophet (peace be upon him), as he was about to depart to Khaybar. They asked to accompany him so as to attend the wounded, and help the Muslims in any way they could. The Prophet (peace be upon him) told them to do so, with God's blessing. One of these women was quite young, and the Prophet (peace be upon him) took her on the back of his saddle. When they stopped next morning to pray, there was menstrual blood in the saddle where the young girl had been sitting. She clinched to the camels back trying to hide it. The Prophet (peace be upon him) saw her and understood the cause of her embarrassment. He said, 'put some salt in the water and wash it, and continue your ride with me.' Such was the character of the Prophet (peace be upon him) easy, natural and quite accommodative to other people. No wonder, he was so dearly loved by the Muslims, and by anybody who happened to meet him. His way with women and young people was most impressive: he needed no time to win over their hearts.

22. THE RETURN OF JAʿFAR AND OTHER MUSLIMS FROM ABYSSINIA (778 A.C.)

Ibn Hishām narrates, on the authority of his sources, that Jaʿfar, and sixteen other men and some women, came back from Abyssinia, the same day on which Khaybar surrendered. The Prophet (peace be upon him) was quite pleased to see Jaʿfar. He embraced him, and kissed him between his eyes, and said: 'I do not know whether I am more pleased with the surrender of Khaybar, or with the coming of Jaʿfar ibn Abī Ṭālib.'

Jaʿfar was the young cousin of the Prophet (peace be upon him), the younger brother of ʿAlī ibn Abī Ṭālib. He looked very much like the Prophet (peace be upon him) himself. He came accompanied with his wife, Asmā' bint ʿUmays, and his son ʿAbdullāh who was born to them in Abyssinia.

Jaʿfar soon lead an expedition to Muʿtah, and fell a martyr in the cause of Islam.

Two years after the Ḥudaybīyah Pact, the Prophet (peace be upon him) led the Muslims into Makkah, performing the ʿUmrah (or lesser pilgrimage). His dream was eventually realized, and he and the Muslims entered Makkah, in peace and without fear, with their heads shaven. In these two years, between Ḥudaybīyah and the performance of the lesser Pilgrimage, Islam spread far and wide, across the Arabian peninsula.

CHAPTER 8

The Conquest of Makkah and its Aftermath

1. THE MOMENTUM FOR PEACE DUE TO ḤUDAYBĪYAH

No doubt, the successful conclusion of the Ḥudaybīyah Pact, and the subsequent peace agreements with the Jews of Khaybar and Fadak, after their defeat by the Muslim forces, created tremendous drive and momentum for peace in Arabia. The Prophet (peace be upon him), whose desire for peace was paramount, drove that momentum to its fullest. He was very clear that, in order to achieve total conversion of Arabia to Islam, he needed a period of peace so that Islam would spread, as a creed and as a way of life. The atmosphere of war was not congenial to the successful dissemination of ideas or religious movements. Once he obtained that period of grace, the Prophet (peace be upon him) lost no time or opportunity to utilize it to the maximum. After the removal of the Jewish opposition, Islam was still left with two adversaries, the Quraysh and the desert Bedouins, especially those in the immediate or reachable vicinity of Madīnah. It was quite true that the Quraysh represented the greatest enemy. But the desert Bedouins were not to be taken lightly. For one thing, they were unpredictable, and quite often they were driven to military exploits by sheer poverty. Since they were not far from Madīnah, they represented a real hazard to the security of the city. Consequently, they had to be watched very closely, and the Prophet (peace be upon him) took good care of that by placing informants amongst them.

As for the Quraysh, the Prophet (peace be upon him) put into effect a number of measures with the objective of further weakening their morale, and striking at their economic livelihood. The Quraysh's trade with Syria was particularly targeted, and the Prophet (peace be upon him) worked out a number of alliances with the Bedouin tribes in order to further isolate the Quraysh politically, and reduce their traditional influence and prestige with the tribes of Arabia at large. All these tactics and designs served as a sort of psychological and intelligence warfare, antecedent to the eventual conquest of Makkah by the Prophet (peace be upon him).

2. THE BLOCKADE OF QURAYSH

As we said before, the Prophet's thoughts were all directed towards Makkah, after the Khaybar's expedition, and the return of the Muslim immigrants from Abyssinia, led by Ja'far ibn Abī Ṭālib. He first performed the 'Umrah (or lesser pilgrimage) as provided for in the Ḥudaybīyah Pact. He carried out the rituals of the 'Umrah, circumambulating the Ka'bah, seven times, and moving between Ṣafā' and Marwah seven times also, then shaving (the hair off) his head. He stayed for three days and nights in Makkah, as provided in the Ḥudaybīyah Pact, and was then asked to leave the city by the Quraysh. He asked them to extend his stay in Makkah, so that he could marry Maymūnah bint al-Ḥārith, sister of Umm al-Faḍl, the wife of the Prophet's uncle al-'Abbās, but they refused. The Prophet (peace be upon him) then returned to Madīnah in Dhū'l-Ḥijjah, 7th A.H. On the way back to Madīnah, God revealed the following verses of the Qur'ān:

> *Allah has indeed fulfilled the vision, He vouchsafed to His Messenger: truly you shall enter the Holy Mosque, if Allah wills, in security, your heads shaved, your hair cut short not fearing. He knew what you knew not, and granted besides this, a speedy victory...*" [al-Fatḥ 48:27]

3. THE PROPHET SENT FIVE RAIDS AGAINST BEDOUINS

Within a month or so of returning to Madīnah, the Prophet (peace be upon him) initiated five raids against the Bedouins around Madīnah. As we said, the Bedouins around Madīnah, had to be kept under constant check and surveillance. They were usually, treacherous and opportunistic, and quick to seize any advantage present to them. Their desire for spoils of war, and for women were boundless, and they moved quickly in pursuit of them. The raids initiated by the Prophet (peace be upon him) were useful also in maintaining a high level degree of alertness and mobilization among the Muslims. The enemy, whether the Quraysh or the Jews, or the Bedouins, might strike at any time, so the Muslims needed to be vigilant and prepared at all times. The raids were also important in keeping up the pressure against Makkah. They helped enforce the psychological and economic blockade of the Quraysh, and gave notice to the Bedouins, who might be considering an alliance with the Quraysh, that the Muslims were now the dominant political and military power in Arabia.

3.1 The Five Raids directed against the Desert Bedouins were as follows:

1. The Raid of Abū al-Awjaʿ on Banū Sulaym (fifty men) most of whom were killed.
2. The Raid of Ghadīsh ibn ʿAbdullāh on Banū Mulayḥ at al-Qadīd.
3. The Raid of Ghālib ibn ʿAbdullāh on Fadak in the north.
4. The Raid of Shujāʿ ibn Wahb to Banū ʿĀmir at al-Sīʿ.
5. And lastly, the raid of Kaʿb ibn ʿUmayr on Dhāt Aṣlaḥ, to the north of Wādī al-Qurā, the north of Khaybar.

4. THE EXPEDITION TO MU'TAH

A much bigger expedition, both in number and military and political significance, was sent to the north, in the southern part of Syria. The

Prophet (peace be upon him) sent an emissary by the name of Al-Ḥārith ibn ʿUmayr al-Azdī, to the governor of Buṣrā, a Ghassānid functionary of the Romans. Al-Ḥārith was killed by the governor Shuraḥbīl ibn ʿAmr al-Ghassānī. The incident weighed heavily on the conscience of the Prophet (peace be upon him), who called the Muslims to battle against the Ghassānī Authority in southern Syria. A force of three thousand responded to this call. For a reason unknown to us, he appointed three men to hold the command in succession, if the first or second was killed then the third would take command. Perhaps the Prophet (peace be upon him) anticipated an intense and prolonged campaign on this new front against the Romans and their clients in Syria. Zayd ibn Ḥārithah, the one-time adopted son of the Prophet; Jaʿfar ibn Abī Ṭālib, the Prophet's cousin; and ʿĀbdullāh ibn Rawāḥah, a well-known Anṣārī, physically fit, dedicated to the cause of Islam, and with a strong love and loyalty to the Messenger of Islam. The Prophet (peace be upon him) was also known to be very fond of them. Zayd ibn Ḥārithah was called Zayd ibn Muḥammad, until the Qur'ān advised against that Arab custom of calling adopted children by the names of their adopters, and ordered them to be called by the names of their biological fathers. As to Jaʿfar, he was strikingly similar to the Prophet (peace be upon him), both in physical appearance and conduct. ʿAbdullāh ibn Rawāḥah often used to recite Islamic poetry in the presence of the Prophet (peace be upon him), and with his consent and approval. Once ʿUmar ibn-al-Khaṭṭāb tried to prevent him doing that, but the Prophet (peace be upon him) intervened on behalf of Ibn Rawāḥah.

When the Muslim army, led by Zayd ibn Ḥārithah, reached the southern border to Syria, they got disturbing news about the huge armies, amassed by the Romans and their Arab Ghassānid clients; a hundred thousand led by Heraclius, the Roman Emperor himself, and another army of one hundred thousand soldiers, led by Mālik ibn Zāfilah, according to Ibn Hishām[1] but, according to Ibn Saʿd, led by Shuraḥbīl ibn ʿAmr.[2] The Muslim army camped in southern Syria, and held a *Shūrā* Council. At first, the prevalent opinion was to inform the Prophet (peace be upon him), and await his advice on what to do in the circumstances, and to request additional forces and equipment, if they were to go forward. But ʿAbdullāh ibn Rawāḥah persuaded the army to move forward, regardless of the huge imbalance between the Muslim and the Roman forces (3000 vs 200,000)! ʿAbdullāh said, 'What you see in front of you, is what you have come forward to meet, either victory or martyrdom!'

The Muslims were swayed by Ibn Rawāḥah's argument, and pushed forward with great enthusiasm and ferocity. When they met the Roman armies, they stationed themselves in a village called Mu'tah, and the bloodiest battle in the history of Islam so far was fought. The first commander, Zayd ibn Ḥārithah, knew that it was a pitch battle, and wrote himself as a martyr, and thus he fought in the most gallant, almost reckless way, not taking any measure to protect himself. He plunged deep into the lines of the enemy, hitting right and left. He even dismounted from his horse and engaged the enemy in hand-to-hand combat. He did not fall a martyr until his whole body was bleeding profusely. Ibn Hishām[3] described the scene saying: 'Zayd fought carrying the banner of the Messenger of God high, until he plunged to death, due to the piercing of his body by the spears of the enemy.'

When Zayd fell, Jaʿfar came forward, and took the banner from him; and he too fought with such courage and fearless determination, that he received more than seventy sword and spear cuts. When his right hand was cut, he took the banner in his left. When that hand too was cut, he took the banner between his two arms. Finally, he received a sword blow that cut him in two halves. Such was the bravery and the dedication of Jaʿfar for his Lord and for his religion! (The Prophet (peace be upon him) later said that he was in Paradise, his two arms replaced by two wings, with which he could fly anywhere he liked, in those lavish gardens of Paradise. For this reason, Jaʿfar became known as Jaʿfar al-Ṭayyār; the flying Jaʿfar.)

When Jaʿfar fell, the third commander, ʿAbdullāh ibn Rawāḥah, came forward and took the banner of the Prophet (peace be upon him), but he hesitated a bit, before he thrust himself forward. It was during that brief hesitation, that he composed his famous poem, in which he persuaded himself to go forward, to meet what was certain death.

These couplets have been rendered into English as follows.

I swear, my soul, you shall come to the battle!
You shall fight, or be forced to fight!
Though men shout and scream aloud!
Why should you spurn Paradise?
Long have you been at ease!
You are nothing but a drop in a worn out skin!
O soul, if you are not killed you will die!
This is the fate of death which you suffer
You have been given what you hoped for
If you do what those two did, you will have been guided a right!
How well it is to enter Paradise
They are very good, and of very cool springs to drink
The Romans are worthy to suffer
Infidels and of bad lineage[4]
If I meet them, I should kill them

The Prophet (peace be upon him) managed to oversee the events of that battle of Mu'tah, by a special kind of revelation, and he described it to his Companions, long before the defeated army returned to Madīnah. Had it not been for the mercy of God, the whole Muslim army might have been routed. Khālid ibn al-Walīd was chosen as a commander by an Anṣārī soldier, who took the banner, after the fall of ʿAbdullāh ibn Rawāḥah. Being very skilled in the art of warfare, Khālid managed to manoeuvre the enemy, attacking them fiercely while he regrouped the Muslim forces. Then when the enemy retreated, he did not pursue them any further, but seized the opportunity to withdraw the Muslims in a safe and orderly way, without incurring further losses.

Although both Ibn Hishām[5] and Ibn Saʿd[6] described the outcome of the battle of Mu'tah as a terrible defeat for the Muslims, the number of casualties does not seem to have been very big. In addition to the martyred three commanders, Ibn Hishām gives the number of those killed among the Muslims as eight. This seems to me to be far fewer than one would have expected in a major battle, described as the worst defeat the Muslims had yet incurred. (We recall that the number of those killed at Uḥud was approximately seventy.)

5. THE PROPHET GRIEVES AT THE DEFEAT OF THE MUSLIMS

The Prophet (peace be upon him) grieved profoundly at the slaying of the Muslims, and he grieved especially for Jaʿfar and Zayd ibn Ḥārithah. It was the practice of the Prophet (peace be upon him) to come and meet the people, after each prayer. That day, when he received the sad news of the defeat of the Muslim army at Mu'tah, the Prophet (peace be upon him) disappeared into his house, without talking to anybody. He did the same in the noon, mid-afternoon, sunset and night prayers. The Muslims sensed that something very grave might have happened, and they grieved deeply and profoundly. However, when the Prophet (peace be upon him) prayed the dawn prayer of the next day, he looked in the direction of the Muslims and smiled. They rushed to him saying: 'When we saw you in grief, and that was showing in your face, we suffered tremendously, and only God knows the extent of our grief for you, may ourselves be your ransom, O Prophet of God!'[7]

The Prophet (peace be upon him) told them that he grieved, because of the slaying of his Companions at Mu'tah. Then he told them that, in his night dream, he had seen them sitting on beds made of pure gold, facing each other in Paradise, and some of them were a little bit behind, seemingly because they hesitated a little bit in front of the swords of the enemy.

'But Jaʿfar I saw as an angel with two wings covered with blood, even the front parts of his wings were painted red with blood, the colour is the colour of blood, but the smell is the smell of Musk!'

The Prophet's grief for Jaʿfar was particularly acute: Jaʿfar was much beloved by the Prophet (peace be upon him), as he was a young, and a staunch fighter in the way of God. For many years, he had been in a voluntary exile in Abyssinia, wanted by the Quraysh. Yet hardly had he returned to safety in Madīnah, he was ready to go forth on a *jihād* against the formidable Roman armies. The way he fought, in absolute self-denial, bravery and dedication, made his memory one of the most cherished of the men who gave their lives in the way of God, to uphold His religion. The young Jaʿfar was so attached to the Prophet (peace be upon him), that his manners and conduct were very much like those of the Prophet, even his physical appearance and his gestures, by long association, started to resemble the Prophet's. Jaʿfar was greatly mourned by his wife, Asmā' bint ʿUmays, and the generality of the Muslims. When the Prophet (peace be upon him) sent for Jaʿfar's children and they came to him, he cuddled and smelled them, with tears on his noble face and beard.[8]

6. THE CONQUEST OF MAKKAH

We have seen that it was a long-term plan of the Prophet (peace be upon him) to take Makkah where the Holy Mosque, built by Abraham and his son Ishmael, is situated. After the Quraysh's failure at the Battle of al-Khandaq, the Prophet (peace be upon him) had taken all kinds of measures to weaken and blockade the Quraysh, politically, militarily, economically and even by psychological warfare. All the raids he made, after Ḥudaybīyah were directed towards that end, and the Quraysh trade routes were effectively disrupted. The city and its regime were cut off from the outside world, with no prosperous trade, and no allies among the Arab tribes, excepting the nearby Banū Bakr, in the Baṭḥā' Desert, around Makkah. It will be recalled that one of the stipulations of the Ḥudaybīyah Pact was that any tribe was free to choose to ally with the Muslims or with the Quraysh, without prejudice to the terms of the Pact. Banū Bakr became the allies of the Quraysh, and Khuzāʿah (partially Muslim) became allies of the

Prophet (peace be upon him). The reason behind these polarizations was the age-old feud in the *jāhiliyyah* (Pre-Islamic Era) between these two tribes. The Ḥudaybīyah Pact itself thus contributed to increase the isolation of the Quraysh, as we have seen. The Muslim rebels, who ran away from the Quraysh, and whom the Prophet (peace be upon him) was initially prevented from admitting to Madīnah, because of the terms of the Pact, became a real menace to their trade routes to Syria. Led by Abū Baṣīr, as mentioned earlier, they were very successful in disrupting and effectively preventing the Quraysh movements, commercial or otherwise. That blockade dealt severe blows to the prestige of the Quraysh throughout Arabia.

Moreover, the defeat of the Jews and their expulsion from Madīnah, together with the conquest of their strong Khaybar strongholds, deprived the Quraysh of their powerful Jewish allies. Also, Ghaṭafān, and their allies among the Bedouins, who had been sympathetic to the Quraysh, were effectively pacified, and no longer contemplated coming to the aid of the Quraysh.

7. THE IMMEDIATE CAUSE FOR THE CONQUEST OF MAKKAH

The immediate cause for the conquest of Makkah however, was the breaching of the Hudaybīyah Pact by the Quraysh, and their Bedouin allies, Banū Bakr. Banū Bakr, taking advantage of the unpreparedness of Banū Khuzāʿah, their traditional enemies, because of the peace granted by the Pact, launched a surprise attack, causing heavy casualties among them. When Khuzāʿah took refuge in the vicinity of the Sacred Mosque, Banū Bakr followed them therein, and continued to inflict heavy casualties on them. They were not inhibited or worried about violating the sanctity of the Sacred Mosque, saying, 'So what? Everybody steals and commits all kinds of crimes in the vicinity of the Sanctuary!' Khuzāʿah dispatched two delegations to the Prophet (peace be upon him) at Madīnah, one led by ʿAmr ibn Salīm of Banū Kaʿb and the other by Budayl ibn Warqā' al-Khuzāʿī. The Prophet (peace be upon him) received them well, and assured them of his full support.

8. THE ARRIVAL IN MADĪNAH OF ABŪ SUFYĀN

The Prophet (peace be upon him) predicted that Abū Sufyān would soon hurry to Madīnah, to mend fences with him. The Prophet's prophecy was soon fulfilled. Abū Sufyān made straight to the apartment of his daughter, Ramlah, the wife of the Prophet. When he tried to sit on the Prophet's bed, she hurriedly rolled it away, so as to deny him that. Abū Sufyān retorted: 'By God' he said, 'since you left me you have been stricken by evil.'[9] Then Abū Sufyān met the Prophet (peace be upon him), but the Prophet would not talk to him. 'If I had so much as an ant, I would fight you with it,' said the Prophet. ʿAlī, the Prophet's cousin, was gentler with Abū Sufyān, no doubt because he anticipated that Islam stood to gain something from the status of Abū Sufyān, as the paramount chief of the Quraysh.

'What shall I do?' asked Abū Sufyān in his predicament. 'Nothing.' replied ʿAlī. 'I don't see anything that can help you with the Prophet (peace be upon him). But you are the chief of Banū Kinānah, so get up and say that you would grant protection between men, (and thus avert a bloodbath in Makkah should fighting erupt there)!'

'Will that make any difference to my situation?' asked Abū Sufyān, anxiously.

'No it won't, but it is the only thing you can do,' replied ʿAlī ibn Abī Ṭālib. Abū Sufyān acted upon the advice of ʿAlī. He knew that he could no longer cling to his former status; times had changed, a new power and authority was soon to take over Arabia as a whole, including Makkah. If he was ever to hold any place in the new authority, he should act immediately and adopt a more pragmatic attitude. He should fit himself to a new role, less than what he was used to, but some measure of authority is better than none at all. So he took himself to the Prophet's Mosque and said what he was advised by ʿAlī to say, that he was extending his refuge and protection to people.

Obviously, the only meaningful protection he could realistically extend would be in Makkah. It is possible that the Prophet (peace be upon him) took that hint and envisaged a role for Abū Sufyān, when Makkah was eventually stormed by the Muslim army, led by the Prophet (peace be upon him) himself!

9. THE PROPHET MAKES PREPARATION TO ATTACK MAKKAH

The Prophet (peace be upon him) seized the opportunity of Quraysh's violation of the Ḥudaybīyah Pact. He had to move to a new and more advanced stage towards achieving the total supremacy of Islam in Arabia. Makkah, the stronghold of Arabian paganism must be overrun and cleansed of polytheism.

So the Prophet (peace be upon him) called the Muslims to mobilize and take up their arms. The streets of Madīnah were accustomed with the familiar cry: 'O horses of God be ready for battle.' The Prophet (peace be upon him), as usual, did not immediately disclose his destination. But when he was about to set out, he indicated that he was moving against Makkah. He prayed: 'O God, take the eyes and ears of the Quraysh, so that we may take them by surprise!'[10]

10. THE EPISODE OF ḤĀṬIB IBN ABĪ BALTA'AH

Ḥāṭib ibn Abī Balta'ah, a Companion of the Prophet of good standing, who had fought at Badr, feared for his son and family, who were still at Makkah. To win some favour with the Quraysh, so that his family would not be harmed, he wrote a letter to them informing them of the intention of the Prophet (peace be upon him) to invade Makkah. Gabriel informed the Prophet (peace be upon him) about the action of Ḥāṭib, and told him about the letter that he had sent with the freed-woman of Banū 'Abd al-Muṭṭalib, who was on her way to Makkah, in such and such location. The Prophet (peace be upon him) sent 'Alī ibn Abī Ṭālib and al-Zubayr ibn al-'Awwām after the woman. She was found and at first denied having the letter. However, when told that she would be stripped naked if need be, she produced the letter which she had hidden in her hair. The letter was taken to the Prophet (peace be upon him), who summoned Ḥāṭib, and asked him why he had done what he did. Ḥāṭib swore that he was a sincere believer, and had only acted as he had acted out of fear for the safety of his immediate family. ʿUmar ibn al-Khaṭṭāb wanted to chop off his head, but the Prophet (peace be upon him) prevented him saying: 'How do you know, ʿUmar, but that God has looked favourably upon those who fought at Badr,' and said: 'Do as you please for I have forgiven you!'

It is on this occasion that God revealed the verses of *Sūrah Al-Mumtaḥanah*.

> *O believers, take not my enemy and your enemy for friends, offering them love, though they have disbelieved in the truth that has come to you, expelling the Messenger and you because you believe in God your Lord, if you go forth to struggle in My way and seek My good pleasure, secretly loving them, yet I know very well what you conceal and what you declare; and whoever of you does that has gone astray, from the right way!*
>
> *If they come to you, they will be enemies to you, and stretch against you their hands and their tongues, to do you evil, and they wish that you may disbelieve. Neither your blood-kindred nor your children shall profit you upon the Day of Resurrection. He shall sort you out. And God sees the things you do.*
>
> *You have had a good example in Abraham and those with him, when they said to their people "We are quit of you and what you worship, apart from God. We disbelieve in you, and between us and you enmity has shown itself, and hatred for ever, until you believe in Allah alone…"* [*al-Mumtaḥinah* 60:1-4].

11. THE PROPHET'S MARCH TO MAKKAH

The Prophet (peace be upon him) set out towards Makkah on the tenth of Ramadan, with ten thousand soldiers, and appointed Abū Umm Kulthūm ibn Ḥusayn al-Fihrī, as governor of Madīnah. He started out fasting, but when he reached al-Kudayd, between Ustān and Amlaj, he broke his fast because of the journey. One unit in the army, led by the Prophet (peace be upon him) himself, was comprised exclusively of the Muhājirīn and the Anṣār only, and called the Green Battalion, because the soldiers were fully dressed in armour and their colours were visible. The tribes of Sulaymān and Muznah each contributed a thousand soldiers, and the rest of the tribes each contributed a thousand soldiers, and the rest of the tribes contributed fewer numbers. The Muslim army encamped at a place called Marr al-Ẓahrān. The Quraysh were still completely in the dark, concerning the march of the Muslim army. But apparently al-ʿAbbās, uncle of the Prophet (peace be upon him) and his principal informant among the Quraysh, had been informed about the march of the Prophet (peace be upon him) towards Makkah. Consequently, he met the Prophet (peace be upon him) at a place called al-Juḥfah with his family, as a Muhājir. Until then, al-ʿAbbās had resided in Makkah, in charge of the traditional privilege of the Hāshimī clan to provide the pilgrims with water. The Prophet (peace be upon him) was content with al-ʿAbbās' staying in Makkah to discharge that vital service of providing water to the pilgrims on behalf of the Hāshimites. Abū Sufyān ibn Ḥarb, and some notable Hāshimites met the Prophet, and became Muslims

Two notable Hāshimites, and relatives of the Prophet (peace be upon him), heard of his march to Makkah, no doubt from al-ʿAbbās, and came out to meet him, and declare their acceptance of Islam. They were Abū Sufyān ibn al-Ḥārith ibn ʿAbd al-Muṭṭalib and ʿAbdullāh ibn Umayyah ibn al-Mughīrah. At first, the Prophet (peace be upon him) refused to see them, because they were offensive to him, and to the Muslims at large. But his wife, Umm Salamah, intervened on their behalf, and the Prophet (peace be upon him) forgave them, and accepted them as Muslims. As to Abū Sufyān ibn Ḥarb, he came out of Makkah, seeking information about the Muslims and their whereabouts. By chance, he met with al-ʿAbbās ibn ʿAbd al-Muṭṭalib, the uncle of the Prophet, who had come out on the white mule of the Prophet (peace be upon him), hoping to advise the Quraysh to surrender. Al-ʿAbbās was worried that if the Muslim army forced its way into Makkah, the Quraysh would be utterly destroyed. He wanted to alert and warn the Quraysh against that eventuality. When al-ʿAbbās met Abū Sufyān, the following exchange took place between them:

'Abū'l-Faḍl?' asked Abū Sufyān.

'Yes I am,' answered al-ʿAbbās.

'What is the matter with you, O Abū'l-Faḍl, may my father and mother be your ransom?' asked Abū Sufyān!

'Woe to Quraysh And woe to you, Abū Sufyān. The Prophet is here with his army,' answered al-ʿAbbās.

'What am I to do, O al-ʿAbbās?' asked Abū Sufyān, quite upset.

'Ride behind me on the mule, so that we may go to the Prophet and ask his protection for you, or your head will be cut-off,' said al-ʿAbbās.

Thus, they rode on, and at every check, the people made way, saying: 'This is the uncle of the Prophet, al-ʿAbbās, riding his white mule.' But ʿUmar recognized Abū Sufyān: 'This is the enemy of God. This is Abū Sufyān. Thanks to God, He has delivered him to us, without agreement or any pledge on our part for him.'[11] Then ʿUmar hastened to the Prophet (peace be upon him), to ask his permission to chop off Abū Sufyān's head. Al-ʿAbbās recalled: 'I drove the mule hard so as to reach the Prophet (peace be upon him) before ʿUmar, so that I might reach the Prophet first and ask his protection for Abū Sufyān.'

Al-ʿAbbās did manage to reach the Prophet (peace be upon him) first: Abū Sufyān declared his conversion to Islam and ʿUmar's embassy was thwarted. The Prophet told al-ʿAbbās to take Abū Sufyān to a place, where he could see the strength of the Muslim army. The Prophet (peace be upon him) obviously wanted to bring home to Abū Sufyān, that it was futile for the Quraysh to resist, and to use Abū Sufyān's influence to convince the Quraysh to surrender peacefully, and in that way save the tribe, and the Holy City, from being stormed and destroyed. As we said before, the Prophet (peace be upon him) did not want to subjugate or destroy the Quraysh and the Holy City.

Al-ʿAbbās took Abū Sufyān to the nose of the valley, its narrowest and highest point, where the mountain projected inwards. Abū Sufyan then saw the Muslim squadrons pass by, with distinct standards, representing the different tribes allied with the Prophet (peace be upon him) at that time, such as Sulaym, Muzanah, and others. Abū Sufyān was impressed, but when the Green Squadron commanded by the Prophet (peace be upon him) himself passed by, he was quite awe-struck.

'Good heavens! ʿAbbās, who are those?'

On being told, he commented: 'Who can withstand them?' Then, turning to al-ʿAbbās, Abū Sufyān said: 'By God, O Abū'l-Faḍl, the authority of your brother's son has become very great.' Al-ʿAbbās then told him it was Prophethood and not mere secular authority that was behind the rise in his nephew's authority, and Abū Sufyān said he had no case against that. By then, al-ʿAbbās told him to hurry to his people, and advise them to surrender peacefully to the Prophet (peace be upon him) because fighting was of no avail and would lead to the destruction of the Quraysh and the City. Acting upon al-ʿAbbās' advice, Abū Sufyān entered Makkah and shouted at the top of his voice: 'O Quraysh! Muḥammad has come to you, with an army that you cannot withstand. Whoever enters the house of Abū Sufyān is safe!' His wife, Hind bint ʿUtbah, having seized his moustaches in her hands, said: 'Kill this fat greasy bladder of lure. What a rotten protector of a people!'[12]

But Abū Sufyān went on unabated: 'Do not let this crazy woman deceive you. For Muḥammad has come with an army that you cannot withstand! Whoever enters my house is safe.' But the people were confused. They said: 'May God slay you, what good is your house (for our masses)?'

Abū Sufyān then made an important amendment to his original announcement: 'He who enters the house of Abū Sufyān is safe! He who enters his own house, and shuts his door is safe! And he who enters the Holy Mosque is safe!'

This time, the crowds obeyed him, and they dispersed quickly and quietly into their homes.

12. LIMITED RESISTANCE BY QURAYSH

The Prophet's army entered the city from all four corners. The Prophet (peace be upon him) entered Makkah from its upper end, at Azkhar, ahead of his green squadron. Khālid ibn al-Walīd entered from the lower end, from al-Līt, his soldiers consisted of the Bedouins of Aslam, Sulaym, Ghifār, Muzaynah and Juhaynah. Al-Zubayr ibn al-ʿAwwām entered from Kudan at the left flank, and Saʿd ibn ʿUbādah from Kadāʾ. Abū ʿUbaydah entered from upper-Makkah, paving the way for the entrance of the Prophet (peace be upon him).

The only resistance offered was at the lower end, where Khālid was coming at al-Khandamah. It was led by ʿIkrimah ibn Abī Jahl, Ṣafwān ibn Umayyah and Suhayl ibn ʿAmr. During that brief and limited fighting, three Muslims fell martyrs, but thirteen were killed from the side of the Quraysh. That is according to Ibn Hishām; however, according to Ibn Saʿd, twenty four men were killed from the Quraysh and four from Hudhayl.

13. SAʿD IBN UBĀDAH DISMISSED FOR WORDS UTTERED[13]

Saʿd ibn ʿUbādah (Chief of al-Khazraj of the Anṣār) was overheard by ʿUmar ibn al-Khaṭṭab, saying: 'Today is a day of war. Today sanctuary is no more!' ʿUmar reported what Saʿd had said. The Prophet (peace be upon him) immediately summoned ʿAlī ibn Abī Ṭālib and said to him: 'Go to Saʿd ibn ʿUbādah and take the command from him. But according to Ibn Saʿd, the Prophet (peace be upon him) dismissed Saʿd ibn ʿUbādah and replaced him with his son, Qays.

14. THE PROPHET ENTERS MAKKAH IN HUMILITY

The Prophet (peace be upon him) entered Makkah with humility, his head cast down in thanks-giving to God, his chest almost touching the saddle of his camel. When he learnt about the fighting in lower Makkah, he protested, 'Did I not tell you no fighting today?' he said visibly annoyed.

The Muslims explained that it was Khālid, who had been attacked, and he had to fight back. The Prophet (peace be upon him) then said: this was God's determination, and it was all right. The Prophet (peace be upon him) then dismounted, and a hut of clay was made for him. When asked why he would not take up residence in his home, he answered: '῾Uqayl did not leave me any home in Makkah,' perhaps meaning that he had sold off the properties.

The Prophet stayed in his hut for a few hours of noon time, then entered the Holy Mosque, and encircled the Ka῾bah on his she-camel, al-Qaṣwā'. As he did so, he destroyed the idols, placed around the Ancient House. Ibn Sa῾d says, there were three hundred and sixty idols. The Prophet (peace be upon him) destroyed them saying: 'Truth has come, and falsehood has vanished, Surely falsehood is perishable.'

The Prophet (peace be upon him) then prayed two *rak῾ahs* at the corner of Abraham and sent for ῾Uthmān ibn Ṭalḥah, the keeper of the Ka῾bah, who kept the keys of the Ancient House. When the keys came, the Prophet (peace be upon him) entered the Ka῾bah and prayed two *rak῾ahs* inside it. Then he came out. People by then had crowded around the Ka῾bah in very big numbers.

15. THE PROPHET'S FAMOUS SERMON AT THE DOOR OF THE KA῾BAH

Standing there, at the door of the Ka῾bah, the people of Makkah converged to him, anxious to know their fate, and the Prophet's decision. It was a moment of truth, and they knew very well in their hearts, what they had made the Prophet (peace be upon him) go through, in the twenty years or so that had elapsed since he announced his Prophethood to them. They could only expect the worst.

The Prophet (peace be upon him) started his sermon by praising God, as was his custom. Then he said:

> I bear witness that there is no God but God, Alone, He has no partner. He has fulfilled His promise, and made His servant victorious, and defeated the Confederates alone! All claims of

privilege or blood or property are abolished by me (lit, are under my feet) except the custody of the House, and the watering of the pilgrims. O Quraysh! God has taken from you the mischief of paganism and its veneration of ancestors:

> *O people, We have created you from male and female, and made you into races and tribes, that you may know one another, of truth the most noble of you in sight of Allah are the most God-fearing.* [*al-Ḥujurāt* 49:13]

'What do you think I am going to do to you?' he asked. They replied: 'Good you are but a noble brother, and son of a noble brother!'

He said: 'Go your way in peace and freedom, for you are the freed ones!'[14]

There was much commotion and rejoicing as the silent, apprehensive crowds suddenly came alive to the prospect of a new freedom, a new beginning and a new all-embracing political and religious order. The Prophet (peace be upon him) then moved from the Ancient House to Mount al-Ṣafā, the very place where he first proclaimed his call to Islam, over twenty years before. ʿUmar ibn al-Khaṭṭāb stood under him for security as well as protocol purposes. The huge crowd of "the freed ones" struggled to reach the Prophet (peace be upon him), touch his hand, pay homage to him and greet him. They wanted to get a glimpse of his beautiful face, which on that great occasion was radiant as if a column of light was focused on it. Above all the Prophet (peace be upon him) loved Makkah as a Holy City and as home of his childhood days. The Prophet (peace be upon him) also loved the Quraysh, Arabs of Makkah, as his own people, whom he never hated, even when they rejected and persecuted him. Deep in his heart, he knew that they would be the ones most qualified to carry the call of Islam and brotherhood to the whole of humanity, only if they would become convinced by the truth of Islam. The Quraysh were heirs to the great Abrahamic legacy, which the Jews, the other Abrahamic tribe or race, had forsaken and abandoned. Most of all, the Quraysh Arabs possessed the great virtues of generosity, sincerity and bravery. Niggardliness, cowardice and hypocrisy were qualities unknown in Makkah. The Prophet (peace be upon him) had hoped, prayed and waited for the Quraysh to come round to Islam. It was for this reason that he never cursed or damned them. Even when the ignorant crowd in Ṭā'if had pelted him with stones and caused his gracious face to bleed, he had refused to damn or curse them, knowing that if a Prophet cursed his people, then terrible chastisement must befall them. Gabriel came to him at Ṭā'if and offered: 'Shall I make the two mountains collapse and press down upon them?'

'No! No! No! Do not do that. Rather, I hope that God will bring forth Muslims from their offspring,' protested the Prophet (peace be upon him) in eagerness, and apprehension.

The Prophet (peace be upon him) again displayed that same compassion that he had felt for the Quraysh on the eve of the conclusion of the Ḥudaybīyah Pact. He had felt dismay and grief at the prospect of the destruction of the Quraysh, by their insistence on war, and hostilities, with him: 'Woe to Quraysh, they have been devoured by successive wars with Muslims! Why don't they leave me to deal with the desert Bedouins? If I perish, that is what they want, but should I succeed, they would enter Islam with dignity and honour. Otherwise, they would fight when they have sufficient power.'

But nowhere did the Prophet (peace be upon him) show greater compassion and magnanimity than at the time when he conquered Makkah:

a. First of all, he sternly instructed his commanders not to resort to any fighting on that day, and showed displeasure when he knew of the battle fought by Khālid, at the lower end of the City, at al-Khandamah, and demanded an explanation for the incident. He was only satisfied, when he learned that Khālid had only fought back against his attackers in self-defence.

b. Secondly, he moved quickly to depose Sa'd ibn 'Ubādah, the chief of al-Khazraj, when it was reported to him that he was threatening to kill the Makkans. Sa'd had said: "Today is the day of war! Today Sanctuary is no more!"

c. The modesty he displayed as he entered Makkah was sufficient to indicate to everybody around, that he was in no mood for revenge or killing.

d. Last, but not least, the great amnesty and forgiveness he gave the Makkans, his former enemies and persecutors, was perhaps unparalleled in history.

The Prophet's understanding that the Quraysh Arabs would play a crucial role in carrying the banner of Islam to mankind, was decisively borne out by subsequent developments. 'Umar ibn al-Khaṭṭāb described the Arabs in general as 'the material force of Islam.' The Quraysh were the elite of the Arabs who epitomized their best qualities of intellect as well as character.

The view that the Arabs were destined to play a major role in the spread of this universal religion is emphasized in the Qur'ān itself. Time and again, God reminds the Arab Muslims of His great favours and blessings upon them: Says God in the Qur'ān:

> *Surely, there has come to you (O Arabs) a Messenger from amongst yourselves (your race). Grieving to him is your suffering, anxious is he over you, gentle to the believers, compassionate.* [*al-Tawbah* 9:128]

As stated by this verse of *Sūrah al-Tawbah* (Repentance), the Prophet (peace be upon him) was very anxious and concerned that the Quraysh, in particular, and the Arabs in general, should enter into the true religion of God and in this way be saved. Thus he called them to Islam in the most vigorous way, argued with them, fought and struggled with them, but, most of all, he hoped, prayed, and waited for them to come round and uphold the banner of Islam because he knew very well that they were uniquely qualified to do so.

In another verse, the Qur'ān also reminds the Arab Muslims of God's greatest favour upon them:

> *Truly Allah was most gracious to the believers when He raised up among them a Messenger from themselves: to recite to them His signs (his verses), and to purify them, and to teach them the Book and the Wisdom, though before they were in manifest error.* [*Āl ʿImrān* 3:164]

The Qur'ān tells us also that this was no mere accident of history, but part of God's grand design for mankind. The commissioning of Muḥammad, descendent of Ishmael, son of Abraham, as the last Messenger to mankind, and the Seal of the Prophets, was in answer to Abraham's most sincere and passionate prayer in Makkah, when he and his son Ishmael finished the building of the Ka ʿbah:

> *And when Abraham and Ishmael with him, raised the foundation of the House. Our Lord, receive this from us, you are the All-Hearing, All-Knowing. And, our Lord, make us submissive (Muslims) to you and of our seed a nation submissive to you, and show us our holy places, and turn toward us (relent to us) you are the All-Relenting, All-Merciful, and, our Lord, you send among them a Messenger, one of them, who shall recite to them your verses, and teach them the Book and the Widsom, and purify them. You are the All-Mighty, the All-Wise.* [*al-Baqarah* 2:127-129].

Although Islam is a universal religion for all mankind, it is, at the same time, the spiritual heritage of the progeny of Ishmael, son of Abraham, of the Arab nation as a whole, and it is their primary and foremost responsibility, duty and privilege to uphold and convey it to humanity at large.

16. A GREAT DAY AND A GREAT MOMENT

As the Prophet (peace be upon him) stood there on Mount as-Safa, his face gleaming with joy and delight, and a great sense of fulfilment, the crowd grew bigger and bigger. The Quraysh were almost certainly there, to a man, as they heard of the great pardon which the Prophet (peace be upon him) had accorded to them. They were suddenly anxious to be part of that great day, part of the moment, and part of the new movement, and new political order. In a sense, the new emerging authority was their own, as Muḥammad himself was their own. Was he not a Qurayshite par excellence? As Abū Sufyān did not find it impossible to reverse his loyalties, who had been the figure-head of the pre-Islamic Arabian aristocracy, the ordinary men of the Quraysh found it even less difficult to do so.

For the Prophet (peace be upon him), who was a direct descendant of Ishmael, son of Abraham, it was indeed the moment of home-coming, of reunion and a great moment of restoration. The great spiritual legacy of Ishmael and the Ancient House of God, rebuilt and raised by his ancestors, Ishmael and Abraham, had now returned to the custody of the sons of Ishmael and Abraham, as cleaned and rescued from the custody of paganism. To reinforce this sense of legitimacy, justice, charity and fidelity, the Prophet called upon ʿUthmān ibn Ṭalḥah, and gave him the keys of the Kaʿbah. 'Here! Take these keys, today is a day of charity and fidelity.' Before that, ʿAlī ibn Abī Ṭālib came along, and asked the Prophet (peace be upon him) to give the Hāshimite the privilege of the custody of the Kaʿbah, in addition to their original privilege of giving water to the pilgrims. But the Prophet (peace be upon him) refused and returned the keys to ʿUthmān ibn Ṭalḥah, of the Banū Shaybah, the original custodians of the Kaʿbah, saying: 'I give you O Hāshimites what will be to you a burden, and an obligation, and not a right or a privilege…'[15]

17. THE PROPHET'S SHORT SERMON AT THE DOOR OF THE KAʿBAH[16]

When he addressed the masses of Quraysh, for the first time after he entered Makkah victoriously, the Prophet (peace be upon him) gave a short but momentous speech. The basic ideas in that speech were meant to herald a new phase in the history of Arabia, a phase that would constitute a total break with the norms of the pre-Islamic *jāhiliyyah* (or age of ignorance). The sermon can be broken down into the following basic notions.

a. All the rites of privileges, blood or property were all discredited and abolished, excepting the custody of the Holy Mosque, and providing water to the pilgrims. This meant a total break with the socio-religious order of Pre-Islamic Arabia, with the privileges of the aristocracy of the Quraysh, and that of the religious order of the oracles of Hubal, and the other allies of Makkah and Ṭā'if. It also meant a ban on the blood feuds that were responsible for so much fighting and suffering in pre-Islamic Arabia, together with usury, fornication and the burial of young girls alive, and last but not least, the worship of idols as well as excessive veneration of the ancestors.

b. The first notion was meant to prevent new outbreaks of war and fighting, the second was meant to curb foul play with arms, leading to accidental and unnecessary loss of life. That is the reason for the heavy penalty of a hundred camels as blood ransom. The Bedouins had to be educated about the value of human life; as it was the gift of God, none should take it but God Himself. Thus if a life was taken by error, a ransom, and a heavy one, must be paid. A hundred camels was a lot of wealth, with fifty of them being pregnant, and served as a good and effective deterrent against such conduct, as led to wanton loss of life.

c. The third notion was that the Holy Mosque should continue to have its sanctity as the House of God, rebuilt and raised by Abraham and son Ishmael. The Holy Mosque was the spiritual heritage of all Muslims, especially of the sons of Ishmael. So the privileges of the custody of the house, and the watering of the pilgrims were not abolished. They continued to be the privilege of the Muslims in general, Banū Shaybah and Banū Hāshim in particular.

d. Racial preference and prejudice were abolished, in particular the *jāhiliyyah* Arabs' arrogant claim to be ethnically or racially superior to other non-Arabs was rejected. In fact, all racial discrimination and cultural chauvinism was declared null and void. The Prophet recited verse 13 of *Sūrah al-Ḥujurāt* (the apartments) the famous verse which rejects outright any kind of discrimination or inequalities among men. All men are equal in the sight of God. They are all the off-spring of Adam, and Adam sprang or was created from dust and clay. God says in this verse:

> *O mankind, we have created you of male and female, and made you into races and tribes, that you may know each other. Surely the noblest among you in the sight of Allah, is the most God-fearing of you. Allah is All-knowing All-Aware…* [*al-Ḥujurāt* 49:13]

18. NAMES OF THOSE DECLARED DEAD, (EVEN IF THEY CLUNG TO THE CURTAINS OF KA'BAH)

In exception to the general amnesty and pardon declared by the Prophet (peace be upon him) to the people of Makkah, there were a few persons who were to be killed, because of the exceptionally terrible crimes they had committed against the Prophet (peace be upon him), Islam and the Muslims. Some managed to meet the Prophet (peace be upon him), before they were killed, and, as was his habit, the Prophet (peace be upon him) pardoned them. But those who did not make it, were seized and killed. Those excluded from the general amnesty were as follows:

a. 'Abdullāh ibn Sa'd, foster-brother of 'Uthmān ibn 'Affān, had been a Muslim and one of the Prophet's amanuenses. But he ran off to Makkah and became an apostate. When the Prophet (peace be upon him) entered Makkah, he was excepted from the general amnesty, and was to be killed. However, he managed to escape to his foster-brother ʿUthmān, and he took him to the Prophet (peace be upon him), who forgave him, after some hesitation.

b. ʿAbdullāh ibn Khatal, who was employed by the Prophet (peace be upon him) to collect *Zakāt*. He had an assistant whom he killed; he himself apostatized and ran away to Makkah with the *Zakāt* money he had collected. He had two slave girls who used to sing abusive songs about the Prophet (peace be upon him). The Prophet (peace be upon him) ordered him to be killed, together with the two slave girls. ʿAbdullāh ibn Khatal was killed, and one of the slave-girls. The other slave-girl made her way to the Prophet (peace be upon him), asked to be forgiven and he forgave her.

c. Al-Ḥuwayrith ibn Nuqaydh, a man who used to follow the Prophet in Makkah and harm him whenever possible. He also followed the daughters of the Prophet, Fāṭimah and Umm Kulthūm, and caused them to fall to the ground by agitating the camels on which they mounted. He was later killed by ʿAlī ibn Abī Ṭālib.

d. Miqyās ibn Ṣubābah who, having killed an Anṣārī Muslim who killed his brother by mistake, had fled to Makkah. He was seized, and killed.

e. ʿIkrimah ibn Abī Jahl was also one those excepted from the amnesty. He fled to Yemen. However, his wife, who was a Muslim, came to the Prophet (peace be upon him), secured amnesty for him, then went to Yemen and brought him back. ʿIkrimah converted to Islam, became a sincere Muslim and fought well in the defence of Islam.

f. Sārah, the slave-girl of ʿAbd al-Muṭṭalib, used to compose abusive poetry about the Prophet (peace be upon him). She was supposed to be killed, but managed to meet the Prophet (peace be upon him), and ask his forgiveness, and he forgave her. All in all, the number of persons executed was very small indeed: three men and one woman, a facet which speaks a great deal about the tolerance of the Prophet (peace be upon him), and the human nature of the religion of Islam.

19. THE PROPHET DECLARED MAKKAH AN INVIOLABLE SANCTUARY

On the second day of his stay in Makkah, the Prophet declared it a Sacred Sanctuary. Banū Khuzāʿah killed some individuals of their former enemies. But the Prophet (peace be upon him) forbade any further killing, and gave an address declaring the Sanctity of the city. He said:

> 'O men, God made Makkah an Inviolable Sanctuary, the day he created heavens and earth. So the City is inviolable until the Day of Resurrection. It is not lawful for anyone, who believes in God and the Hereafter, to shed blood in it or to cut a tree. It has not been lawful for anyone before to violate its sanctity and it is unlawful for anybody after me to do so. It has been made violable to me this day as an exception, because God is angry with its inhabitants. But now it has returned to its sanctity again. If anybody would say otherwise and point to my killing some persons in it these days, tell him that God had made it violable for the Prophet, only as an exception.'

20. THE PROPHET REASSURES THE ANṢĀR

The Prophet (peace be upon him) stayed in Makkah, after its conquest, for eighteen days and nights, praying as a traveller would pray, two *rakʿahs* instead of four. He was evidently enjoying his stay in Makkah. He used to frequent the Holy Mosque to pray and to make *Ṭawāf*. Then he would go to Mount Al-Ṣafā, and meet the delegations. One day he was sitting there, and ʿAbdullāh ibn Umm Maktūm walked between Al-Ṣafā and al-Marwah, reciting poetry on the love of Makkah.

The Anṣār became uneasy. They feared that Muḥammad might now prefer to stay in Makkah. One day, he was deeply engulfed in his supplications at Mount Al-Ṣafā, a group of the Anṣār crowded around him, by now very anxious for the Prophet (peace be upon him) whom they loved more than they loved their own kith and kin. They said to each other, 'now that the Prophet has settled nicely at Makkah, and found his beloved ones, do you think he would go to Madīnah again?' When the Prophet (peace be upon him) finished his prayer he addressed them. 'What is it that you were saying?' asked the Prophet.

'Nothing, O Messenger of God, nothing,' answered the Anṣār. But the Prophet (peace be upon him) insisted on hearing what they were whispering about, and so they told him. Then he said: 'God forbids, God forbids! The living, is your living and the dying is your dying,' meaning that he would live and die with them in Madīnah! Then he prayed passionately that God will shower this Mercy on the Anṣārs and their future generations.[17]

21. THE ERROR OF KHĀLID IBN AL WALĪD

Khālid ibn al-Walīd was sent to Banū Judhaymah ibn ʿAmr ibn ʿAbd Manāt ibn Kinānah as a *dāʿiyah*, that is, to teach, not to fight, together with a number of the Muhājirīn and Anṣār. When he reached them, he called out. 'Put down your weapons, if you people have embraced Islam.'

The men put down their arms, but then Khālid seized and killed them by surprise. When ʿAbudllāh ibn ʿUmar ibn al-Khaṭṭāb and Sālim, the freed man of Abū Ḥudhayfah, attempted to stop him, he yelled at them. When the Prophet (peace be upon him) heard of the incident, he was very upset indeed. He faced the Holy Mosque, and raised his two hands towards heaven and prayed.

'O God, I am innocent before you of what Khālid had done.' He said that phrase and repeated it three times. Then he dispatched ʿAlī ibn Abī Ṭālib, with a lot of money, to pay blood money for the deceased men, considered killed by mistake. ʿAlī apologized on behalf of the Prophet (peace be upon him) for the terrible error committed by Khālid.

22. THE SECURE STATUS OF THE FIRST MUSLIMS (*AHL AL-SĀBIQAH*)

When Khālid returned, he had an argument with ʿAbd al-Raḥmān ibn ʿAwf, who protested against the killings. When the Prophet (peace be upon him) met Khālid, he rebuked him for the killing, and also for his quarrel with ʿAbd al-Raḥmān ibn ʿAwf. 'Leave my Companions alone, O Khālid. By God, if you have a mountain of gold and you spend all of it in the way of God, you would not reach a reward of a morning or evening travail of one of them…'

The status and the contribution of the first Muslims is quite secure in Islam, in the Qur'ān as well as in the *Sunnah* and the *Sīrah*.

These were the pioneering Muslims, who accepted Islam when that acceptance put their whole life in peril and jeopardy. ʿUmar ibn al-Khaṭṭāb, when he organized his government, composed a comprehensive register of all Muslims in the state, according to the criteria of:

a. precedence in entering Islam.

b. making the two *Hijras* to Abyssinia and to Madīnah.

c. participating in the expeditions (battles).

Even stipends were determined according to the above criteria. The Prophet (peace be upon him) declared that there would be no *Hijrah* after the conquest of Makkah, but sincerity in religion and *jihād* in the way of God.

He stayed in Makkah for about eighteen days and nights, receiving men and women who came to pay homage to him. On the day he was receiving women, Hind bint ʿUtbah, wife of Abū Sufyān, the one who had chewed the liver of Ḥamzah, came in disguise, fearing for her life. The Prophet (peace be upon him) took the woman's pledge to witness that there is no god but God, that Muḥammad is His Messenger, that they would obey Him for better or worse, and that they would not steal or fornicate.

'O Messenger of God, does a free woman fornicate?' asked Hind in surprise.

The Prophet recognized her voice: 'Is that you Hind bint 'Utbah?'

'Yes, Messenger of God, I bear witness that there is no God, but God, and that you are His Messenger.'

The Prophet (peace be upon him) laughed, and forgave her the heinous crimes she had committed against him, Ḥamzah and the Muslims. Hind then migrated to Madīnah, while her husband Abū Sufyān and her son Mu'āwiyah joined the *jihād* expeditions.

CHAPTER 9

After the Conquest of Makkah, Ḥunayn and Tabūk

The chief tribes residing in the territories to the east of Makkah were Hawāzin, and Thaqīf of Ṭā'if. When they heard about the conquest of Makkah, they called for a gathering to consider their position vis-à-vis the Prophet (peace be upon him) and the Muslims. That gathering was attended by the chiefs and leaders of Hawāzin, Thaqīf and some lesser tribes like Naṣr, Jusham, Sa'd ibn Bakr and some clans of Banū Hilāl. The powerful clans of Ka'b and Kilāb of Banū Hudhayl stayed away from the gathering, which was largely organized by Mālik ibn 'Awf, the unwise or inexperienced chief of Hawāzin at large. Thaqīf attended, but they had no paramount chief, and were represented by their elders and apparently accepted the overall presidency of Mālik ibn 'Awf, the chief of Hawāzin. The meeting was also attended by the famous knight and poet Durayd ibn al-Ṣimmah, of Banū Jusham.

The strategy of Mālik bin 'Awf was to confront the Prophet (peace be upon him) half-way between Makkah and Ṭā'if. He encamped at a valley called Awṭas, having ordered every soldier to bring with him his family and wealth, mainly camels and sheep. The old and experienced Durayd ibn Abī al-Ṣimmah did not like Mālik's strategy for the battle. He asked:[1] 'O Mālik, you are the chief and leader of your people, and this is a very important day, which will have grave consequences. Why, for goodness sake, did you order the men to bring their women, children and animals?'

'I wanted every man to have his women, children and wealth with him, so that he would know what it is he is defending,' replied Mālik.

'Stop! By God, you are nothing but a shepherd of sheep! Does anything stop one who is fleeing the battle? If the war goes in your favour, you would have no use except for a warrior with a sword or spear, but should it turn against you, you would be disgraced and lose your families and wealth as well.'

When Durayd further learnt about the absence of Kaʿb and Kilāb, the two most powerful clans of Hawāzin, he said sadly 'Both bravery and strength are absent.' Then Durayd added: 'This is a day which I have not witnessed (as a warrior) nor did I miss altogether.'

Durayd then composed poetry, which can be translated into English as follows: 'Would that I were young again, I would ride forward gently leading long manned steeds like young antelopes.'

Durayd then advised Mālik to change his strategy, send the women, children and animals home, meet the advancing Muslims on horse-back, and be ready to manoeuvre according to the fortunes of battle. But Mālik insisted on his strategy, even threatening to kill himself, if Hawāzin did not obey him. In this way, he got his way, and the battle was fought as he planned.

1. ANGELS SEEN FIGHTING WITH THE MUSLIMS

Mālik sent out a reconnaissance force which came back broken and defeated: 'What happened?' asked Mālik. 'We met white men riding on black horses, wearing turbans and they struck at us such as you see!'

2. THE PROPHET SENT A SPY

When the Prophet (peace be upon him) learnt of the encampment of the enemy, he sent one ʿAbdullāh ibn Hadrad al-Aslamī to infiltrate their ranks, and bring exact information as to their numbers, weapons and dispositions for battle. Ibn Hadrad did as commanded, and came back with the information, undetected and unharmed. The Prophet (peace be upon him), no doubt, made good use of that information.

3. THE PROPHET BORROWED WEAPONS

The Prophet (peace be upon him) borrowed some weapons from Ṣafwān ibn Umayyah, still a non-believer at that time. Ṣafwān was pardoned by the Prophet (peace be upon him), and given the option to remain an unbeliever for some time, was ready and willing to lend the weapons. In all, he gave about a hundred steel shields, as well as camels to carry them.

4. THE PROPHET MARCHED TO ḤUNAYN

The Prophet (peace be upon him) then marched to Ḥunayn, his army consisting of twelve thousand soldiers; ten from Madīnah and two thousand who had joined at Makkah. 'Utbah ibn Usayd was appointed governor of Makkah in the absence of the Prophet (peace be upon him).

This army reached through a narrow and steep side of the valley of Ḥunayn, when it was still dark before dawn. Here the Muslims were taken in a severe ambush by Hawāzin, who had concealed themselves among the rocks and defiles of the valley. The Muslims' lines were shattered in a few hours of fighting, and they ran for their lives in every direction. But the Prophet (peace be upon him), just as in Uḥud, held his ground, with a few Muslims around him. Al-'Abbās, uncle of the Prophet, and who had a strong voice, was instructed by the Prophet (peace be upon him) to shout at the top of his voice: 'O Anṣār! O comrades of the Acacia Tree (of the Pledge of Riḍwān)!'

They answered: 'Here we are O Prophet! Here we are, O Prophet!'

The Anṣār rallied to the Prophet (peace be upon him), about a hundred of them. They dismounted from their fleeing camels, which they could not control. Around the Prophet (peace be upon him), only a few Companions stood their ground. They included:

1. Abū Bakr al-Ṣiddīq.
2. ʿUmar ibn al-Khaṭṭāb.
3. ʿAlī ibn Abī Ṭālib.
4. Al-ʿAbbās ibn ʿAbd al-Muṭṭalib.
5. Abū Sufyūn ibn al-Ḥārith ibn ʿAbd al-Muṭṭalib.
6. Jaʿfar ibn Abī Sufyān ibn al-Ḥārith.
7. Al-Faḍl ibn al-ʿAbbās ibn ʿAbd al-Muṭṭalib.
8. Rabīḥ ibn al-Ḥārith.
9. Usāmah ibn Zayd.
10. Ayman ibn ʿUbayd, the son of Barakah, the Abyssinian maid of the Prophet who was martyred that day.

Some of the new Muslims from *al-Ṭulaqāʾ* (the freed ones) were secretly pleased with the defeat of the Muslims. Abū Sufyān ibn Ḥarb said, jestingly, 'These fleeing Muslims can only be stopped by the Red Sea!' Another, by the name Jabalah ibn al-Ḥanbal, brother of Sufyān ibn Umayyah (then still an unbeliever), said: 'Today, the magic spell has been broken.'[2]

But one Quraysh fighter told them to shut up, saying, 'Be quiet or I will strike your face! By Allah, to have as a master one of the Quraysh is more to my liking than to have a master from Hawāzin.'

5. THE PROPHET CHARGES AGAIN

When about a hundred men, mostly from the Anṣār, had assembled around the Prophet, he again charged the enemy, his face red with the fire of courage and determination shouting: 'I am the Messenger of Allah!'

The Muslims charged with the Prophet (peace be upon him), and the fortunes of the battle were reversed by a tiny minority. When the Muslims had felt secure in their big numbers, and boasted about them, they were defeated. They had said. 'We will not be defeated today because of deficiency in our numbers.' But when they were a sincere and steadfast minority, they won the battle. Allah says in the Qur'ān: *How often a little company has overcome a numerous company by God's leave, and God is with the patient.* [*al-Baqarah* 2: 249]

Umm Salīm bint Milḥān, and her husband Abū Ṭalḥah, were among those who held their ground around the Prophet (peace be upon him). Umm Salīm had a dagger in her fist. When the Prophet (peace be upon him) saw her, he called out to her: 'Umm Salīm! Umm Salīm!'

'Yes, O Prophet,' she said: 'Shall I kill those who ran away from you, as I kill those who attacked you, O Prophet?' she asked.

'No! No!' said the Prophet. 'Is Allah not sufficient unto us, O Umm Salīm?'

The Prophet (peace be upon him), when surveying the casualties and the captives of Ḥunayn, found a dead woman. 'Who killed this woman?' he asked.

'It is Khālid ibn al-Walīd who killed her, O Messenger of Allah,' they said.

'Tell Khālid that the Prophet prohibits killing women, children or slaves.'[3]

6. AL-SHAYMĀ', THE FOSTER SISTER OF THE PROPHET, TAKEN CAPTIVE

Al-Shaymā', the foster-sister of the Prophet(peace be upon him), was taken captive, among many women, after the defeat of Hudhayl and Thaqīf at Ḥunayn. She told them that she was the foster-sister of the Prophet (peace be upon him), when he was with his nurse (Ḥalīmah al-Sa'diyyah of Banū Zuhrah). They took her to the Prophet, and the Prophet (peace be upon him) asked her how she would prove that she was actually his foster-sister. Al-Shaymā' then showed him a scar on her back, which was a result of a bite by the Prophet (peace be upon him), when he had ridden on her as a child. When the Prophet (peace be upon him) saw the scar, he remembered the incident, and was greatly moved by pity and compassion for her. He gave her the choice, either to stay with him, in good standing and good company, in affection and honour, or join her own family and people with gifts and presents. She chose the latter option. The Prophet (peace be upon him) gave her a male servant, and a female servant. She had the two marry, and their children continued to live with and serve her family, for a long time afterwards.

7. THE MARTYRS OF ḤUNAYN

The number of those killed at Ḥunayn, among the Muhājirīn and Anṣār was very small indeed. Ibn Hishām gives only four names, the most notable among which was Ayman ibn ʿUbayd, maternal brother of Usāmah ibn Zayd. Their mother was Barakah, the Abyssinian, the wet nurse of the Prophet (peace be upon him). Ibn Saʿd, gives only three names, but he says that a good number of the Bedouins of Banū Naṣr, and Banū Rabāb were killed. So much so that a Muslim, apparently of the latter tribe, said, 'Alas, the Banū Rabāb have all perished!' The Prophet prayed for them: 'O Allah, reward and compensate the Banū Rabāb in their calamity.' It would appear that the Bedouins of Banū Rabāb bore the brunt of the casualties, because they were the front battalions of the Muslims' army, attacking Ḥunayn. It is these Bedouins who took to flight, when the battle started, thus causing the initial defeat of the Muslim army. So, it would seem that they were not listed as casualties, because their names were not known by the historians.

8. THE EXCLUSION OF THE ANṢĀR FROM THE DISTRIBUTION OF THE SPOILS

The accumulated spoils of the battle of Ḥunayn were huge. The tribes of Hudhayl, Thaqīf and their allies were among the richest in

Arabia. Their wealth was only matched by that of the Jews of the north, especially Khaybar and Fadak. Their region was famous for its orchards, agricultural produce, camels and sheep, gold and silver. Moreover, the ill-conceived strategy of the leader of Hudhayl had made them bring all their wealth and families behind their fighting lines. For all these reasons, the spoils were tremendous and very great: Ibn Saʿd gave the following list:

a. Six thousand captives, men, women and children;

b. Twenty-four thousand camels;

c. More than forty thousand head of sheep;

d. Four thousand ounces of silver.

The Prophet (peace be upon him) distributed the bulk of the war spoils before he left the battlefield. He gave large portions to the 'freed ones' of the Quraysh, but gave nothing to the Anṣār and Muhājirīn. Among the Quraysh who received spoils were:

a. Abū Sufyān ibn Ḥarb: a hundred camels, and forty ounces of silver. He said, 'And my son Yazīd?' And he was given another hundred camels and forty ounces of silver. He said, 'And my son Muʿāwiyah?' And was given a further hundred camels and forty ounces of silver.

b. Ḥakīm ibn Ḥizām: a hundred camels. He asked again and got another hundred camels.

c. Suhayl ibn ʿAmr (the chief negotiator of the Quraysh at Ḥudaybīyah): a hundred camels.

d. Al-Naḍr ibn al-Ḥārith: a hundred camels.

e. Al-Ḥārith ibn Hishām: a hundred camels.

f. Ṣafwān ibn Umayyah (who had just became a Muslim): a hundred camels.

g. Ḥuwayṭib ibn al-ʿUzzā: a hundred camels.

h. Makhramah ibn Nawfal (also from the Quraysh): fifty camels.

i. ʿUmayr ibn Wahb al-Jumaḥī (from the Quraysh): fifty camels

j. Hishām ibn ʿAmr, ibn Yarbūʿ and ʿUdayy ibn Qays: all got fifty camels each. From his gift, the Prophet (peace be upon him) gave ʿUsayd ibn Jāriyah and al-ʿAlā' ibn Ḥārithah each a hundred camels.

The Prophet (peace be upon him) also distributed some of the spoils, indeed substantial shares, among the heads of the Bedouin tribes, that fought with the Muslims. However, nothing was given either to the Anṣār or the Muhājirīn, who felt unfairly dealt with. Especially among the Anṣār, feelings of resentment were running high: 'The Prophet was favouring his own kith and kin from the Quraysh, who had done all they could to harm the Prophet and the Muslims, and who obstruct the cause of Islam, who had not become Muslim, until there was no other option for them, but to submit to the overwhelming power of a victorious Islam,' the Anṣār complained bitterly.'

The Prophet (peace be upon him) heard about those murmurings and resentments of the Anṣār. He called them for a meeting. When they were assembled in his council, he began:[4] 'O men of the Anṣār, what is this statement I have heard of you? And what is this resentment in your hearts against me? Did I not find you poor, and Allah made you rich? Were you not enemies of one another? And Allah softened your hearts towards each other, and gave you peace and reconciliation?

The Anṣār answered: 'Yes indeed, Allah and His Messenger are most kind and generous.'

The Prophet continued: 'Why don't you answer me, O Anṣār?'

'How can we answer you O Prophet of Allah? Kindness and generosity belongs to Allah and His Messenger,' said the Anṣār.

The Prophet changed his tone so as to elicit a franker answer from the Anṣār, who did not speak their minds, out of love, respect and veneration for the Prophet (peace be upon him). The Prophet then said: 'Had you so wished, you could have said with truth: 'You came to us discredited, and we believed you; deserted and we helped you; a fugitive, and we harboured you; are you angry with me, because of these trivialities of this world (meaning spoils), which I gave to these people (i.e. the new Muslims) hoping to win over their hearts to Islam, while entrusting you to your faith and conviction? Are you not satisfied that men should take away flocks and herds, while you take back with you the Messenger of Allah? By Him, in whose hand is the soul of Muḥammad, but for the migration (the *hijrah*), I should like to have been one of the Anṣār myself! If all men take one way, and the Anṣār another, I will take the way of the Anṣār, May Allah have mercy on the Anṣār, their sons, and their sons' sons.'

The people wept until tears ran down their beards, as they said: 'We are indeed satisfied with the Messenger of Allah as our lot and portion, O Messenger of Allah.'

9. A DEPUTATION FROM THE VANQUISHED HAWĀZIN VISIT THE PROPHET

A deputation from the vanquished tribe of Hawāzin came to the Prophet (peace be upon him). They asked him to set free their captured men and women. They said, 'These included the people of your foster mother, Ḥalīmah as Saʿdiyyah,' for Banū Saʿd were a clan of Hawāzin. The Prophet's heart softened, and he was very lenient with them. He at once ordered all those captives in his own custody to be set free. But some of the captives were dispersed among the allied tribes. So the Prophet (peace be upon him) asked the delegation of Hawāzin to come back when the people assembled for the noon-prayer. The Muslims assembled, and when the prayer was over, the delegation made their request again, acting in this way, on the advice of the Prophet (peace be upon him). They mentioned the fact that among the captives were the foster-aunts and uncles of the Prophet (peace be upon him) himself. Then the Prophet stood up and declared all the Hawāzin's captives at his disposal set free. The Anṣār and the Muhājirūn did the same. Then most of the Bedouin tribes also did likewise, except for a few of them. When the Prophet (peace be upon him) requested them to free their captives, promising them good compensation in the future, all the remaining captives were set free, and the majority of Hawāzin entered Islam, as a result of that magnanimous and generous act of the Prophet (peace be upon him).

10. THE SIEGE OF AT-ṬĀ'IF

The Prophet (peace be upon him), after Ḥunayn, marched towards Ṭā'if. He laid siege to that city for seventeen or twenty days, but was unable to overcome its resistance. The city was well fortified, with huge and strong doors, well guarded by skilful bowmen. The Prophet (peace be upon him) used a catapult to shell the city, but to no avail. Then he tried to storm it with wooden vans, filled with men, and pushed up to the walls; the vans were covered with leather so as to protect the men from the enemy archers on the towers of the fortress. But Thaqīf was able to destroy their vans, by pouring hot iron down on them, and in this way setting them alight. A number of the Companions of the Prophet were killed by archers, and the Prophet's army was forced to retreat a considerable distance, beyond the reach of the bowmen.

The Prophet (peace be upon him) saw that no good was going to come of that siege. Ṭā'if was a very rich city, and had food provisions that might last them many months, possibly years. Moreover, it would have been very costly, in terms of casualties, for the Muslims as well as for the enemy, if he were to take the city by force. There was no point in that, because Thaqīf would eventually have no option, but to become Muslims, as Arabia as a whole, and the two major tribal groupings, Quraysh, and Hawāzin, had already accepted Islam. So, the Prophet (peace be upon him) called upon his army to depart.

Before marching to Madīnah, the Prophet (peace be upon him) entered Makkah, once more, this time to perform the rites of the *ʿUmrah*, or the lesser pilgrimage.

After that, he hurried on to Madīnah, where the site of his government, and the home of his larger family, and his Mosque were all situated. The city of Madīnah was destined soon to be the focal point for the visitation of almost all the tribes of Arabia from near and far, in the peninsula. The year of deputations lay ahead. Before that there was the unfinished military confrontation with the Romans, and their Arab clients of Banū Ghassān. It must be recalled that the battle of Mu'tah was far from being decisive, and apparently the Roman military build-up did not ease, on the northern boundaries of the Muslim state of Madīnah.

11. THE PROPHET ARRIVES IN MADĪNAH AND THE ADVENT OF KAʿB IBN ZUHAYR

The poet Kaʿb ibn Zuhayr, son of the famous pre-Islamic Arabian poet Zuhayr ibn Abī Salmah, one of those whose poems was among the seven Muʿallaqāt hung on the walls of the Kaʿbah, had written poetry against the Prophet (peace be upon him), and against Islam and the Muslims. When Islam had spread far and wide in Arabia, and the Quraysh and Hawāzin were subdued, Zuhayr hurried to Madīnah, and hid in the house of one of his friends, until he could come to the Prophet (peace be upon him), and secure his pardon. Then he composed his famous and most charming poem, known as *al-Burdah*, because the Prophet (peace be upon him) liked it so much, that he gave his own green mantle (*Burdah*) as a reward to Zuhayr, and he himself put it on him.

Kaʿb ibn Zuhayr ibn Abī Salmā praised the Prophet (peace be upon him) and praised the Muhājrīn, but he did not praise the Anṣār, because an Anṣārī almost killed him when he was trying to enter the council of the Prophet (peace be upon him). It was even believed that he had censured them, when referring to them as 'the black folks.' It is reported that, had it not been for the Prophet's honouring him, they might have killed him. To amend this, the Prophet (peace be upon him) advised him to praise the Anṣār, and he composed another poem, later on, on the virtues of the Anṣār and they were satisfied. The gist of what Kaʿb ibn Zuhayr had said in the above poem has been translated by A. Guillaume,[5] as follows:

> 'Suʿad is gone, and today my heart is love-sick enthralled to her
> Unrequited, bound with chains and as to Suʿad, when she came forth
> On the morn of departure
> Was but as a gazelle
> With bright black downcast eyes
> When she smiles, she lays bare
> A shining row of side-teeth
> That seems to have been bathed
> Once and twice in (fragrant) wine

Kaʿb ibn Zuhayr continues the long poem, until he says:

> I was told that the Messenger of Allah threatened me (with death)
> But with the Messenger of Allah
> I have hope of finding pardon!
> Gently! May you be guided by Him
> Who gave you the gift of the Qur'ān
> Wherein are warnings and a plain setting out (of the matter)
> Do not punish me, when I have not sinned, on account of what is
> Said by the informers,
> Even should the (false) sayings about me be many
> I did not cease to cross the desert
> Plunging betimes into the darkness
> When the mantle of night is fallen
> Till I laid my hand, not to withdraw it, in
> The hand of the avenger
> Whose word is the word of truth
> Truly, the Messenger is a light
> Whence illumination is sought
> A drawn Indian sword,
> One of the swords of Allah!
> Amongst a ban of Quraysh!

This is only a small part of *al-Burdah*. It is simply beautiful, but its beauty cannot be conveyed in any language, other than its own Arabic. Later on, the mystic-poet al-Buṣayrī of Egypt, composed a poem in the praise of the Prophet (peace be upon him), in which he tried to match the rhythm and rhyme of Zuhayr's *Burdah*. Al-Buṣayrī's poem was so popular, that it came to be called *al-Burdah* of al-Buṣayrī, though composed much later in time than the original *Burdah* of Kaʿb Ibn Zuhayr.

12. THE TABŪK EXPEDITION

After his return from Ḥunayn and Ṭā'if, the Prophet (peace be upon him) stayed in Madīnah for almost eight months, from Dhū'l-Ḥijjah until Rajab of the ninth year of the *Hijrah*. He then disclosed his intention of marching against the Romans in Rajab. That was unusual, since it was the Prophet's habit not to disclose his military objectives. Why did he depart from his custom on this occasion? It is thought that he did so, because he would be waging war against the formidable Romans and he wanted the people to make the necessary preparations. The expedition of Tabūk was also unique because the distance was so great, and it was summer time, with heat scorching, crops not yet harvested, and the people needing to harvest. It was in such testing circumstances that the Prophet (peace be upon him) ordered his people to prepare to march to Tabūk, to engage the Romans.

The hypocrites were very active in discouraging people from joining up. They themselves gave the most strange and unacceptable excuses.

12.1 The Excuse of al-Jidd ibn Qays

One of the leaders of the hypocrites, al-Jidd ibn Qays, came to see the Prophet (peace be upon him). The Prophet (peace be upon him) asked him to join the expedition.But al-Jidd had the most extraordinary excuse:

'You know, O Messenger of Allah, nobody loves women more than I do; and they say that the women of the Romans (Byzantines) are so beautiful, so I am afraid that I shall be infatuated by them.'[6]

The Prophet (peace be upon him) accepted his apology, but Allah did not, and the Qur'ān condemned the man in very severe terms: Says Allah, in the Qur'ān:[7]

> *Some of them they are that say: 'Give me leave and do not tempt me,' Truly, such men have fallen into temptation, and surely Hell fire encompasses the unbelievers.* [*al-Tawbah* 9:49]

12.2 Another Group asks Leave because of the Heat

Another group asked the Prophet (peace be upon him) to excuse them from fighting, because of the scorching heat. The Qur'ān also rejected their excuse as unacceptable. Says Allah in the Qur'ān, referring to those hypocrites:

> *They said, 'Go not forth in the heat', Say Hell Fire is hotter. Do they not understand? Therefore, let them laugh little, and weep much in recompense for what they have been earning.* [*al-Tawbah* 9:81-82].

13. THE PROPHET ORDERS THE HOUSE OF SULAYM THE JEW, TO BE BURNT

The hypocrites used to assemble in the house of Sulaym, a Jew from Madīnah, to jest and joke about the orders to mobilize for war against the Romans. They discouraged the people against going out to meet the Romans, making fun of the Muslims' confidence that they could beat them. The Prophet (peace be upon him) ordered that house to be burnt down. It was burnt down with the hypocrites assembled inside: Many of them sustained wounds because of the fire, one of them jumped out of the window, breaking his leg in the process.

14. THOSE WHO WEPT BECAUSE THEY HAD NOTHING TO RIDE ON

Some poor Muslims wanted to join the expedition of Tabūk. As they had nothing to ride, they asked the Prophet's help, but he excused himself. They went back to their houses weeping, because they were unable to join the Prophet in the *jihād* against the Romans. They were:

a. Salīm ibn ʿUmayr,

b. ʿUtbah ibn Zayd,

c. Abū Laylā, ʿAbd al-Raḥmān ibn Kaʿb,

d. ʿAmr ibn Humām ibn al-Jamūḥ,

e. ʿAbdullāh ibn al-Muqaffaʿ,

f. Harim ibn ʿAbdullāh,

g. ʿIrbāḍ ibn Sāriyah al-Fazārī.

15. THE STORY OF THE THREE MUSLIMS WHO FAILED TO JOIN THE EXPEDITION

Three Muslims, of good standing with the Prophet (peace be upon him) and the Muslims, failed to join the expedition, for no good reason, and they stayed behind. They were described as *al-mutakhallifin* i.e. those who stayed behind, for no good reason.

They were:

a. Kaʿb ibn Mālik,

b. Murārah ibn al-Rabīʿ,

c. Hilāl ibn Umayyah.

On his return, from Tabūk, the Prophet (peace be upon him) ordered a boycott, which meant that nobody would deal with the three men, or even talk to them. For it was a great sin indeed not to join in *jihād*, when an expedition was being waged against the enemy. After some time, he ordered them separated from their own wives, and forbade them to touch them. Life became very hard for those three Muslims, especially for Hilāl, who was an old man. Hilāl's wife came to the Prophet (peace be upon him), and asked for special permission to serve him, because he was too old to serve himself. The Prophet (peace be upon him) agreed, but cautioned her not to let him approach her sexually. To that she replied that Hilāl was too old for that.

The boycott was also especially hard for Kaʿb ibn Mālik, a young man, who had participated in all the previous battles. Because Kaʿb loved the Prophet (peace be upon him), he could not abandon the congregational prayers. He would enter the Mosque, and give the greeting, but nobody would reply to him, even the Prophet (peace be upon him) used to look the other way, which hurt him the most. The other two Muslims stayed locked in their homes, until Allah pardoned them, and verses were revealed declaring that pardon, but not accepting their action of staying behind the Prophet (peace be upon him). Says Allah in the Qur'ān:

> *Allah has relented (turned) towards the Prophet and the Muhājrīn and Anṣār, who had followed him in the hour of difficulty, after the hearts of some of them well-nigh were aside, then He relented towards them, surely Allah is Gentle to them, and All-Compassionate. And to the three who were left behind, until when the earth became very small for them, for all its breadth, and their souls became tight for them, and they thought that there was no shelter from Allah, except in Him. Then He relented (turned) towards them, that they might also repent, surely Allah is Relenting, and is All-Compassionate.* [*al-Tawbah* 9:117-118]

The boycott lasted for fifty days, in the last ten days of which the boycott was total, including the boycott of their wives. The severity of the boycott served to indicate how grave a sin it is for a healthy and able-bodied Muslim, not to take part in *jihād* with the Muslims, marching to the battlefield. It also served to show that no exception was possible for anyone not to join in *jihād*, because Hilāl was an old man, and yet was not exempted or executed, nor was Ka'b ibn Mālik, who had participated in all previous battles except Badr.

16. THE PROPHET TOLD ABŪ DHARR OF LONELY DEATH

Abū Dharr al-Ghifārī was not able to keep up with the pace of the advancing army to Tabūk, because his camel was old and weak. Eventually, he abandoned it and came running on foot. He caught up with the Prophet (peace be upon him), when the army was encamped for some rest. When the Prophet (peace be upon him) saw a solitary figure coming in the distance, he made a wish – 'Be Abū Dharr,' the Prophet (peace be upon him) wished and it was Abū Dharr. When he approached, the Prophet (peace be upon him) said to him: 'May Allah's mercy be on Abū Dharr; he walks alone, dies alone and he will be resurrected alone.'

As a matter of fact, Abū Dharr died alone. Only his wife and an attendant were with him at a place in the desert called Al-Rabdhah, to which he was exiled by 'Uthmān ibn 'Affān, because Abū Dharr disagreed with the Caliph 'Uthmān over the way he was running the state. The Prophet's prophecy for Abū Dharr was realized. The Prophet used to praise Abū Dharr and said of him: 'The earth has not borne, nor the heaven has under its roof anyone more truthful than Abū Dharr.'

17. THE MOSQUE OF DISSENSION

This Mosque was built by the hypocrites of Madīnah to oppose the Prophet, and to rival his Mosque. It was denounced by the Qur'ān, in the strongest possible terms, and the Prophet (peace be upon him) was forbidden to pray in it, by Allah. It was described as the Mosque of *Ḍirār*. That mosque was built by twelve men of the hypocrites. Their names are given by Ibn Hishām. They finished building the mosque when the Prophet (peace be upon him) was about to depart on his way to the Battle of Tabūk. They came to the Prophet (peace be upon him) and said: 'O Messenger of Allah, we have built this mosque for the sick, the busy, and for rainy or cold nights, when we cannot join you, and come to your mosque! We would like you to come and pray in it.'

The Prophet (peace be upon him) wished them well, and said that he was about to set out for the Battle of Tabūk, but that when he will be back, he would come and pray with them, in their mosque. But when the Prophet (peace be upon him) marched for about an hour, and encamped at a place called Dhū Awān, Gabriel came and told him about the true purpose of the new mosque: that it was a mosque of opposition, and that he was forbidden by Allah to pray in it. At that point, the Prophet (peace be upon him) ordered a group of the Anṣār to go to Madīnah and burn down that mosque. The group was headed by Mālik ibn Dukhshum of the Anṣār. The mission was carried out immediately and efficiently, and the mosque was burnt down with the hypocrites assembled inside. The Qur'ānic verses revealed on the Mosque of the Opposition, run as follows; said Allah in the Qur'ān:

> *And those who have taken a mosque in opposition and unbelief, and to divide the believers, and as an outpost for those who fought Allah and His Messenger before-time. They will swear; 'We desire nothing but good.' And Allah testifies that they are truly liars; stand there never! A mosque that was founded upon God-fearing from the first day, is worthier for you to stand in, therein are men who love to cleanse themselves, and Allah loves those who cleanse themselves. Why, is he better, who founded his building upon the fear of Allah and His good pleasure, or he who founded his building upon the brink of a crumbling bank, that has tumbled with him unto the Fire of Hell? And Allah guides not the wrong-doers. The building they have built will not cease to be a (cause of) doubt within their hearts, unless (until) their hearts are cut into pieces. Allah is All-Knowing, All-Wise.* [*al-Tawbah* 9:107-110]

18. THE OUTCOME OF THE EXPEDITION OF TABŪK

When the Prophet (peace be upon him) arrived in Tabūk, there was no fighting. He was met by the rulers of the region, seeking peaceful agreements with him: Yuḥannā ibn Ru'bah, the ruler of Īlyā, came first. He made peace with the Prophet (peace be upon him) and paid *jizyah*. He was followed by the rulers of Jaba' and Adhrush, who also made peace and paid *jizyah*.

18.1 The Agreement with Ibn Ru'bah

Ibn Hishām gives the text of the peace agreement between the Prophet and Yuḥannā ibn Ru'bah, as follows:

> In the Name of Allah, the compassionate the Most Merciful
>
> This is a guarantee from Allah and Muḥammad, the Prophet and Messenger of Allah to Yuḥannā ibn Ru'bah and the people of Īlyā, for their ships and their caravans by land and sea. They and all the men with them, in Syria, and Yemen, and their seamen, all have the protection of Allah, and Muḥammad, the Prophet. Should any one of them, break the treaty by introducing new factors, then his wealth shall not save him, it is fair prize of him who takes it. It is not permitted that they shall be restrained from going down to their wells, or using their roads by land or sea.

18.2 Khālid ibn al-Walīd and the Ruler of Dūmah

Ukaydir ibn ʿAbd al-Malik, was the Christian client of the Romans, and the ruler of Dūmah. The Messenger of Allah (peace be upon him) dispatched Khālid ibn al-Walīd, in a suitable military contingent for him. The Messenger of Allah (peace be upon him) told Khālid: 'You will find Ukaydir hunting wild cattle.'

Khālid found Ukaydir, as predicted by the Messenger of Allah, and took him completely by surprise. He brought him to the Prophet (peace be upon him), his gown embroidered with pure gold. The Prophet (peace be upon him) spared his life and made a peace treaty with him. Ukaydir agreed to pay *jizyah* and recognize the overall authority of the Prophet in Arabia. The Prophet (peace be upon him) stayed in Tabūk for ten days, before he made his way back to Madīnah.

18.3 Peace at last: Thaqīf Converted to Islam

The Prophet (peace be upon him) returned to Madīnah in good cheer. The Muslim authority in Madīnah was no longer threatened by any power in Arabia at large. The north borders with the Romans were by then thoroughly pacified, and made to recognize the authority of Allah and his Messenger. The only exception to this was the enclave of the Thaqīf in Ṭā'if.

As the Prophet (peace be upon him) had foreseen, the position of Thaqīf was no longer tenable. They themselves became remorseful, especially after the killing of their tribal leader, ʿUrwah ibn Masʿūd, after his conversion to Islam. Gradually, Thaqīf came to realize their isolation in Arabia, as well as their increased inability to deal with the tribes around them, since those tribes had converted to Islam. Their business interests were severely curtailed, as nobody was prepared to deal with them. Gradually, they became prisoners in their own city, unable to venture outside, with nobody visiting them. Moreover, they lost much of their labour force, when a good number of their slaves ran away to the Prophet's encampment when he was laying siege to at-Ṭā'if, and converted to Islam, and they were declared free men.

So, Thaqīf gradually awoke to the gravity of their situation. Since all other Arab tribes had adopted Islam, they could not contemplate war or conflict with them. One of their chiefs, ʿAmr ibn Umayyah, was the first to analyze the situation and understand that something had to be done to end the isolation of Thaqīf, vis-à-vis the Arab tribes, and the state of the Prophet (peace be upon him) in Madīnah. He conferred with another chief, ʿAbd Yalayl ibn ʿAmr ibn ʿUmayr, who agreed that the position of Thaqīf was no longer tenable. They recognized that they were not secure in their own quarters, nor able to venture outside their own town, except at a great risk. They decided to go to Muḥammad at Madīnah and accept Islam. ʿAbd Yalayl ibn

ʿAmr was appointed to lead the embassy to the Prophet (peace be upon him), to declare the surrender of Thaqīf and Ṭā'if to Islam.

19. THE DELEGATION OF THAQĪF TO THE PROPHET

The delegation of Thaqīf consisted of six men, representing the different clans of the tribe, headed by ʿAbd Yalayl:

1. ʿAbd Yalayl ibn ʿAmr ibn ʿUmayr,
2. Al-Ḥakīm ibn ʿAmr,
3. Shuraḥbīl ibn Ghaylān/confederates of Thaqīf,
4. Abān ibn Abī al-ʿĀṣ
5. Aws ibn ʿAwf/Banū Mālik,
6. Numayr ibn Kharashah.

As the delegation approached Madīnah, they found al-Mughīrah ibn ʿAbī Shuʿbah looking after the camels of the Prophet (peace be upon him). The task of tending the camels of the Prophet (peace be upon him) was rotational, and it was the turn of al-Mughīrah ibn Abī Shuʿbah. When he saw the delegation and understood their intention, he ran towards Madīnah to tell the Prophet (peace be upon him) the good news, leaving the delegation at his station. On the way, he was met by Abū Bakr, who insisted on being the one to bring the good news to the Prophet (peace be upon him). He implored al-Mughīrah to let him take the news to the Prophet (peace be upon him), and al-Mughīrah agreed.

When the Thaqīf's delegation was eventually standing before the Prophet, they asked him for some concessions:

a. that their beloved idol, al-Lāt, should not be destroyed for three years.

b. that they be excused from the *Ṣalāt* (Prayer).

c. that they should not be required to break their idols themselves: the Prophet must appoint somebody else to do so, should it come to that.

The Prophet (peace be upon him) refused the first two demands, but conceded the third . They tried to get a lesser concession with regard to the first demand. They asked to keep al-Lāt for two years: the Prophet (peace be upon him) again refused; then they suggested one year, again the Prophet (peace be upon him) refused; then three months, again he refused. Then they asked him to leave al-Lāt for a month or even a few days, but the Prophet (peace be upon him) was adamant that al-Lāt be destroyed, at the first possible opportunity. As for *ṣalāt*, he told them that it was the prime pillar of Islam. Whoever failed to perform prayer, would not be regarded as a Muslim.

As for the third demand, which the Prophet (peace be upon him) had conceded, he appointed al-Mughīrah ibn Abī Shuʿbah, and Abū Sufyān ibn Ḥarb, to carry out the destruction of al-Lāt and all the other idols of Thaqīf. The Prophet (peace be upon him) also appointed Abān ibn Abī al-ʿĀṣ, as the Amīr over Thaqīf. He was very young, but most learned in the Qur'ān and *sunnah*. The Prophet (peace be upon him) also wrote them a letter, containing instructions to be followed by them in Ṭā'if.

CHAPTER 10

The Year of Deputations: The Advent of Peace in Arabia

The political implications of the surrender of the Quraysh, signalled a new era in Arabia. After the return from Tabūk, and Thaqīf's acceptance of Islam, the Prophet (peace be upon him) became the unquestioned master and ruler of Arabia as a whole. The Arabs, and the Bedouin tribes of the desert, knew very well the political implications of the surrender of the Quraysh. After all, the Quraysh were the leaders of the Arabs and their respected guides and chiefs. They were, moreover, the guardians of the Ancient Sanctuary, and the pure stock of Ishmael, son of Abraham. When the Quraysh were subdued, the Arabs knew that a new political force had come into Arabia, and that they could not fight the Messenger of God, or show enmity towards him. Consequently, they entered in the religion of God in throngs, as God says in the Qur'ān, and they converged on Madīnah from all directions. This has been underscored in the Qur'ān, in *Sūrah al-Naṣr* (Help) as follows:

> *When comes the victory of Allah, and the conquest, and you see men entering God's religion in throngs, then proclaim the praise of your Lord, and seek His forgiveness, for He is Most Forgiving.* [*al-Naṣr* 110:1-3]

The Arabs arrived in 'throngs' from the remotest corners of Arabia, to pay homage and recognize the new authority. They entered into the religion of Islam in 'throngs' as the Qur'ān reports. The first delegation to call on the Prophet (peace be upon him) was that of the tribe of Banū Tamīm. Banū Tamīm called out loud from outside.

Banū Tamīn were desert Bedouins, coarse, ignorant and ill-mannered. They called out loudly from the street: 'O Muḥammad, come out to meet us!'

The Prophet (peace be upon him) did not like to be summoned in this way, but with his accustomed gentleness and courtesy, he said nothing and showed nothing. Banū Tamīm went on: 'O Muḥammad, we came to compete and boast the glory of our tribe. So, give permission to our orator and our poet to speak praise of our pride and glory.' The Prophet (peace be upon him) reluctantly gave permission to this *jāhiliyyah* custom of boasting. So, he consented to play the game, according to their rules, taking great care not to put them off at that initial encounter.

Then the Banū Tamīm's orator, 'Uṭārid ibn Ḥājib, got up and said: 'Praise belongs to God, for His favour on us, and He is worthy to be praised, who had made us kings, and had given us great wealth, wherewith we are generous, and has made us the strongest people in the east, the greatest in numbers and the best equipped, so who, among mankind, is our equal? Are we not the princes of men and their superiors? He who would compete with us, let him enumerate what we have enumerated. If we wished, we could say more, but we are too modest to say much of what He has given us, and we are well known for that. I say this, that you may bring forward the likes of us anything better.' Having said his piece, 'Uṭārid ibn Ḥājib sat down.

The Prophet (peace be upon him) then asked Thābit ibn Qays ibn al-Shammās, of the Khazraj, to reply to the orator of Banū Tamim. Thābit got up and said:[1] 'Praise belongs to God, who created the heavens and earth, and established His rule therein! His knowledge embraces His Throne. Nothing exists but by His Bounty. By His power, He made us kings and chose the best of His creation as Messenger, honoured with lineage, made him truthful in speech, and favoured him above all that He had created. He was God's choice from the worlds, and sent down to him His Book, and entrusted him with it above all that He has created…'

Then al-Zibriqān ibn Badr got up and said: 'We are the nobles; no tribe can equal us. From us, kings are born, and in our midst churches are built. In time of dearth, we feed meat to the hungry. Guests coming to us are well-satisfied with food. We forbid others, but none forbids us.'

The Prophet asked his poet, Ḥassān ibn Thābit, to answer az-Zibriqān ibn Badr. Hassān got up and recited a long poem, in which he praised the Prophet (peace be upon him), and his Companions, both as virtuous and brave people and of noble birth, going back to Fihr, the ancestor of the Quraysh. Banū Tamīm were duly impressed by Ḥassān's poem, and felt obliged to acknowledge the superiority of the Prophet's position. Az-Zibriqān, then got up and said:

'By my father, this man has a ready helper! His orator and his poet are better than ours, and their voices are sweeter than ours!'

In the end, Banū Tamīm accepted Islam, and the Prophet (peace be upon him) honoured them, accorded them very generous hospitality, and gave them valuable gifts on their departure.

All of this duly recorded, in the Qur'ān, in *Sūrah al-Ḥujurāt* (The Apartments or Rooms). As a matter of fact; this *Sūrah* gave a whole set of rules and moral principles and an elaborate code of mannerism of how a Muslim should behave and act, when in the gracious presence of the Prophet (peace be upon him).

It is significant that the Prophet (peace be upon him) agreed to deal with them in their own idiom. Although the Prophet (peace be upon him) was known to dislike boasting and arrogance, yet he had to work within the accepted customs of the pre-Islamic Arabs. Large and prestigious tribes, like Banū Tamīm, were very proud of their tribal poets and orators. Good, eloquent and pure Arabic speech and poetry were highly valued by them. Banū Tamīm did not expect the Prophet (peace be upon him) to have with him such eloquent orators and poets. They were greatly impressed by them, and decided to embrace Islam for that reason. Thus one of the Prophet's strategies was to work within the cultural and political systems of Pre-Islamic Arabia, and use them prudently to spread Islam.

1. THE UNSUCCESSFUL PLOT ON THE LIFE OF THE PROPHET

ʿĀmir ibn al-Ṭufayl, and Arbad ibn Qays came to Madīnah, planning to murder the Prophet (peace be upon him). The plot was that ʿĀmir would distract the Prophet (peace be upon him) and Arbad would strike him with his sword and kill him.

ʿĀmir did his part as planned, but Arbad failed to move against the Prophet (peace be upon him). When they came out, ʿĀmir scolded Arbad for his failure to perform his part. Arbad explained that every time he had tried to strike against the Prophet, he saw his friend ʿĀmir standing between him and the Prophet (peace be upon him) so that if he struck at the Prophet he would kill only his own friend ʿĀmir. The Prophet (peace be upon him), knew of their evil intention, (Gabriel told him), and he prayed to God Almighty to punish and destroy them. ʿĀmir fell ill after contracting the plague, and died on his way home. Arbad reached his people, but was killed by a thunderbolt, a short time afterwards.

2. ḌIMĀM IBN THAʿLABAH, THE QUICK-MINDED DEPUTY

Ḍimām ibn Thaʿlabah was sent by his people, the Banū Saʿd ibn Bakr, to find out about the Prophet (peace be upon him). Being a man of quick mind and keen eye, he recognized the Prophet (peace be upon him) as such, asked him a few questions and set out on his way home.

When the people assembled around him, he told them that Islam was a true and noble religion from God Almighty, that Muḥammad was truthful and that idol-worshipping was indeed a false and irrational religion. Being respected and trusted by his tribe, they all converted to Islam on his advice. This incident tells us something about the wisdom of the pre-Islamic Arabs. The notion that they were all only coarse, unruly and foolish is not very fair. The story of the long-haired Ḍimām ibn Thaʿlabah shows that they were capable of good sense, seriousness of purpose, and had sound judgement, since they followed the advice of the person they had chosen and trusted. The incident also shows that their leader, Ḍimām ibn Thaʿlabah was a firm and serious man. Once he thought he had discovered the truth about Muḥammad (peace be upon him), he lost no time taking that discovery to his people. This is evident from the fact that he only spent a few hours in the company of the Prophet (peace be upon him). He did not want to waste the time of his people or their chance of becoming one of the first tribes to embrace the new religion of Islam, and support the new Arab state.

3. THE COMING OF AL-JĀRŪD IBN ʿAMR

Al-Jārūd ibn ʿAmr ibn Ḥanash accepted Islam, because he was moved by the generosity and fairness of the Prophet (peace be upon him). When a member of his tribe asked the Prophet (peace be upon him) to pay off his debts, the Prophet (peace be upon him) immediately agreed. But when al-Jārūd himself asked him permission to take into his possession any stray camels on the road, the Prophet (peace be upon him) refused and warned against that, because he had no right to take hold of them.

4. ZAYD AL-KHAYL BECAME ZAYD AL-KHAYR

Zayd al-Khayl was the chief of the tribe of Ṭayy, famous for their generosity. Their all-time honoured chief Ḥātim al-Ṭā'ī, was legendary in his generosity, considered to have been the most generous pre-Islamic Arab, whoever lived. Whenever guests came, he would slaughter a camel. On one occasion when guests came, and he did not find any camel to slaughter, he slaughtered his own transport and favourite she-camel. The Prophet (peace be upon him) used to collect information about the chiefs of the Arab tribes, so that he would know how to treat them, and how to win them over to Islam. On this account, the Prophet (peace be upon him) is reported to have said:

> No Arab has ever been spoken of in high terms but that, when I have met him, I have found him to fall below what was said of him, except Zayd al-Khayl, who exceeded all that has been said about him.'

Zayd al-Khayl (i.e. Zayd of the horses) was so-called because of his bravery. The Prophet (peace be upon him) liked him very much, and when he became a Muslim, on the invitation of the Prophet (peace be upon him), he renamed him Zayd al-Khayr (i.e. Zayd of the good). The Prophet (peace be upon him) then gave Zayd al-Khayr gifts and allotted to him a piece of land, by name of Fayḍ, and other land, and wished him a safe journey home. However, and quite sadly, Zayd al-Khayr fell ill on the road and died, before reaching his destination.

5. THE CONVERSION TO ISLAM OF THE CHRISTIAN ʿADIYY IBN ḤĀTIM

This was the son of the famous Arab chief of the tribe of Ṭayy, Ḥātim al-Ṭā'ī. He was a Christian, and he said he felt a consuming hatred for the Prophet of Islam, when he first heard of him. When Muḥammad's army was advancing against Ṭayy, ʿAdiyy ibn Ḥātim fled to Syria. But his sister, who was taken captive by the Muslim soldiers, and subsequently freed, went to him in Syria and praised the Prophet (peace be upon him). She told him that it was not befitting of him, being the chief, and the son of a chief, to be on the run abroad. She asked him to come back, and meet the Prophet (peace be upon him) and find out for himself about Islam. Nobody was going to compel him to accept it. It was his free choice, and if he did not like Islam, he could walk away with dignity. But should he accept Islam, he would be reinstated as the chief of his people Ṭayy.

6. ʿADIYY MEETS THE PROPHET

On receiving his sister, and listening to her advice, ʿAdiyy decided to go and meet the Prophet (peace be upon him) in Madīnah. He was intent on checking up on the Prophet (peace be upon him) to determine whether he was a true Prophet or not. The Prophet (peace be upon him) took ʿAdiyy ibn Ḥātim to his own house, and was host to him, since he was very keen to see him become a Muslim, because of his high social standing among his tribe and people. Should ʿAdiyy become a Muslim, all the tribe would convert to Islam. ʿAdiyy, who was closely watching the Prophet (peace be upon him), said: 'As we were making for the house, there met him an old feeble woman, who asked him to stop, and he stopped for a long time, while she told him her needs. I said to myself, "This is no King." Then he took me into his house, took hold of a leather cushion stuffed with palm tree leaves, and threw it to me saying, "sit on that," and he insisted that I sit on it, which I did, while he sat on the ground in front of me, and I said (to myself), "This is not the way a King behaves."'

ʿAdiyy, then, said that the Prophet (peace be upon him) addressed him:[2] 'Are you not a Christian, O ʿAdiyy?'

'Yes, I am', I said.

'But why then do you take a quarter of the stock of your people? That is not permitted to you by your religion.'

'Quite true, O Prophet', I said. ʿAdiyy then reached the conclusion that indeed Muḥammad was not a king, but a true, genuine Prophet, since this question of ʿAdiyy taking a quarter of the stock of his people was not generally known. ʿAdiyy became a Muslim, after listening to a passionate and moving speech by the Prophet (peace be upon him), as follows: 'O ʿAdiyy, why do you not accept Islam? It may well be that the poverty you see among the Muslims prevents you from joining this religion, but, by God, wealth will soon flow so copiously among them, that there will not be people to take it. But perhaps, it is that you see how many are their enemies, and how few we are? But, by God, you will hear of a woman unaccompanied coming on her camel from Qādisiyyah to visit this Scared House unafraid. But perhaps it is that you see that others have the power and sovereignty, but, by God, you will soon hear that the White Castles of Babylon have been opened to them: (The Muslims).' The Prophet (peace be upon him) thus addressed ʿAdiyy, very much eager, and hopeful to win him over to Islam.

ʿAdiyy, on hearing the Prophet's moving speech, and because of what he saw of the modest manners, and behaviour of the Prophet (peace be upon him), became a Muslim. ʿAdiyy said that he lived on until two promises and prophesies of the Prophet had been achieved: the opening of the White Castles of Persia, and that women began to come to Makkah from Qādisiyyah on camel back, quite safe and sound. The third promise of abundant wealth was realized later on, during the reign of the fifth Caliph ʿUmar ibn ʿAbd al- ʿAzīz, of the Umayyad Dynasty.[3]

7. THE COMING OF AL-ASHʿATH IBN QAYS THE KING OF KINDAH

The kings of Kindah were probably the strongest kings of Yemen, Haḍramawt and the eastern parts of Arabia, whereas the Quraysh were the kings and nobility of Ḥijāz, and the western region of Arabia. From Kindah came the famous poet, Imra' al-Qays, who is said to have exploded the Arabic language, that is, added so many words, expressions, idioms, rhymes and rhythms that it became very rich and wide in scope. From Kindah too came the famous philosopher and physician, Abū Yaʿqūb Isḥāq al-Kindī, who was the first Arab philosopher to study and transmit Aristotle's logic and philosophy. The kings of Kindah were rich and civilized people. They wore elaborate striped robes embroidered with silk. They made their hair in a very beautiful way and they put *kohl* in their eyes to enhance their looks. When the Prophet (peace be upon him) saw them, he did not like their lavish costumes, especially he did not like the wearing of silk. He therefore asked them, if they had accepted Islam, and when they answered in the affirmative, he added, 'Why do you wear silk, then?'

implying that wearing silk is not allowed for men! At that point, they tore them off immediately, and threw them to the ground!

That incident is quite significant. First, it indicates the practical behaviour orientation of Islam, and the Prophet's method of insisting that Islamic principles be observed, right from the start. The incident is also significant in indicating the Arab's readiness to change their ways and behaviour, and modify their life-styles to fit the orientation and principles of the new state of Madīnah. That incident also says a great deal about the flexibility and wisdom of those pre-Islamic Arabs.

Then the kings of Kindah, headed by al-Ashʿath ibn Qays, tried to remind the Prophet (peace be upon him) that they and the Prophet were relatives, at least on their maternal side. Al-Ashʿath said: 'We are the sons of the Eater of Bitter Herbs and so are you.' The Prophet smiled cordially, but added, 'You want to say that to my uncle al-ʿAbbās.' Of course al-ʿAbbās was a merchant, and used to travel quite a lot among those Arab tribes, especially to the east and south of Makkah. And to secure his safe passage, he would remind those Arabs that he was the son of the Eater of Bitter Herbs. The Prophet (peace be upon him) then added that he was the descendant of al-Naḍr ibn Kinānah, and that a man should be linked, genealogically speaking, to his paternal side, and not maternal ancestors and, no offence meant, 'one must not disown one's father.' On hearing this, al-Ashʿath turned to his men of Kindah, and warned them that if they should ever mention anything about the Eater of the Bitter Herbs, he would deal them eighty strokes of the cane! Now, it is of course, quite true, that the Eater of Bitter Herbs, was one of the great-grand fathers of the Prophet, from his maternal side, the Banū al-Najjār, of Yemen, who were then living in Yathrib (Banū al-Ashhal of Khazraj).

8. THE DEPUTATION OF THE KINGS OF ḤIMYAR (YEMEN)

After returning from the Battle of Tabūk against the Byzantines (Romans), the Prophet (peace be upon him) received the embassy of the kings of Ḥimyar of Yemen. He wrote them a detailed letter explaining the Five Pillars of Islam, giving details of the *Zakāt* and *jizyah*. He also sent the knowledgeable Muʿādh ibn Jabal with them, to teach them the principles of Islam and Qur'ān. Muʿādh ibn Jabal was a close and beloved Companion of the Prophet. He was quite young, handsome and very knowledgeable in Islamic jurisprudence and *daʿwah*, with a sharp mind and an easy and friendly disposition. So the Prophet's choice was not at random. The Prophet (peace be upon him) knew the importance of the Yemen as a region, and he knew the calibre of the Yemeni people. Later on, history proved the far-sightedness of the Prophet (peace be upon him), as the Yemenis came to form the core of the Muslim armies that conquered extensive territories, and spread Islam from the borders of China and the Himalayas to the plains of Muslim Spain.

'How would you judge and govern those people of Yemen?' the Prophet (peace be upon him)[4] asked Muʿādh.

'By the Book of God, Almighty!' answered Muʿādh.

'But suppose you didn't find anything (by way of guidance) in the Holy Qur'ān?' added the Prophet (peace be upon him).

'Then I will invoke the *sunnah* of the Prophet,' answered Muʿādh.

'But suppose you didn't find any help there, either, what will you do?'

The Prophet (peace be upon him) confirmed his questioning of Muʿādh, to measure-up, the extend of his knowledge and wisdom!

'Then I will seek out my best judgement, and spare no effort to find the right ruling.' replied Muʿādh emphatically.

'Praise be to God, Almighty, Who has guided the messenger of the Apostle of God to what would please God', said the Prophet (peace be upon him), quite impressed and pleased with the wisdom and prudence of Muʿādh ibn Jabal.

This exchange became a hallmark of Islamic jurisprudence, because it demarcated the three foundational pillars of Islamic jurisprudence. The basic sources of all Islamic legislation are :

a. The Qur'ān;

b. The *sunnah* of the Prophet (both verbal, and situational, i.e. his approvals or lack of them);

c. *al-Ijtihād*, i.e. the enlightened, educated and knowledgeable opinion of the executive ruler, and his *Shūrā* Council.

What is meant by the 'enlightened, educated and knowledgeable opinion', is that this opinion must follow rules of deduction '*Istinbāṭ*'. It should not be based on mere subjective or whimsical judgement. The objective rules of deduction, as developed by a Shāfiʿī and other jurists, stipulate that any 'reasoned', or 'deduced' opinion must be ultimately based on a text (*naṣṣ*) of the Qur'ān or the *sunnah*. Thus, juristic deduction proceeds by analogy (or *qiyās*), either strict and narrow *qiyās* or wide-ranging, 'general' *qiyās*. By strict or narrow *qiyās* is meant *qiyās* based on a text (i.e. directly or indirectly). By 'general' *qiyās* is meant an appeal to the basic or universal aims of the *sharīʿah* or Islamic law. These general aims of the *sharīʿah* are termed. '*Al-Maqāṣid al-Kulliyyah*', i.e. the universal goals of the Islamic law at large.

The Islamic law generally aims at realizing utilities and benefits for mankind, and avoiding unbeneficial and harmful behaviour. That is to say, it generally aims at realizing the legitimate and proven interests of humanity. For instance, Islamic law generally aims at preserving:

a. Life,

b. Money and property,

c. Honour and integrity of man,

d. The soundness of the intellect,

e. The sanctity of religion.

Any ruling that is deemed consistent with those general objectives or universal goals of *sharīʿah* is considered to be desirable from the standpoint of the Islamic law. This is what is meant by 'general' *qiyās* or general analogy. Al-Shāfiʿī warned quite emphatically against views or opinions based merely on personal preferences.

After this rather long digression, which is quite relevant and important, we must now return to our historical scene and describe, in gist, what had gone between the Prophet (peace be upon him) and those kings of Ḥimyar.

It appears that the Prophet (peace be upon him) had given the matter of spreading Islam quite a lot of thought. Firstly, he had chosen the best of the Muslims' jurists and learned ones to be dispatched to Yemen, they were five of them:

1. Muʿādh ibn Jabal, leader of the delegation.
2. ʿAbdullāh ibn Zayd.
3. Mālik ibn ʿUbādah.
4. ʿUqbah ibn Nimr.
5. Mālik ibn Murrah

Obviously, there were others (lesser jurists) to whom the Prophet (peace be upon him) had alluded by the expression 'and their companions.' The Prophet (peace be upon him) commended those jurists, and their companions very highly and advised the kings of Ḥimyar to respect them, and treat them in the best manner. He praised them as pious and knowledgeable men, the best of his people.

Further, the Prophet (peace be upon him) had written, for the nobles of Ḥimyar, an elaborate document addressed to the kings, to teach them their religious duties and obligations, and how to discharge them. He ordered them to practise the following pillars of Islam:

a. To perform *ṣalāh*, as best as it should;
b. To pay *zakāt,* and the fifth of the booty;
c. To perform *ḥajj* (pilgrimage to Makkah) whenever possible.

Anyone who did more than those fixed pillars of Islam (which no doubt included fasting), would have done so to his own merit.

The document also mentioned the obligation to uphold Islam, and bear witness that it is the true religion of God Almighty.

It also stressed the believers' obligation to uphold the *farīḍah* (Obligatory nature) of *jihād*, and that was by helping their fellow believers against the idol worshippers or polytheists of Yemen.

Last, but not least, the document advised the nobles of Ḥimyar to treat their people well and not to be false or treacherous, because the Messenger of God (i.e. Muḥammad) was the friend of both the poor and the rich of them. That important document, which the Prophet (peace be upon him) dictated in an elaborate and thoughtful way, was concluded by the following significant words:[5]

> Mālik [Mālik ibn Murrah, one of the dispatched jurists] has brought the news concerning the conversion of the kings of Ḥimyar to Islam, and kept secret what is confidential, so I order you to treat him well. I have sent to you some of the best of my Companions, pious and learned men, and I order you to treat them well, for they must be respected. Peace be upon you, and the mercy and the Blessings of God.

It was most significant that the Prophet (peace be upon him), in his letter to the kings of Ḥimyar should emphasize the importance of receiving those 'pious and learned men' with respect and good treatment. That was intended to underscore the importance of knowledge and enlightenment, in the new Islamic order and society. Secondly, it is also significant that the Prophet (peace be upon him) should remind the nobles of Ḥimyar to treat their people, poor and rich alike, with fairness and compassion. That new policy was intended to bring about a change for the better in the life of the people under the New Islamic Order. The document contained elaborate details about *Zakāt*. *Zakāt*, together with booty and charity, constituted some of the revenue sources of the new Muslim State, without which it could not function well, hence the need both to emphasize the importance of *Zakāt*, and educate the nobles of Ḥimyar on how to go about collecting it, together with *jizyah* and booty.

Another significance of the Prophet's emphasis on the collection of *Zakāt* has something to do with the fact that the Muslim State has an obligation towards the poor, the needy and the dispossessed. It caters for such things as their safety, their health and education and that of their children. Not only this, but also if they are travelling they become entitled to *Zakāt* allowances, even if they are rich at home, because they are termed *'Ābir Sabīl* (wayfarers). Another category recipients of *Zakāt*, is those termed *'Al-Ghārimīn'*, i.e. those who have incurred debts which they cannot repay. Thus, in a sense, an Islamic State is a welfare state, catering for the basic needs of the under-privileged. It has an Islamic responsibility towards the poor and the dispossessed. Having compassion and mercy towards the weak and the needy, is a basic feature of an Islamic State. The Qur'ān tells the Prophet Muḥammad (peace be upon him) that he has been sent by God Almighty as a Mercy unto Mankind: *We have not sent you except as a Mercy unto Mankind.* [*Al-Anbiyā'* 21:107]

We saw earlier that the Prophet (peace be upon him) ordered the nobles of Kindah not to wear silk clothes. This is another aspect of how Islam organizes economic and financial matters. The basic philosophy behind this system of Islamic Economy is that of wealth-preserving and wealth-sharing between the rich and the poor. Wealth shall not to be the monopoly of the rich few, nor should it be allowed to be squandered through foolish and irrational extravagancy and indulgence in meaningless luxury! Lavish spending, and those engaged in it are condensed in the most harsh and uncompromising way. They are singled out as the cardinal cause of the destructions of townships and cities. The Qur'ān rules against the monopoly of wealth by the rich people:

> *What God has bestowed on his Apostle, (taken) from the people of the township, belongs to God, to His Apostle, and to the kindred and the orphans, the needy and the wayfarer... In order that it (wealth)*

may not merely make a circuit between the wealthy among you. [*Al-Ḥashr* 59:7]

Hoarding of money, gold or silver is strictly forbidden in Islam. Also, all kinds of misuse of funds are likewise forbidden, like the squandering of wealth or extravagance (as is extracted by the wearing of silk by the kings of Ḥimyar. It is for this reason that men are not allowed to wear silk or use gold as an ornament, though, these are allowed, in a limited scale, to women!

9. THE DEPUTATION OF BANŪ AL-ḤĀRITH OF NAJRĀN (YEMEN)

It would appear that Banū al-Ḥārith of Najrān (Yemen) were late to dispatch their deputation to Madīnah. So, the Prophet (peace be upon him) dispatched his famous Companion and general, Khālid ibn al-Walīd, to them. He told him to call on the Prophet and accept Islam, and he gave them a respite of three days. If they accepted Islam, he was ordered to treat them well, and stay for some time to teach them the principles of Islam as well, as some sūrahs of the Qur'ān. But should they refuse to accept Islam, he was ordered to attack them. He did this, and then asked them to name their delegation to meet the Prophet (peace be upon him).

When they came before the Prophet (peace be upon him), he asked them how it was that they always fought so well and were never defeated. They explained that they were never divided, but always fought united, and that they never initiated hostilities or acted as aggressors.

The Prophet (peace be upon him) described them as looking like Indians. No doubt they resembled Indians as they were living on the edge of the Indian Ocean.

10. CONCLUDING REMARKS

The year of deputations witnessed the total submission of the whole peninsula of Arabia to the authority of the Prophet (peace be upon him) and the state of Madīnah. That was the logical consequence of the collapse of the authority of the Quraysh, who were the leaders of the Arabs and their notables. They had been a stumbling block in the way of the other Arabs, who might otherwise have accepted the authority of the Prophet (peace be upon him) much earlier. It would also appear that some of those Arabs were not at liberty to come to the Prophet (peace be upon him), and offer their political and religious allegiances, or that they were hesitant to do so, as shown by the Christians of Najrān. However, it appears that the Prophet (peace be upon him) demanded that they come, and recognize his overall authority, in the entire Arabian Peninsula. Those who tarried somewhat or hesitated, were reminded that it was incumbent on them to come, and offer their political and religious allegiance, to the authority of the Prophet (peace be upon him). The Prophet used the occasion of these meetings to become acquainted with them, and they had the chance to get acquainted with the new political order of Islam. He also used the occasion, to teach them the principles of Islam, paramount among them was *Ṣalāt* and *Zakāt*. Those deputations were very colourful occasions, and a great deal took place during them. The Prophet (peace be upon him) showed an excellent understanding of the names and characters, of the chiefs of the major Arab tribes, and he used that knowledge to endear Islam to them. He also treated them very well, and confirmed them in their positions as tribal chiefs or kings as the case was. That was what he did with the kings of Kindah, and the kings of Ḥimyar of Yemen. It was certainly a very wise policy to recognize the positions of men, and confirm them in their status. The year of deputations marked a new stage in the history of Islam, and the state of Madīnah. The Prophet (peace be upon him) started to look beyond Arabia, in particular to think about the threats and challenges coming from the North (the Romans) and the East (the Persians).

CHAPTER 11

Epilogue

1. CAN A POWERFUL ISLAMIC STATE COEXIST PEACEFULLY WITH OTHER POWERS?

Some Western orientalists used to argue that a powerful Islamic State cannot coexist peacefully with other non-Muslim States, because Islam does not recognize other regimes or ideologies, and resists and fights such regimes. According to these orientalists what *jihād* (or holy war) is designed for is to wage war against the infidel states. Those orientalists further claim that Islam is an inherently violent religion. It was spread by the sword in the early stages of its inception, and would be violent again if it became strong enough. If Muslims are not doing this now, it is because Islam is weak. This view has been expressed recently by such figures as Richard Nixon, the former American President, and Samuel Huntington.[1] According to these orientalists Muḥammad, as ruler of the Islamic State at Madīnah became a despot, and Islam itself became a violent and belligerent religion. Khadduri[2] claimed that even the Qur'ān changed its peaceful accent and reconciliatory language. He claimed that the Qur'ānic verses which advocated tolerance and religious coexistence and liberties were superseded by what he called the Sword Verse(s). Among the Qur'ānic verses that advocate freedom and religious tolerance are such verses as:

Let there be no compulsion in religion: truth stands out clear from falsehood. Whoever rejects tyranny, and believes in Allah has grasped the strong rope that never breaks. [*al-Baqarah* 2:256]

And say: The truth is from your Lord, let him who he chooses to will believe, and let him who chooses to disbelieve do so, at will. [*The Cave* 18: 29]

Fight in the cause of Allah those who fight you, but do not initiate aggression. For Allah loves not the aggressors. [*al-Baqarah* 2:190]

Therefore remind them (by giving admonitions) for you are just a reminder. You are not a controller over them. [*al-Ghāshiyah* 88:21-22]

Could you compel people to become believers (in Allah)? [*Yūnus* 10:99]

We know best what they say, and you are not a controller over them: so admonish with the Qur'ān whoever fears My warning... [*Qāf* 50:45]

All these Qur'ānic verses are *Muḥkam* verses, i.e. definite, not allegorical. They are not known to have been abrogated, so they naturally hold. No reason exists at all to think that they have been overruled. But orientalist Khadduri says that the so-called sword verse has abrogated them.

According to Khadduri, the verses of the sword are verse numbers 5, 29 of *Sūrah al-Tawbah*:

When the sacred months are passed, then fight and slay the idolaters, whenever you find them, and seize them, and beleague them and ambush them by every possible strategem (of war).
But if they repent, and establish regular prayers, and give Zakāt, *then make way for them, for God is All-Forgiving, All-Merciful.*
[*al-Tawbah* 9:5]

This is the verse of the sword indeed, but its military is in response to that of the idolaters of the Quraysh. It was the Quraysh who persecuted Prophet Muḥammad (peace be upon him), and his followers in Makkah and eventually forced them to leave the Holy City of their homeland, leaving behind their wealth and property. But even here, the way in which this verse finishes off, advocates tolerance, and forgiveness, should those polytheists of the Quraysh change their way, and repent their former insolence. If they indicated their peaceful intentions, their desire to take refuge in the camp of the Muslims or their desire to listen to the Qur'ān, then they should be allowed to go freely, Says God in the immediate next verse:

> *If one of the idolaters ask you for asylum, grant it to him; so that he may hear the Word of God, then escort him to where he can be safe and secure, that is because they are men without knowledge'.* [*al-Tawbah* 9:6]

As we have said before, this verse expresses the peacefulness of Islam and the Prophet's basic desire for peace; that peace is the rule, hostilities are the exception, even with former belligerents and enemies such as the Qurayshites, peaceful coexistence is preferable, should they be willing. The idea is that an enemy may fight the Muslims out of ignorance and hatred, unfounded hatred. Therefore every chance for peace and reconciliation must be seized to educate him, and remove the subjective factors of hate and prejudice.

Immediately following these verses (7 and 8 of *Sūrah al-Tawbah*), verses which advocate war against the Quraysh idolaters. These say that Qurayshite idolaters have no respect for their covenants or pledges which they made to the Muslims. They were the ones that started aggression and hostilities, and should they prevail over the Muslims, they would destroy them, heeding neither the bonds of family, nor any pledges or covenants they had made with them. That the advocacy of hostilities against the Quraysh idolaters was a special case, governed by specific circumstances, and historical relations between the Muslims and those idolaters. So any attempt to generalize from that or infer from it that Islam is a violent religion does not hold. In particular, to infer from it that verse 5 (which advocates tolerance and peaceful coexistence) has been abrogated is quite unjustifiable.

Khadduri also gave another verse of *Sūrah al-Tawbah* which he counted as the second and principal verse of the sword:

> *Fight those who believe not in God, nor the Last Day, nor hold that forbidden which has been forbidden by Allah and His Messenger, nor acknowledge the religion of Truth (Islam), from those who are the People of the Book, until they pay* Jizyah, *with willing submission, and until they feel themselves subdued.* [*al-Tawbah* 9:29]

There are a number of remarks which we must first make with reference to the above verse:

Although the verse refers to the People of the Book, in a way, that refers both to the Jews and Christians of the time, yet the Arabic text clearly indicates that this reference is not absolute or general. The Arabic expression (*minal-ladhīna*) clearly indicates that the reference here is to a certain faction, from among the People of the Book, who are characterized as:

- Not believers in God;
- Not believers in the Last Day;
- Non-practising (i.e. they did not observe what God had made forbidden);
- Not acknowledging or recognizing anything in common with (the religion of Truth namely Islam).

If we put this verse in historical perspective, it becomes quite clear whom it is referring to. It is definitely not referring to the Christians in Arabia at that time, who were described elsewhere as believers in God and the Last Day, who uphold religious values and obligations. Most importantly, these People of the Book maintained peaceful and even cordial relations with the Prophet of Islam, and from the start opted for and accepted the citizenship of the Madīnah State. Those were the Christians of Najrān in the Yemen, to the south, and the Christians of the Banū Taghlib to the north of Madīnah. Both Christian groups were of Arabic stock, visited the Prophet (peace be upon him) in his Capital, and were very well received by him. Indeed, when the Christians of Najrān came, the Prophet (peace be upon him) attended to their needs, with special cordiality and kindness, and permitted them to perform their Christian rites and prayers in his own mosque. He conducted very elaborate dialogue with them, and when they indicated their desire of sticking to their faith, he accepted and respected their decision and choice in good faith and cheer, and bid them farewell, with warm feelings and even gifts. For their part, they accepted the peace of Islam, and declared themselves citizens of the new Muslim State, as well as their willingness to pay the *jizyah* tax. There were never any ill-feeling between the two groups. This was also the case with the Christians of Banū Taghlib to the north of Madīnah. History does not record any such misunderstanding or tension between the Prophet (peace be upon him) and those Arab Christians of Najrān or Taghlib; never a single incident of conflict or discord. Most probably, those Arab Christians tolerated the new Islamic authority in Madīnah because they recognized that it was closer to them than the Roman authority of Syria or the Persian Authority of al-Ḥīrah, in southern Iraq. Moreover, the Islamic State was not aggressive, but quite tolerant towards them, as Christians.

However, with the other People of the Book, namely the Jews, the story was quite different: First of all, the Jews of Madīnah and other enclaves to the north of Madīnah were not of Arabic stock. If anything, they showed nothing but arrogance, intransigence, and contempt towards the Arabs, as an ignorant and backward lot.

Although they entertained friendly relations with the Prophet (peace be upon him) and the Muslims in the first days of the inception of the Muslim State, and even signed an accord with the Prophet (peace be upon him) (*the Ṣaḥīfah of Madīnah*) they later violated that accord. Not only that, they declared themselves as allies of the Qurayshite idolaters, and did all they could to incite them to engage in hostilities with the Prophet (peace be upon him) and Muslims.

From the other perspectives, those Jews of Madīnah were characterized with haughtiness. They were not particularly religious people either, and some of them took Judaism as a sort of nationalism. Together with this, they were given to belligerency and conflict. They were quite rich, but a substantial source of their wealth came from the fact that they were makers and traders of weaponry. So it was in their interest to fan wars and military conflicts, out of which they stood to gain handsome dividends. They were also quite lax in their way of living, given to wine drinking, and the practice of usury. Therefore, it was quite obvious that the Jews of that time and place were the ones meant in the above verse, and not the Arab Christians. The advocacy of hostilities with them was dictated by their belligerent and aggressive attitudes towards the Prophet and the Muslim State of Madīnah! In a way, it is a reaction to their misdeeds, and scheming, against the Muslims.

This reading of those verses which Khadduri called the 'sword verses' and which he claimed abrogated the verses advocating tolerance cited above, is not borne out by the facts of history. Moreover, Khadduri has never demonstrated that these verses were abrogated. Khadduri's failure to read those verses in their historical perspective is responsible, in a large measure, for his inability to read correctly the Islamic theory of international relations. In addition to this, he failed to take into account the cordial relations that existed between the Prophet (peace be upon him) and the Christians of Najrān and those of Banū Taghlib.

It is really surprising that Khadduri should fail to read the Qur'ān in a more comprehensive and objective way, given that he was of Arabic stock, and knew the Arabic language and culture. For there is an abundance of Qur'ānic verses which admonish the Muslims to maintain cordial relations with the People of the Scripture generally, so long as they do not wage war on, or start hostilities with the Muslims. We will quote just one clear and comprehensive Qur'ānic verse as an example:

> *God forbids you not, with regard to those who did not fight you because of your faith, nor did they drive you out of your homes,*

> *from dealing kindly and justly with them, for God loves those who are just! God only forbids you, with regard to those who fought you, because of your faith, drove you out of your homes, and supported others in driving you out that you turn to them for friendship and protection…* [*al-Mumtaḥinah* 60:8-9]

These verses 8 and 9 of *Sūrah Al-Mumtaḥinah*; (the woman examined), made it quite clear that there was nothing wrong if the Muslims befriended the Jews or Christians, so long as these remained pacific in their intentions and actions.

The conduct of the Prophet (peace be upon him) and his Caliphs after him, give ample evidence of the tolerant and relaxed way, with which People of the Book were treated, by the Muslim State and society: Muslims used to visit the Jews of Madīnah (before the breaking out of hostilities), have dialogue, and shared food with them, marry their girls, and have commerce with them. It is known that the Prophet (peace be upon him) married a Jew from Khaybar, namely Ṣafiyyah bint Ḥuyayy ibn al-Akhṭab, the daughter of the vanquished chief of Khaybar. Although she was indeed beautiful, the Prophet (peace be upon him) had married her out of compassion, seeing that both her husband and father had been killed in the fighting. She came to him seeking his help, to avert falling into slavery, as was then the custom that slavery was the lot of captives of war. We have already discussed above the dream (narrated in Muslim historical sources: Ibn Hishām, Ibn Saʿd and others) of Ṣafiyyah, long before the battle of Khaybar took place. When she came to him, the Prophet (peace be upon him) offered to marry her, and she consented without hesitation. Although Ṣafiyyah's family tried to poison the Prophet (peace be upon him) immediately after the battle, offering him a poisoned shoulder of roast lamb, knowing it to be the Prophet's favourite dish, the Prophet (peace be upon him) was not deterred, and the marriage took place. The Prophet held Ṣafiyyah in high esteem, cherished and loved her. ʿĀ'ishah, who was said to be quite jealous of her, once remarked: 'I wonder how you can love this dwarf-sized Jewess!'

The Prophet was angered by her remark.

'O ʿĀ'ishah you have just uttered a word that, if it were mixed with the ocean, it would have made it dirty! Moreover, how could you call her a Jewess when she has embraced Islam, and become a good Muslim!'

The Prophet (peace be upon him) used to treat the Jews of Madīnah, who opted to stay after the banishment of their settlement, with obvious compassion and care. He continued to have commercial dealing with them, including borrowing money from them. It was said that when the Prophet (peace be upon him) died, his shield was mortgaged to a Jew. When the Prophet was living in Makkah before the *hijrah,* he had a Jewish neighbour, who used to throw garbage in the Prophet's yard, almost every day. Then the throwing stopped for some time. The Prophet (peace be upon him) went to visit his Jewish neighbour, to see what was wrong with him, that he stopped throwing garbage in his yard, and he found him ill in bed. The Prophet continued to visit him and send gifts to him, until he became well again. The Jew was so moved by the Prophet's behaviour that he embraced Islam.

The Prophet's second Caliph, ʿUmar ibn al Khaṭṭāb, found one old Jew begging in the streets of Madīnah. He was moved by compassion, at this sight, that he ordered for a permanent pension from the state treasury. The Caliph ʿAlī ibn Abī Ṭālib, the fourth Caliph, contested the ownership of a shield with a Jew, who had actually stolen it from him. But the Muslim judge, finding the evidence advanced by ʿAlī inconclusive, gave his verdict in favour of the Jew.

It is not our purpose here to enter into a lengthy discussion of the status of non-Muslims in a Muslim State. That status is outlined by the Qur'ān itself, and detailed in the sunnah of the Prophet (peace be upon him), but the subject lies beyond the scope of the present study.

The Qur'ān stipulates that both marriage to women of the People of the Book, and eating their food are lawful for the Muslims.

2. THE SPECIAL STATUS OF THE PEOPLE OF THE BOOK

That the People of the Book have a special status in Islam is well-known. It is indeed a very privileged status. A Muslim will not be a Muslim, if he does not believe in the Prophethood of both Moses and Jesus Christ. Further, he is enjoined to show great veneration, respect and love for them. The Prophet (peace be upon him) used to allude to Moses and Jesus Christ as 'my dear brothers'. So with such a conceptual, religious and legal framework, it would indeed be very odd for the Prophet (peace be upon him) to have waged unprovoked war against the People of the Book. The only feasible explanation for the outbreak of hostilities between the Prophet (peace be upon him) and the Jews of Madīnah, must be the political one. The responsibility for these hostilities must be placed squarely on the shoulders of the Jews themselves.

Some orientalists cite the invasion of Byzantine and Persian Empires by the Muslims, as a conclusive proof that Islam is an aggressive and belligerent religion. However, it is well known that the Romans, in particular, were a massing huge forces on the northern frontier of the Muslim State of Madīnah. They had stationed large forces to invade Madīnah, for this reason the Prophet (peace be upon him) mounted the Mu'tah and Tabūk expeditions.

The hostile intent of the Romans is borne out, not just by their amassing of soldiers, but by encouraging opposition inside Madīnah itself. Apparently, they were able to monitor events inside Madīnah, through their agents and spies:

a. When Jabalah ibn al Aytham apostatized, they summoned him to Constantinople and he went there. They were obviously monitoring every small event in the Muslim State.

b. When Ka'b ibn Mālik, one of the three Muslims who failed to join the Tabūk expedition, and who was subsequently boycotted by the Muslims on the orders of the Prophet (peace be upon him) and the instructions of the Qur'ān, the Roman secret agents came to him in Madīnah, with gifts and money, and told him that their Caesar would offer him political asylum with dignity and honour, if he chose to come to Constantinople.

As to the Persians, they were attacking Muslim forces in Yemen, Ḥadramawt and in Iraq. They too were amassing large numbers of troops at Qādisiyyah and al-Madā'in, to the east of the river of Dajlah. Their aggressive designs and intentions against the Muslims were also manifested by the way in which Chosroes received the ambassadors of the Prophet. He ordered them to be killed, and he tore up the letter of the Prophet (peace be upon him).

3. THE NECESSITY OF WAGING WAR AGAINST TYRANTS

Quite apart from those considerations mentioned above, Islam makes it an obligation and privilege of Muslims to fight tyrants who are unjust and oppressive to their subjects. The objective of fighting these tyrants is not to convert them to Islam, or even to convert their followers. It is solely to liberate humanity at large, and rid it from oppression and tyranny. It is to make religious freedom an overriding ideal and obligation for all religions, be that Islam, or other faiths.

4. THE QUR'ĀN STRONGLY URGES MUSLIMS TO FIGHT TYRANNY AND OPPRESSION

God said in the Qur'ān:

> *And what is wrong with you, that you do not fight in the cause of God, and for those who, being weak and powerless, are ill-treated and oppressed among men, women and children, who cry out: Our Lord! Rescue us from this town, whose people are oppressors; and raise for us from You, one who will protect us and raise from You one who will help us.* [*Al-Nisā'* 4:75]

Muslims are commanded never to accept or even tolerate oppression practised against them or against others (non-Muslims). God says, in the Qur'ān:

> *Permission to fight is given to those against whom war was waged (to fight back), because they have been wronged, and surely Allah is able to make them victorious. [They are] those who have been expelled from their homes, without justice, [for no cause] except that they say: 'Allah is our Lord.' For had not God checked some people by means of others, there would have been destroyed (many) monasteries, churches, Synagogues, and Mosques, in which the name of God is much commemorated* [*al-Ḥajj* 22:39-40]

This verse above makes it abundantly clear that the objective of waging war in *jihād* is not to convert people to Islam, it is merely to assure religious freedom for all: to protect churches, synagogues, monasteries as well as mosques. It is indeed significant that mosques are mentioned at the end of the list. It is also very significant that waging of *Jihād* is made sanctionable, in the beginning, in self defence. The Muslims were given permission to fight back, because they were wronged, persecuted and driven out of their homes, for no cause except that they worshipped the One, True God – Allah! The call for religious freedom for all, Muslims, Jews, Christians and others, is reflected also in another Qur'ānic verse which was also directed to the People of the Book. God says in the Qur'ān:

> *Say (O Muḥammad); 'O people of the Book, come to a word that is common between us and you: That we worship none but Allah, that we associate no partners with Him, and that none of us shall take others as gods, besides Allah!'* [*Āl 'Imrān* 3:64]

The Qur'ān, in its endeavour to establish some accord among the Muslims and the People of the Book, makes two very simple demands:

a. To acknowledge and worship God alone;

b. Not to associate tyrants or overlords with God. The purpose of those two demands is to assure religious freedom and to combat tyranny and resist oppression.

Islam is very accommodating and conciliatory towards other religions. It acknowledges Moses and Jesus Christ, as true and authentic Apostles of God Almighty. Muslims are allowed to mix freely with the People of the Book:

- To eat their food;
- To visit their homes and invite them into their Muslim homes;
- To marry their women, without requiring them to convert to Islam and;
- To be kind and charitable to them, so long as they maintain peaceful relations with the Muslims. Many Qur'anic verses emphasize these notions.

In addition, the Qur'ān advises courteous dialogue, and friendly and kind exchanges with the People of the Book:

> *Do not argue with the People of the Book unless you do so in the fairer way – except in the case of those of them who do wrong, and say, we believe in what has been revealed unto us and what has been revealed unto you, and our Lord, and your lord is One and the same and we are submissive unto Him.* [*al-ʿAnkabūt* 29:46]

The emphasis here is on dialogue, and not conflict, emphasizing what is shared rather than what is controversial, valuing friendly relations, rather than hostilities. Islam commends exchange of views and dialogue and not clash between societies and civilizations, knowing very well that the luminous truth will triumph at the end of the day: Says God, in the Qur'ān:

> *It is Him who has sent His Messenger with the true guidance, and the true authentic religions that He will make prevail (over all religions) despite the displeasure of the associationists.* [*as-Ṣaff* 61:9]

Subḥānaka Allāhumma wa biḥamdika, Ashhadu an Ilāha Illā Anta…

Notes and References

CHAPTER I

1. Verse 39 of *Sūrah al-Ḥajj* was revealed in the tenth year of *Hijrah*.
2. A fifth expedition against Quraysh was led by Zayd ibn Ḥarithah al-Kalbī, in the third year of the *Hijrah*, after Badr.

   He intercepted a caravan belonging to Quraysh, led by Ṣafwān ibn Umayyah, won all the caravan and captured one of its men, by the name of Furāt ibn Ḥayyān, who later became a Muslim. The same Zayd is said to have led and of having won a caravan on the Red Sea Coast in the sixth year of *Hijrah*.
3. Vide. Majid Khadduri, *War and Peace in the Law of Islam,* John Hopkins Press, Baltimore, 1955.
   a. Muḥammad ibn al-Ḥasan as-Shaybānī *Siyar*, Translated by M. Khadduri, titled as: *The Islamic Law of Nations*, John Hopkins Press, Baltimore, 1966.
   b. Joseph Schacht,*The Origins of Muhammadan Jurisprudence* Oxford University Press, 1979 (paperback).
4. Khadduri believes that Muslim states were forced into coexistence peacefully by other nations, i.e. by their own weakness. The theoretical level, Muslims remain committed to the Verse of the Sword *al-Tawbah* 9:29.
5. Vide, Dr. Abdul Hamid Abu Sulayman, *The Islamic Theory of International Relations.* International Institute of Islamic Thought, Washington, USA, 1987.

   Dr. Abu Sulyman's account seems to be more tilted in the direction of emphasising the temporal aspect of *Sharīʿah* and discounting, in an unwarrantly degree, the more basic eternal divine aspect in dealing with the issues of war and peace in the Prophet's early stage of Islamic history.
6. Vide: Yusuf Talal De Lorenzo's translation of Muhammad al-Ghazali's work: *Remembrance and Prayer. The Way of the Prophet Muhammad.* Islamic Foundation UK, 1986, pp. 184.

7. This *ḥadīth* is narrated by Muslim.
8. This *ḥadīth* is narrated by Imām Aḥmad ibn Ḥanbal, Imām Abū Dāwūd and Imām al-Ḥākim al-Tirmidhi.

   It is significant to note that both the Qur'ānic verse (8:60) of *Sūrah al-Anfāl* (War Spoils) and the *aḥādīth* of the Prophet, referred to above, footnotes 30, 31, consist of warning against the enemies and their designs, and they seem to imply that (a) those enemies are prone to aggression against the Muslims because of the latter's proclamation of religious freedom and their stance against *Ṭawāghīt* (tyrants and oppressive forces), (b) that weakness is an open invitation for the invaders and aggressors, (c) that a cardinal strategy of defence is to be strong and appear strong; this will deter the enemy, (d) these texts of Qur'ān (8:60) and *aḥādīth* of the Prophet (peace be upon him) do not incite the Muslims to initiate wars and conflicts, but merely to prepare and be ready for them and to intimidate the enemy that, if that enemy is speculating aggression against them, aggression will not go unpunished, that the Muslims are both able and willing to retaliate. These considerations, together with what we called the lenient Qur'ānic text, which command kindness and compassion towards the People of the Book and forbid the Muslims to use harsh words in their debate, seem to mitigate against what I called 'the militant understanding' of the verse of the sword as the final ruling over the issue of how to deal with the People of the Book.

   The verse of the sword was revealed on the occasion of the Battle of Tabuk against the Romans who initiated hostilities against the Muslims, firstly by killing the Prophet's ambassador al-Ḥārith ibn ʿUmayr al-Azdī, and secondly by a massing soldiers on the northern borders of the Muslim state, first at Mu'tah and then at Tabūk.

CHAPTER II

1. Ibn Hishām, Ibn Saʿd, al-Wāqidī, al-Ṭabarī and Ibn Kathīr.
2. Conflict and war, in the Qur'ānic conception of things, are ways and means which sometimes becomes necessary, to defeat and vanquish the forces of evil and Satan, which otherwise could not be defeated. Just war becomes an important and legitimate instrument by means of which God propels (*yadfaʿ*) some people by the means of others. This is the '*Dafʿ' Allah*' to which the Qur'ān refers more than once. See, Zakaria Bashier: *Sunshine at Madinah*, The Islamic Foundation, Leicester, 1990.
3. Ibid, p. 144. However, al-Wāqidī gives another/other versions of the number of those killed and captured at Badr, from among the Quraysh unbelievers version, puts the number of those killed at 45, while another puts number

of those killed at 73. There is similar disagreement as to the numbers of captives.

4. Ibn Hishām, *Sirā*, al-Ḥalabī, Cairo, 1955 Vol. 111, p. 644.
5. al-Anfāl 8:65-66.
6. Ibn Hishām, vol. III, al-Ḥalabī, Cairo.
7. Zakaria Bashier, *Sunshine at Madinah*, Islamic Foundation, Leicester, 1990.
8. Zakaria Bashier, *Hijrah, Story and Significance*, The Islamic Foundation, Leicester, 1983.

CHAPTER III

1. Ibn Hishām, vol. 11. Al-Ḥalabī edition, p. 43, 644.
   Witness the statement of Salamah ibn Salamah when entering Madīnah after the Battle, with the Prophet, in reply to the congratulations of the Madīnans, that the war was too easily won, 'as the army of the Quraysh consisted of no more than bald-headed old soldiers.' See also the statement of Abū Sufyān ibn al-Ḥārith and ʿAbd al-Muṭṭalib of Banū Hāshim when asked by Abū Lahab, 'How was it, son of my brothers?' Abū Sufyān ibn al-Ḥārith said: 'I do not blame Quraysh for the defeat, for by God, we met men in white costume, riding on piebald horses between the sky and the earth. For by God, nothing could stand in front of them, and nothing could escape their blows.' Somebody present, by the name of Abū Rāfiʿ, commented: 'These are indeed angels.' Abū Lahab hit him hard, and when Abū Rāfiʿ repeated his statement about the angels' interference, Abū Lahab threw him on the ground, and sat on top of him, hitting as hard as he could in his mad anger. Ibn Hishām, Vol. 11, p. 647.

   These verses were revealed in the wake of the affair of the Jews of Banū Qaynuqāʿ, and it refers to the intercession of both ʿAbdullāh ibn Salūl, the head of the Madinan hypocrites, and Saʿd ibn ʿUbādah, the Companion of the Prophet and head of the Khazraj, who was an age old ally of Jews. Henceforth, the Muslims were forbidden to take friends and confidants from among the Jews of Madīnah, since it was then total war between two groups. The verses strongly condemned the intercession of Ibn Salūl but that of Ibn ʿUbādah was pardoned, coming as it did out of good faith and good intentions, as Ibn ʿUbādah, together with many other Muslims, at the time still harboured love and friendship to their Jewish compatriots, unaware of their guiles and schemes against Muslims – hence the Qur'ānic reminders and educational remarks signalling the need for a new orientation on the Jewish question.

Another Qur'ānic verse which singled out the Madīnan Jews as foremost among the enemies of Muslims must have been revealed at that time, when relations between Muslims and Jews reached their climax of mistrust, hostility and enmity. 'You will find, (Muḥammad), the most hostile of men to those who believe are the Jews and the polytheist, and you will find the nearest of them in affection to those who believe are those who say: "Surely we are Christians that is because, there are among them priests and monks, and because they were not proud."'

This verse, if read in conjunction with verse 5:51 raises the question of whether this hostility between Muslims and Jews is an eternal one, or one merely anchored in historical accidents related to the Madīnan Jew? Or is it perhaps anchored in an ever-lasting clash between cultural identity of the two groups? One factor militating against the second possibility is that the Muslims and Jews of Madīnah did enjoy an interval of peace, mutual love and friendship in the pre-Badr period. That this did take place is, in part, attested to by the Qur'ānic injunctions to the Muslims to cease regarding the Jews of Madīnah as friends and confidence, injunctions to which we have been referring. Another reason, which tends to mitigate against the second possibility, is also provided by the status of *Ahl al-Kitāb*, accorded to the Jews by the Qur'ān itself. However, this issue is a complex one, and it could very well turn out that the hostility in question is not a passing façade, but of some groups, as a matter of fact. Though, theoretically speaking, peaceful coexistence remains an open possibility.

2. In the first year of the *Hijrah*, The Prophet (peace be upon him) made a pact with the Jews of Madīnah, laying down the following terms:
   a. Anyone of the Jews, who joined us (as a citizen of Madīnah), will be defended, protected and helped, on equal footing with other citizens, not wronged or abandoned.
   b. The Jews will contribute towards the expenditure of war, and will join as fighters if they so-wished.
   c. The Jews will be part of the *Ummah* of Islam, as citizens; however they will be free to practise their religion, as will the Muslims.
   d. The Jews will be free to have followers, and alliances, except those who committed a crime or a wrongdoing against the Muslims.
   e. However, should the Jews opt to go out of Madīnah, they should secure the permission of the Prophet, before they do so.
   f. The Jews will be obligated to come to the help of the Muslims, should an enemy attack Madīnah, and they bear the expenses, in doing so, as will the defenders among the Muslims also bear their expenses.
   g. The parties to this '*Ṣaḥīfah*' will help and support each other against anybody who fight the People of this *Ṣaḥīfah* (be they Muslims or

non-Muslims). They shall advise each other and consult each other, they will help each other in good charitable deeds, but not in evil or wrong deeds.

h. Yathrib will be a Ḥaram (an inviolable sanctuary) for all parties to this pact.

i. A neighbour is exactly like the self, not harmed, or stand accused without reason.

j. Anyone committing a crime will not be given a sanctuary in Yathrib, without the permission of his family and people.

k. Should any disagreement or conflict arise between parties to this pact, it should be referred to God and to the Prophet (peace be upon him) as Judge and arbiter.

l. This pact should be accepted freely and with full approval, as God and His party from among the Mu'minun have freely and gladly accepted it.

m. Parties to this pact will not give refuge to anyone from the Quraysh, or to anyone who is a supporter of the Quraysh.

n. Parties to this pact will all come to the defence of Yathrib, should it be attacked by any enemy, and if the people of Yathrib should decide to conclude a peace agreement with anyone, the Jews should uphold that peace agreement alongside with the Muslims.

The text of this pact is given by Ibn Hishām, in Vol. 2, p. 149-150 of the version of Dār al-Qalam, Beirut (No date given).

3. Ibn Hishām, the edition of Dār al-Qalam, Beirut, (No date given) vol. 3, p. 50.
4. Al-Ṭabarī ibn Jarīr: *Jāmiʿ al-Bayān ʿan Ta'wīl āy al-Qur'ān* (Arabic), Dār al-Fikr, Beirut, 1982 vol.3, p. 60-65.
5. Sayyid Quṭb *Fī Ẓilāl al-Qur'ān*, Dār al-Shurūq, Cairo, 1973 Vol.1, p. 431-435.
6. Ibn Hishām, Dār al-Qalam edition, Beirut, (No date given) vol.3, page 55.
7. Ibn Hishām, Dār al-Qalam edition vol, 3, page 50.
8. *Al-Tawbah* [9:99].
9. *Al-Tawbah* [9:99] which reads; 'and of the Arab Bedouins, there is that who believes God, and the Last Day, and takes that which he expends and also the prayers of the Messengers as acceptable offering in the sight of God; surely, it is an acceptable offering for them. God will bring them into His Mercy. Surely God is Forgiving, Merciful.'
10. Al-Tawbah 9:97, 98, verses that denounce these hypocritical Bedouins are live in the Qur'ān, viz. Verses 49:14:101. Verse 49:14 of *Sūrah al-Ḥujurāt* records as follows: 'The Arab Bedouins said we believe Say (O Muḥammad). You

do not (as yet) believe but say "We surrender" for belief has not yet entered your hearts.' It is such Qur'ānic verses which seem to give a very strong impression that, in the Qur'ānic scheme of things, civility and urbanism are by far the favourite mode of living and his constant condemnation of civility and city-dwelling in his famous *Muqaddimah.*

11. Al-Wāqidī: *al-Maghāzī*, Vol. 1 (No date given) see his account of the Battle of Uḥud.
12. Ibid.
13. Ibid, (al-Wāqidī –vol.1).
14. Ibn Hishām, vol. 3, page 68 (al-Qalam edition).
15. Al-Wāqidī vol. 1.
16. Ibn Saʿd *al –Ṭabaqāt al-Kubrā*, vol. 2, page 40, Dār Ṣādir, Beirut (No date given).
17. It is narrated by some *sīrah* sources, that the Prophet (peace be upon him) vowed, in the wake of the martyrdom of Ḥamzah, his uncle, and the mutilation of his body by Hind bint Abī Sufyān, to mutilate the bodies of thirty of the Qurayshite polytheists, but God forbade him from doing so. Vide, *Sūrah al-Naḥl* (16:126); also ibn Hishām, vol. 3, page (101).
18. Ibn Saʿd: *al-Ṭabaqāt al-Kubrā*, vol. 2, page 44, Dār Ṣādir, Beirut, (No date given).
19. Ibn Hishām, vol. 3, p. 85.
20. Ibn Hishām, vol. 3, page 89; Al-Qalam edition.
21. Ibid, p. 86.
22. The Prophet's beautiful, radiant face turned into a hardness, like that of steel, when he became angry, and his eyes became red, and none could then dare look him in the face.
23. The Prophet's bravery was amply demonstrated in the battles of Uḥud, and Hunayn, being rare occasions, on which he did actual fighting. ʿAlī ibn Abī Ṭālib, legendary for his bravery, said that, when the battles reached their most fierce moments, they used to protect themselves by fighting from behind the Prophet, taking him as a protection shield.
24. Ibn Hishām, al-Qalam edition vol. 3, p. 79.
25. Ibid, vol. 3, p. 79.
26. Ibn Hishām, vol. 3, p. 99.
27. Ibid, vol. 3, p. 99.
28. Ibid, vol. 3, p. 104.

CHAPTER IV

1. Ibn Hishām; vol. (II) al-Ḥalabī edition, 2nd impression, Cairo, 1955, p. 169.

2. Ibn Hishām; vol. (II), al-Ḥalabī edition, 2nd impression, Cairo, 1955, p. 183.
3. Ibn Hishām; vol. (II), al-Ḥalabī edition, 2nd impression, Cairo, 1955, p. 86.
4. M. H. Haykal: The *Life of Muḥammad*, Translated by Ismail Faruqi, The North America Trust Publications, 1976 U.S.A., p. 281-285.
5. Ibn Hishām; vol. (III), Dār al-Fikr, Damascus (n.d), p. 187.

CHAPTER V

1. Ibn Hishām narrates (vol 3, p. 225) that when the Qurayshite polytheists asked the Jews of Banū al-Naḍīr whether Muḥammad's new religion was better or their idol-worshipping, the Jews replied without hesitation:

   'Your religion is better, and you are more worthy of the true religion than him.'

   Furthermore, the Jews vowed to the Qurayshites to fight with them against Muḥammad and his Muslim followers until they were completely exterminated.

   The Qur'ān *al-Nisā'* 4:54, attributes this state of the Jews to their envy and invidiousness, because Prophethood used to be among the descendents of Jacob (Israel), but Muḥammad was Arabian of the seed of Ismā'īl, son of Abraham through Hājir, the Egyptian former slave-girl.
2. Ibn Hishām narrated that some of the hypocrites excused themselves from participating in the digging of the Trench, or worked without any vigour or enthusiasm, or even slipped out of the camp, secretly and without taking permission from the Prophet (peace be upon him). But the Qur'ān exposed their ill designs. Says Allah in the Qur'ān, exposing the hypocrites' misdeeds of slipping out of the camp without being noticed, and without taking permission from the Prophet (peace be upon him): 'God knows those of you who slip away surreptitiously; so let those who against His command beware, lest a trial befall them, or there befall them a painful chastisement.' (*al-Nūr* 24:63).

3. Ibn Hishām, Dār al-Qur'ān, Beirut (no date given) vol. 3, p. 231.
4. Ibn Sa'd al-*Ṭabaqāt al-Kubrā*, Dār Ṣādir, Beirut (no date given) vol. 2, p. 69.
5. Ibn Hishām, Dār al-Qalam, Beirut (no date given) vol. 3, p. 24.
6. Ibid., vol. 3, p. 242.
7. Ibid., vol. 3, p. 245.
8. Ibid., vol. 3, p. 247.
9. Ibid., vol. 3, p. 249.

CHAPTER VI

1. Guillaume, A., *The Life of Muhammad: A Translation of Ibn Ishaq's Sirat Rasul Allah*. Oxford, Oxford University Press, 5th impression, 1978, p. 469.
2. Ibid., p. 468.
3. Ibid., p. 469.
4. Ibid., p. 469.
5. Ibid., p. 486.
6. Ibid., p. 491.
7. Ibid., p. 493.
8. Ibid., p. 495.
9. Ibid., p. 496.
10. Ibid., p. 496.
11. Ibid., p. 497.
12. Ibid., p.496.
13. Ibid., p.494.
14. Ibid., p.496.
15. Ibid., p.496.
16. Ibid., p.496.

CHAPTER VII

1. Guillaume, A., *The Life of Muḥammad: A Translation of Ibn Ishaq's Sīrat Rasūl Allāh*. Oxford, Oxford University Press, 5th impression, 1978, p. 500.
2. Ibid., p. 504.
3. Ibid., p. 507.
4. Ibid., p. 511.
5. Ibid., p.510-511.

CHAPTER VIII

1. Ibn Hishām, Dār al-Qalam edition, vol. 4, p. 17.
2. Ibn Saʿd, Dār al-Fikr, vol. 2, p. 129.
3. Ibn Hishām, Dār al-Qalam , vol. 4, p. 19.
4. Ibid., vol. 4, p. 20.
5. Ibn Hishām, (He gives less than twenty the number of Muslims who were Martyred at Mu'tah), vol.4, p. 30.
6. Ibn Saʿd, Dār Ṣādir, Beirut, (No date), vol. 2, p. 129-130.
7. Ibid., vol. 2, p. 129.
8. Ibid., vol. 4, p. 22.

9. Ibid., vol. 4, p. 38.
10. Ibid., vol. 4, p. 39.
11. Ibid., Vol. 4, p. 45.
12. Ibid., p. 47.
13. Ibid., p. 49.
14. Ibid., p. 55.
15. Ibid.
16. Ibid., vol., 4, p. 54.
17. Ibid., vol.4, p. 59.

CHAPTER IX

1. Guillaume, A., *The Life of Muḥammad A Translation of Ibn Isḥaq's Sīrat Rasūl Allāh*. Oxford, Oxford University Press, 5th impression, 1978, p. 566.
2. Ibid., p. 569.
3. Ibid., p. 576.
4. Ibid., p. 596.
5. Ibid., p. 598, 599.
6. Ibid., p. 602.

CHAPTER X

1. Guillaume, A., *The Life of Muḥammad A Translation of Ibn Isḥāq's Sīrat Rasūl Allāh.* Oxford, Oxford University Press, 5th impression, 1978, p, 629.
2. Ibid., p. 639.
3. Ibid., p. 641.
4. Ibid., p. 643.
5. Ibid., p. 644.

CHAPTER XI

1. Author of (The Clash between Civilizations, and the Remaking of the New World Order).
2. An American Orientalist and author of Lebanese origin: Some of his famous books are:
   a. Khadduri (Majid); *The Islamic Law of Nations (Shybahi's Siyar)* Baltimore; John Hopkins Press, 1966.
   b. Khadduri (M): *The Islamic Conception of Justice*; Batlimore; John Hopkins Univ. Press (1984).

Index

Ustān, 228
ʿUtārid ibn Ḥājib, 268
ʿUtbah ibn Abī Muʿādh, 53
ʿUtbah ibn Abī Waqqāṣ, 83
ʿUtbah ibn Ghazwān, 87
ʿUtbah ibn Rabīʿah, 40, 53, 59, 67
ʿUthmān ibn ʿAffān, 196, 204, 239, 261
ʿUthmān ibn Ṭalḥah, 232, 237
ʿUyaynah ibn al-Ḥiṣn al-Fazārī, 170, 171

Waddān, 11
Wādī al-Qurā, 207, 218
Waḥshī, 82, 83
Walīd ibn ʿUtbah Al-, 53
Wāqidī Al-, 53, 77, 79, 80, 86, 87
Waṭīh, 210

Yāsir, 211, 212
Yathrib, 58, 77, 149, 275
Yemen, 7, 211, 240, 263, 274-276, 278, 279, 281, 282, 286, 292
Yuḥannā ibn Ru'bah, 263

Zachariah, 33
Zakwān ibn 'Abd Qays, 79, 80
Zayd al-Khayl, Zayd al-Khayr, 271, 272
Zayd ibn al-Arqam, 79, 172
Zayd ibn al-Dathinah, 129
Zayd ibn Ḥārithah, 74, 87, 138, 219, 220, 222
Zayd ibn Muḥammad, 74, 219
Zayd ibn Thābit, 79, 135
Zaynab bint Jaḥsh, 54, 55, 138, 139, 140, 141, 176
Zibriqān ibn Badr Al-, 269
Zubayr ibn al-ʿAwwām Al-, 85, 88, 92, 108, 211, 226, 231
Zuhayr ibn Abī Salmā, 255, 257